In the Steps of Timothy

In the Steps of Timothy

Lance Pierson

Inter-Varsity Press

INTER-VARSITY PRESS
38 De Montfort Street, Leicester LE1 7GP, England

First published 1995

British Library Cataloguing in Publication Data
A catalogue record for this book is available from the British Library.

ISBN 0–85110–977–7

Set in Palatino

Typeset in Great Britain by Parker Typesetting Service, Leicester

Printed in Great Britain by Cox & Wyman Ltd, Reading

*Inter-Varsity Press is the book-publishing division of the Universities and
Colleges Christian Fellowship (formerly the Inter-Varsity Fellowship), a
student movement linking Christian Unions in universities and colleges
throughout the United Kingdom and the Republic of Ireland, and a member
movement of the International Fellowship of Evangelical Students. For
information about local and national activities write to UCCF, 38 De
Montfort Street, Leicester LE1 7GP.*

Contents

Preface 7

Introduction 9

1 Child 19

2 Youth 33

3 Missionary 54

4 Son 78

5 Letter-writer 99

6 Go-between 124

7 Wimp? 141

8 Heir? 175

9 Saint and martyr? 193

Notes 215

Preface

I've come more and more to feel that every book is a team effort, calling for as long a list of credits as a TV play or film. To say that this one is 'by' Lance Pierson is a gross oversimplification, and robs others of the honour due to them. I say more about this at the end of chapter 5.

I suppose it's unrealistic to list every contributing influence on the front cover. So here on an inside page is my roll of honour for *In the Steps of Timothy*.

Virtually every line and sentence has grown out of reading, hearing or discussing what someone else has said. I've tried to record most of these debts in the Notes. But there must still be places where I've absorbed somebody's idea without realizing it. Where this has happened, sorry – and thanks.

I've read more commentaries on Paul's letters to Timothy than I can list; but more helpful than any of them for my purposes were Dick Lucas' expositions of 1 and 2 Timothy at St Helen's Church, Bishopsgate, London, in 1986 and 1988.

Two early influences on the book were the Orientours 'In the Steps of St Paul' party in May 1989, led by David Hayden; and St Helen's, Bishopsgate's, 'Really Arty Weekend' in January 1990, led by Nigel Styles, which produced the musical 'The Sanctified Diary of Our Brother Timothy Aged $39\frac{3}{4}$'. My understanding of Timothy has been happily marinaded in ideas and phrases from both groups.

Dr Rosalind Love translated out of Latin for me the earlier Lives of Timothy by Polycrates and Metaphrastes.

Anne Atkins listened patiently to early versions of several of the chapters and criticized them astutely. In summer 1993 I received detailed comments on the first draft of the book from Andrew Cornes, Nigel Denton, Angie Edge (who also checked and corrected the Bible references), Andrew Graystone, Alec Motyer, Chris Powell and Jeremy Thomson (who has also consistently encouraged me with thoughts and references from his latest reading and his insistence that the book was worth writing). I have rethought and rewritten every paragraph, almost every sentence, in the light of their reactions. In one or two places I have been so pig-headed as to reject their advice. Perhaps that's one benefit of attributing the book to only one author; its blemishes are my fault, no-one else's.

A final tribute to the two hardest workers. My assistant Yasmin Muttiah has repeatedly protected, corrected and updated the document on an ageing and ailing computer; she has outwitted all its attempts to frustrate our wishes. And IVP's editor Colin Duriez has seen the whole project through from concept to press with unfailing patience, courtesy, resilience and encouragement.

What a team! (And there are of course others I haven't mentioned.) It has been my privilege to enjoy their help. If you like the book, please join me in thanking them. They have made it what it is.

I dedicate this book to several 'Timothys' in my life:

– my own dear children Joy and Robin, with my love and prayers that they will remain true children in the faith;

– any and all younger Christians I may have been able to help grow in their love and loyalty to Jesus;

– my series of seven work assistants: Esther Back, Anne Ballard, Katherine Cornes, Marion Machin, Alison Wilkinson, and Yvonne Kane as well as Yasmin Muttiah;

– the memory of David Rowe: despite constantly encouraging me to keep working on the book, he rightly feared that he might get to heaven before it was published, and so demanded an early version of it to comment on;

– my wife Sue, the best and longest-suffering helper of all;

– and finally someone actually called Timothy, my nephew Tim Williams.

Lance Pierson

Introduction

I haven't come across any other biography of Timothy.[1] I don't think he has inspired any famous paintings.[2] I *have* heard of two St Timothy's Churches, but they appear to be the only two in the whole Church of England.[3] Timothy doesn't seem a major New Testament character like Paul or Peter or John.

Indeed, he's an elusive figure to get to know. The Bible's spotlight doesn't often fall on him. Whenever Timothy comes on stage in Acts, Luke tends to turn his attention to someone else! Or Timothy goes off to do something that Luke then tells us nothing about.[4] And most people conclude from the two letters Paul wrote to Timothy that he was a bit of a weak character.[5]

Why?

So *why* write a biography of Timothy? Well, at first sight, his seeming nonentity makes a rather encouraging contrast to the Bible characters who usually get books written about them. Abraham, David, Paul and company are certainly inspiring, but they can seem a bit daunting to ordinary mortals like us. Of course we can learn a lot from them, but most of us will not end up as a patriarch or king or leader of a pioneer mission team. They may make us feel a little inferior, as if God – and Christian biographers – were really interested only in the high-fliers.

But someone who gets only nine verses of the Acts of the Apostles to himself (well, actually most of those are shared with at least one other person),[6] someone who is a background, rather than front-stage, character to God's story-book, sounds much more like the rest of us. I find him more approachable.

In fact, though, while he's no giant and remains in the shadows, he's more significant than you might suppose. H. V. Morton's classic book of travel and history, *In the Steps of St Paul*, introduces him like this: 'Timothy was to play a great part in the subsequent

---

[1]These small numbers in the text refer to the further comments in the Notes, starting on p. 215.

development of Christianity.'[7] Think for a moment and you can see what he means.

Timothy was Paul's closest assistant and regular companion from the beginning of his second missionary journey (AD 48) till his Roman imprisonment (AD 62–64). These sixteen years cover chapters 16 – 28 of Acts and most of the New Testament letters – a uniquely important phase in the foundation of Christianity. Timothy is mentioned by name in all Paul's letters except Galatians, Ephesians and Titus (though, as we shall see, he was well aware of those three as well).[8] And as the story of Acts ends, Paul appoints Timothy his representative in Ephesus – perhaps the biggest church at that time, and certainly the one most fully reported in the New Testament for us to learn from.

This doesn't turn him into a spiritual giant; it shows that God can make use of – even give critically important tasks to – ordinary, unspectacular people like you and me, and Timothy. Paul valued and loved him so highly, he came to look on him as his son.[9] He wasn't just a hanger-on, or a footnote to Paul's story, as many people have regarded him. He was *the* major relationship in the life of a man who seems to have had no wife and no children of his own.[10] That's why I think he's worth writing and reading about. People have paid less attention to him than they should.

But there is another, even more important, reason for writing about him. He's an 'ordinary' Christian in another and more important way. Unlike Peter, James and John, and even Paul, he wasn't in the first generation of Jesus' followers; he wasn't present on the day of Pentecost; he wasn't an apostle. Like us, he became a Christian as a result of the apostles' work. He was one of the first 'ordinary' or 'typical' post-apostolic Christians. There are of course others in the New Testament, like his own grandmother Lois, or Luke, or Lydia. But he is by far the most fully recorded of them all.[11]

As I have tried to find out about Timothy, it has felt like restoring an ancient wall painting. He has remained hidden by centuries of people facing the other way. They simply haven't noticed him. But as I've stared and scraped away at the paintwork, a definite picture has emerged; still faint and shaded in places, but far more of it than I had imagined.

Completely against my expectations, I have been forced to a

conclusion I haven't heard anyone else even hint at. Timothy is the third most fully documented and ever-present character in the New Testament, after Jesus and Paul. Indeed, in some respects, we have better material for his biography than we do for that of Jesus! There are fewer big gaps in his story than in anyone else's. For which other New Testament character can we map out a fairly detailed *c.v.* from infancy to late thirties?

From one angle this conclusion seems preposterous. Everyone 'knows' Peter far better than they know Timothy. We endlessly hear and read sermons or stories about Peter, but seldom about Timothy. Yet the New Testament covers a much smaller part of Peter's lifespan than Timothy's. It gives us some thirty incidents taken from about eight years of Peter's life; four sermons or speeches; and two letters (which tell us very little about Peter himself). We have no idea how old he was; we can't put together any itinerary for him after Acts 11. The difference is that he was a strong personality, a natural leader of the apostles, an upfront character whenever he was on stage. Timothy was quieter, in the crowd, backstage.

How?

So *how* can we set about reconstructing a biography of Timothy? Writing a life story from such slender material is a precarious business. We shall be constantly sifting and shifting between four distinct levels of narrative:

1. What the Bible clearly tells us, so that we *know*: for instance, that Timothy's father was a Greek and not a Jew.[12]

2. Very strong likelihoods which we can *deduce* from the Bible record: for instance, that Timothy's father wasn't a Christian. Acts 16:1 tells us that Timothy's mother, *who was also a Christian*, was Jewish, but his father was a Greek. Luke doesn't spell out in so many words that the father was not a Christian; but it's a very strong likelihood from the way he includes the mother's Christian faith as part of the contrast with her husband.

Likelihood becomes virtual certainty when Paul doesn't include Timothy's father among his forebears who came to faith.[13]

3. Probable implications which we *infer* from the Bible record: for instance, that Timothy's father was dead by the time Paul co-opted Timothy in AD 48. This is an inference from the word Luke

11

uses, which could equally well be translated, 'all the Jews . . . knew that Timothy's father *had been* a Greek'.[14]

4. Reasonable speculation based on the Bible and other research which enables us to form an educated *hunch*:[15] for instance, that Timothy's father had belonged to a wealthy family. Neither Luke nor Paul states this in the New Testament. It's only my hunch; but it is a well-founded and supported hunch. Lystra was a remote rural town in Galatia, not Greece. Its native inhabitants were not Greeks, but what we today call Anatolians.[16] In 6 BC, the Emperor Augustus made Lystra a Roman colony as part of a string of defences against local warlike tribes. Greek inhabitants were the better-educated class in society, employed by the Roman officials or trading with them.

The fact that his wife was Jewish makes it likely that Timothy's father was not only well educated but also well off. Sir William Ramsay's researches into first-century customs in this part of the Empire led him to conclude that 'there can be little doubt that the Jews married into the dominant families'.[17]

This gets further support from the way Timothy's family was so well known ('*all* the Jews who lived *in those places* [*i.e.* beyond just his home town] knew that Timothy's father was Greek').[18]

In telling the story I shall use all four levels of narrative; but I shall try always to make clear which level we're working with.

Another example of building up the picture from tiny scraps of information is Timothy's age. What we are *told* (level 1) is that when he was supervising things in Ephesus he was still 'young'.[19] That needn't mean he was a babe in arms. The Greek word can range from childhood through apprenticeship to early adulthood, much as the English word 'young' does today. Irenaeus, a Christian leader and writer in the second century, states that you could fairly be called 'young' up to the age of forty.[20] So Timothy could have been any age up to forty when Paul wrote his first letter to him. The date of writing was almost certainly (level 2) AD 64, 65 or 66.[21] If Timothy was forty or under in AD 64, we're safe in saying he wasn't born before AD 24.

We're also told[22] (level 1) that he left home and joined Paul on the missionary expedition in AD 48. It's most unlikely (level 3) that his mother (and grandmother!) would let him go before he was sixteen or seventeen at the youngest. So it's reasonable to assume he wasn't born after AD 32.

12

There's no way of knowing in which year between 24 and 32 he was born. But to make the book more coherent and less vague, I've plumped as a hunch (level 4) for AD 30.[23] In this case Timothy would have been eighteen when he left home and perhaps thirty-four when he took responsibility for sorting things out at Ephesus. Paul's second letter to him, summoning him back to Rome, came two or three years later.

Eighteen to thirty-six or thirty-seven – a highly formative, active phase of life,[24] a span of years which for most of us marks major growth towards stable, adult maturity and usefulness. We all make plenty of mistakes on the way; rightly handled, these can help us to learn. Timothy seems to have learned from his share of mistakes, and we can learn from them too. Perhaps that's a further reason for writing a biography about a rather unremarkable young man to whom God gave a most remarkable life.

How the book works

I hope what I've said about different levels doesn't sound too much like hard work! Timothy was an 'ordinary' Christian and I want this book to appeal to ordinary readers. So I've tried to keep the story moving along. This means I can't stop and explain *every* deduction, inference and hunch at the time. So I've put my reasoning into the Notes at the end of the book. The small numbers you keep coming across tell you where in the Notes to find the further comment if you want it. Most readers won't need to bother. But if you're puzzled or worried by what I've said, do look it up. (Chapter 5, on his contribution to Paul's letters, and chapters 6 and 7, on his failures, are particularly controversial.) And if you can spare the time to follow me in putting the fragments together piece by piece, much of the most important and interesting material is in the Notes. I've tried to include there everything that explains why I think as I do. That's also where you'll find chapter and verse for the bits I quote from the Bible and other books.

I don't think anyone else has tried to write a full life of Timothy for over 900 years. So in places you'll be aware that what I'm saying is my opinion only. Much of the time, I'm trying to straighten out the facts. But I start each chapter with a short episode from the story, written as if it were part of a novel. The rest of the chapter tries to give the evidence for my version of events. So if the beginning of the chapter is not how you remember hearing or imagining the story before, read on and see if you're convinced. And if you aren't convinced by one chapter, give the next one a fair trial. Each takes a different stage of Timothy's life.

There's a further chance for you to get involved at the end of each chapter. You'll find two sets of questions, one headed 'Reflect', the other 'Share'. They're not totally watertight compartments; but generally the first set are more suitable for private thought, the second for group discussion. Above the questions there's a list of the main Bible passages the chapter is based on, in case you want to refer to them.

The Bible quotes come from the Good News Bible (unless I say otherwise) because I find it easy to read. But to save forever giving its name in full, I refer to it simply as GNB.

A reconstruction of Timothy's life

This chart shows the outline of Timothy's life that this book follows. The 'Paul' column sets the context. In the 'Event' column, the bold type shows what seems certain from the Bible. The rest is deduction, inference or hunch. You will find the relevant section of it at the beginning of each chapter.

Paul	Date	Age	Event
	30?	0	Born in Lystra **of mixed parents (Acts 16:1).**
34/35 Conversion (Acts 9).	30–45	1–15	**Childhood: mother Eunice and grandmother Lois teach Scriptures (2 Tim. 3:14–15).**
46–47 1st missionary journey (Acts 13–14).	46	16	Paul at Lystra: preaching, healing, stoned (Acts 14:6–23; 2 Tim. 3:11). ? Lois, Eunice, Timothy converted (2 Tim. 1:5; 1 Tim. 1:2; 2 Tim. 1:2). ? Timothy baptized (1 Tim. 6:12; 2 Tim. 1:6?).

Paul	*Date*	*Age*	*Event*
	46–48	16–18	**Grows as Christian, respected in area (Acts 16:2).**
? Writes Galatians. Jerusalem Council (Acts 15).	48	18	Timothy and Lystra church among recipients of Galatians.
48–51 2nd missionary journey (Acts 15:40–18:22)			**Paul at Lystra: circumcises Timothy (Acts 16:3)**; commissions him to join team (1 Tim. 1:18; 4:14?). Phrygia, Galatia, Mysia, Troas (Acts 16:4–10).
	49	19	Macedonia: Philippi, Thessalonica, Berea (Acts 16:11–17:12). Helps preach and teach in Thessalonica (1 Thes., 3:2, 4). **Stays with Silas in Berea while Paul escapes (Acts 17:13–15).**
Achaia: Athens, Corinth (Acts 17:16–18:4).	50	20	**Arrives in Athens with Silas (Acts 17:16; 1 Thes. 3:1). Sent to Thessalonica to encourage persecuted Christians (1 Thes. 3:2–6). Arrives in Corinth with Silas (Acts 18:5).**
18+ months in Corinth (Acts 18:5–18).	50–51	20–21	**Helps write 1 and 2 Thessalonians (1 Thes. 1:1; 2 Thes. 1:1). Helps preach gospel in Corinth (2 Cor. 1:19).**

Paul	Date	Age	Event
Return via Ephesus, Caesarea and Jerusalem to Antioch (Acts 18:18–22).	51–53	21–23	Stays on in Corinth? With Paul? Returns home to Galatia till Paul collects him?
53, 3rd missionary journey begins: Galatia, Phrygia (Acts 18:23).	53	23	Travelling with Paul.
54–57, Ephesus (Acts 19).	54–56	24–26	Based in Ephesus with Paul.
	56/57	26/27	**Sent with Erastus to Macedonia (Acts 19:21–22).**
			Sent to teach Corinthians (1 Cor. :14–17; 16:10–11); apparently unsuccessful.
57–59, Troas, Macedonia, ? Illyricum and Achaia (2 Cor. 2:12–13; Acts 20:1–3; Rom. 15:19).	58	28	Most of the preaching in Troas? (2 Cor. 2:13). **Helps write 2 Corinthians (1:1).**
	58–59		**Paul's fellow-worker at Corinth (Rom. 16:21).**
Macedonia, Troas, Miletus, Jerusalem (Acts 20:3 – 21:17).	59	29	**Accompanies Paul on start of journey (Acts 20:4–5).** Goes to Jerusalem (1 Cor. 16:3).
59–61, arrested in Jerusalem, imprisoned in Caesarea (Acts 21:18 – 24:27).	59–62	29–32	? Goes on elsewhere from Jerusalem/Caesarea.

Paul	*Date*	*Age*	*Event*
61–62, appeal to Caesar and journey to Rome (Acts 25:1–28:15)			
House arrest in Rome (Acts 28:16–31).	62–64	32–34	**Accompanies Paul as senior and valued assistant (Phil. 2:20–22). Helps write Colossians (1:1), Philemon (1:1), Philippians (1:1).**
	63/64	33/34	Goes to Philippi for news? (Phil. 2:19, 23).
64 ? Released; further travels (1 Tim. 1:3, *etc.*).	64/65	34/35	**Left in Ephesus as Paul's delegate (1 Tim. 1:3).**
	65/66	35/36	**Receives 1 Timothy: instructions for dealing with crisis.**
Traditional date for re-arrest and martyrdom in Rome.	66/67	36/37	Probably still at Ephesus, **receives 2 Timothy: final instructions, including summons to Rome.**
	before 70	under 40	**Imprisoned and released: still travelling (Heb. 13:23).**
	95?	65	'Bishop' in Ephesus.
	96?	66	Receives Revelation (2:1–7).
	96/97	66/67	? Martyred in Ephesus in reign of Domitian/Nerva.

1
Child

Paul gradually came to, and opened his eyes. A circle of faces surrounded him. Was this heaven? He remembered praying, just before he fell unconscious, 'Lord Jesus, receive my spirit.'[1]

He moved his head to look round the faces. Aaargh, no – not heaven! His body ached and throbbed in every limb. The stones had pounded him almost to death. Yet here he still was . . . among enemies, or friends? Not daring to move his neck again, he steered his eyes round the faces, trying to make them out in the dark . . .

Suddenly he was wide awake. That pale, thin, anxious face furthest from him, peeping from behind the men . . . this was Lystra; that was Timothy. He'd baptized him last night. Timothy was safe!

He must get up. He moved and braced himself for the pain. The onlookers gasped. Barnabas rushed forward to hold him. Paul sat, then knelt, then stood. He could! The pain was all over his body, but standing wasn't impossible.

'No bones broken, I think,' he said, swaying slightly.

'Praise God!' breathed Barnabas. 'We thought you'd gone. The Jews left you for dead.'

Paul leant on him. 'We must leave,' he said. 'If we stay, the crowd will turn on the new believers for sheltering us.'

'But will you make it to Derbe? It's over fifty miles.'

'I can walk,' insisted Paul. He shuffled forward, slowly but firmly, to prove it.

'We can lend a cart,' said one of the men. 'I'll harness a donkey.'

'Not now.' A gentle but commanding lady moved forward and put her arm round Paul's shoulder. 'Dear Paul, you need rest. We'll nurse you.'

'No, Eunice. I must go, to spare you – and Timothy. The Lord Jesus has rescued me from the Jews once again. He has raised me up; *he* will heal me.'

'Just one more night. We'll be safe in the dark. Leave at first light if you must. But give us this last chance to serve you.'

Paul felt the ground swaying under him. He looked at her and

at the thin boy at her side. He saw the tears in Timothy's eyes.
   'All right,' he said. 'Just for tonight.'

The 'level 1' facts[2] recorded in the Bible about Timothy's early life
are simple and few. He lived in Lystra. He was born to a Jewish
mother and a Greek father. He wasn't circumcised at birth as a
Jewish boy; but he *was* taught the Old Testament Scriptures. And
he later became a Christian in the wake of his mother Eunice and
grandmother Lois.[3]

   But if we dig down to levels 2, 3 and 4 (deduction, inference and
hunch), we find out a great deal more.

Timothy's early life

Paul	*Date*	*Age*	*Event*
	30?	0	Born in Lystra **of mixed parents (Acts 16:1).**
34/35 Conversion (Acts 9).	30–45	1–15	**Childhood: mother Eunice and grandmother Lois teach Scriptures (2 Tim. 3:14–15).**
46–47 1st missionary journey (Acts 13 – 14).	46	16	Paul at Lystra: preaching, healing, stoned (Acts 14:6–23; 2 Tim. 3:11).
			? Lois, Eunice, Timothy converted (2 Tim. 1:5; 1 Tim. 1:2; 2 Tim. 1:2).
			? Timothy baptized (1 Tim. 6:12; 2 Tim. 1:6?).

A divided home?

Our starting-point in reconstructing Timothy's early home life is
the simple record, 'his mother was Jewish, but his father was a
Greek'.[4] Their marriage was racially and religiously mixed. This
was not as common as it has become in some circles today; but

neither was it unique. For Jews who lived outside Palestine, it was difficult to form Jewish ghettos. Marrying Gentiles became quite acceptable, especially in the more 'upwardly mobile' families. Eunice and Lois are Greek names, not Jewish; so Eunice may have been following her mother's example, even a family tradition, in marrying a Greek. She was clearly not the sort of Jew who cut herself off from the rest of society.

As for Timothy's father, there's no reason to doubt that he shared the religious tolerance of most 'Roman Greeks' at that time. He would smile indulgently at the native Lystrans adding the Greek Zeus and Hermes into their galaxy of local gods. He may even have attended sacrifices at Zeus's temple outside the town gate, but he wouldn't have believed in him. If his wife was a Jew and believed in her God, that was fine, so long as he wasn't expected to join in.

Branded

You might think so far that Timothy was born and bred in a tolerant religious atmosphere. But the full picture is less rosy. For one thing, the Jewish neighbours disapproved of Timothy. When he first introduces him to us, Luke says, 'all the Jews in those places knew that Timothy's father was Greek'; and they objected to it.[5] His Greek father disqualified him in their eyes from being an evangelist to Jews. He simply wasn't kosher. To strict, conservative Jews, marrying a Gentile was sin. Hadn't Moses forbidden it? Hadn't Ezra forced erring Jews to divorce their foreign wives and turn their children away? Hadn't the prophet Malachi voiced God's continuing displeasure at intermarriage?[6]

They would have made no allowance for Timothy as the 'innocent victim' of a mixed marriage. They had only two categories for the human race and he fitted neither. If he'd been an outright Gentile, at least they could have despised him as an inferior being. But he wasn't; he was the son of a Jewess. As the inheritance passes through the mother, he was a Jew. And yet he wasn't really that either, because he wasn't circumcised.

It's hard to overestimate the emotional importance of this badge of Jewish manhood.[7] 'Uncircumcised' was their stock insult for all Gentile men. It meant unclean, impure, unblessed. No doubt they said it of the boy Timothy, and blared it in his face. He wore the provocative foreskin of his father's race for all to see. There was no hiding it, even if his Jewish upbringing made him want to. In the Greek culture of those days, men's 'private parts' were much less private even than now. Swimming and athletics took place without benefit of trunks or running shorts; and the loos were a communal experience. They probably called him worse things than just 'uncircumcised'. He was, in all respects, deeply illegitimate. He must have been like the Samaritans of Jesus' day, all the more despised for being half-caste.

So much is virtually certain (level 2). Beyond this we may be right to infer (level 3) that he bore this stigma alone; there is no mention of any brother or sister, so he may well have been an only child. And probably he could share none of the burden with his dad, because dad had no Jewish blood or sympathies to understand what was so hurtful.

Instructed

The pain of disapproval might have been easier to live with if the family had all been wholeheartedly non-Jewish, if Eunice had turned her back on her heritage and thought it didn't matter. But she hadn't. She rigorously taught her child the Old Testament. Paul later reminded Timothy to

> continue in the truths that you were taught and firmly believe. You know who your teachers were, and you remember that ever since you were a child, you have known the Holy Scriptures . . .[8]

This wasn't just sentimental nostalgia for Eunice's national folklore. She instructed Timothy as her disciple (the sense of the word 'teacher'). He came to 'know' and love the Old Testament (the word 'know' means intimate friendship); he became firmly convinced of it. Custom required a faithful Jewish mother to teach her son the law from the age of five. But it seems that Eunice didn't wait so long. Timothy knew the Scriptures ever since he was a *baby*, as the word for 'child' means literally; it sometimes refers even to an unborn foetus. Tiny Tim sucked in Old Testament faith with his mother's milk.[9]

The home, without a Jewish father, may not have celebrated the Old Testament festivals. The town may have had too few Jews to build a synagogue with a sabbath school for Timothy to attend.

But verse by verse, law by law, story by story, he learnt to read and understand God's words. He was conscious of being a Jew born of a Jew, and he 'firmly believed' it was good. This will have made the taunts of 'Gentile dog' hurt all the more, but will have opened him at the same time to the Gentile sneers of 'Jewish pig'. Timothy can hardly have found his parents' mixed marriage a piece of progressive enlightenment; it looks as if it may have brought him constant grief.

Fought over

And still we haven't reached the worst of Timothy's troubles at home. Let's return to the big puzzle, the stumbling-block Luke stresses. *Why* hadn't he been circumcised? Eunice taught him the Jewish Bible and bathed him in an atmosphere of reverence and prayer from eight days old and before, but she didn't give him the Jewish 'birthmark' prescribed for that tender age.[10] She may have had blind spots in the Scriptures, as we all do; like many others she had soft-pedalled the command to marry another of God's people. But she could hardly have missed the command to circumcise boy-children, so deeply is it embedded in Jewish consciousness. As she clearly cared for her son's spiritual well-being, she can't have *deliberately* withheld his birthright. To her it would seem a form of abuse to leave a Jewish boy uncircumcised. Circumcision was the passport to acceptance by the local Jews,[11] yet through childhood Timothy's body remained defiantly Gentile.

It's hard to see any possible reason for this except that Timothy's father refused his permission. 'I don't mind what stories you tell him on your lap, but I'm not having him scarred for life.' To him, the abuse would have been in *letting* the boy be snipped. Probably the ceremony disgusted him; to the Greek pride in maleness and physical beauty, the Jewish mutilation made them look deformed. Perhaps he also mistakenly hoped to protect his son, to keep him religiously neutral, safe from the hatred Jews have so often attracted.[12]

The child of a mixed marriage sometimes proves a mixed blessing. A baby can trigger conflict because he draws out the differences between his parents. They both think he's important and worth fighting over. He grows up in an atmosphere of disagreement, instantly sensing it and sickening of it, however much the parents try to cover it up. In Timothy's case, circumcision can hardly have been the only battleground. The Bible stories may have seemed harmless enough at the start; but, as the boy became a firm believer in them, it would be a remarkable father who didn't feel threatened. That sort of religious commitment was so different from his own culture which made a virtue of being *non*-committal.

It would be a remarkable father too who could stop words of disappointment and sarcasm slipping out. He probably faced another irritant in his own home. It's almost certain from social custom, and from Paul's memory of the household,[13] that 'her mother came too'. Lois lived in; she shared Eunice's Jewish faith, and she would have shared in Timothy's upbringing. She may have put extra effort into the Bible teaching to make up to the lad for his lack of circumcision. To the father it would seem that his wife's family and faith were having a more than equal say in Timothy's education.

Aptly named

We may even see a relic of the parents' clash of values in Timothy's name. A Bible-teaching mother must have had moments of fancying an Old Testament hero's name for her boy – David perhaps, or Joseph or Daniel. It was not to be.[14]

But as Greek names went, 'Timothy' offered scope. To the Greeks it meant 'honoured by the gods' or 'revering the gods'; but her mind would substitute for 'the gods' the one true God of Israel. 'Timothy', valued by God and worshipping God in return – that was a worthy target for her prayers and her training of the child.

If he ever stopped to think about it, Timothy too could have found comfort in his name. However much or little his parents fought over him, he will have suffered damage. As he read the stories of Ishmael and Isaac, asking what 'circumcise' meant and why it hadn't been done to him, he would sense the disagreement. To know that your parents dispute even one point of what they want you to be breeds insecurity and confusion. 'Which of them is right? Which must I side with? Am I my mother's son, or my father's?' Timothy's eventual firm alignment with his mother's Scriptures and faith cannot have been quick or easy to reach. 'Why doesn't dad agree with this? Is it girlish to believe it? What will dad say and do if I go mum's way?' These doubts can eat away at the roots of your self-image. 'If mum and dad come to blows over me, I must be a problem, a nuisance, a threat to their relationship. They would find life easier if I'd never been born. Perhaps one day they'll get rid of me.'

Whether or not it dawned on him, his name carries the only full compensation for the failings of our human parents. In whatever ways *they* may have let us down or misled us, 'Timothy' means that *God* values us to the full; we find real security only in our heavenly Father. My parents divorced when I was a baby, and I never met my father till I was thirty-three. Many times during the years in between I ached to know him. I missed the guidance and help my friends found in their fathers. I felt as if I'd had an arm or leg amputated. So the discovery that God was my perfect, ever-present Father has often been my favourite part of the Christian Good News.

Orphaned

Another great thing about our Father God is that he can't die. By contrast, it seems probable that during Timothy's childhood his human father died. When Luke says, 'all the Jews . . . knew that Timothy's father *was* Greek', he implies that he was no longer alive at this stage of the story.[15] The fact that Paul never refers to Timothy's father suggests to me (level 3) that he never met him, and that he was already dead before Paul's first visit to Lystra (when Timothy was, by my count, sixteen). But even if I'm right, we've no idea how long he'd been dead, or whether Timothy lost him in early childhood or mid-teens. My hunch (level 4) is that it was fairly recent, for Timothy was still uncircumcised. Surely Eunice would have had him made a Jew in infancy if she'd become a free agent then; whereas in his teens Timothy would have felt a tug of loyalty in wanting to respect his father's wishes.

Whenever exactly it happened, it seems that Timothy lost his father in his formative years. This would bring another set of problems to a young kid. At just the stage when he needed a male adult to copy and to mould his own development, that 'role model' was taken away. And almost certainly his father died still unhappy with Timothy's choice of race and faith. The boy would have to cope with an unfinished relationship – no chance to make it up to dad or win him over. Such bereavement can take years to work through.

Scarred . . . but not discarded

If I'm right in deducing a home divided in this way, it helps to explain Timothy's sensitive, insecure nature, which dogs his story. I remember the flash of insight I had one day at school when I realized that three boys I liked because they were shy and quiet like me, had also all lost their fathers, like me.

There's nothing unique or even unusual about this experience. Sadly, thousands of children today live in bereaved or broken homes. But the wounds they carry are no less real for being widespread. If you're one of them, I hope you find comfort from this person in the New Testament who knew what it feels like. You can certainly take him as an inspiration. For even these early glimpses into Timothy's life simply highlight God's astonishing ability to turn bad beginnings to good. For this unlikely youngster was to become right-hand man to the most outstanding leader in Christian history, St Paul. His bumpy, bruising childhood was no bar to God using him later on. Forget any ideas that you're at a permanent disadvantage if you've had a difficult start in life.

This good news is not only for children, but also for Christian parents, especially mothers and grandmothers. There are many Christian wives today married to husbands who aren't Christians. Their position is often uneasy. As well as tensions in the relationship with their partner, they may find themselves in a spiritual tug o' war over the children. Boys naturally associate the macho qualities they want with their father's unbelief; his non-participation in bedside prayers or church services speaks a 'loud, silent' message. But girls are affected too; they can see the strains Christianity brings to their mother, and it's understandable if they want no part in it. It's easy in these circumstances for mum to give up hope.

Increasingly today there are also Christian one-parent families. Some of these parents are widows, as Eunice was; others are separated, divorced or unmarried. They too can come to feel that the responsibilities of a Christian parent are too much to cope with.

Eunice brings a flood of reassurance. With prayers and patient teaching she saw Timothy securely grounded in the Scriptures he firmly believed. Much in Timothy's early life was unsatisfactory and hurtful, but his mother's efforts to nurture him on God's book

26

were entirely wholesome. Paul's sketch of Timothy's upbringing ends with the comment, 'the Scriptures . . . are able to give you the wisdom that leads to salvation'.[16] And that was just the Old Testament, whose prophecies prepared Timothy for Christian faith to fulfil the Jewish. *We* have the huge advantage of the New Testament as well. There is supernatural potential in a home where a child learns the Bible in a climate of faith and prayer. It can outweigh the natural tendency for a boy to pick up his dad's lack of Christianity; and it can lay the foundation for a lifetime of Christian faith and ministry. Parents and home are the most powerful influences on us for the rest of our lives.

Even when the child shows no sign of responding, pray on with faith; the foundation is still there. Some become 'firsthand' Christians in their teens, like Timothy; others are adults before they return to the faith of their roots.

And where neither parent is a Christian, there's great scope for Christian grannies, aunties, godmothers (not to mention their male counterparts!), children's leaders at church and family friends. God can use their prayers, their loving friendship with the child, their presents of Bible stories, games and other pointers to Jesus, as a seedbed for the wisdom that leads to salvation.

One Bible teacher, inspired by this part of Timothy's story, ran a 'Lois and Eunice' course to excite and equip Christian mums and grandmas for their ministry to children. It's an idea worth a few offspring of its own.

A visiting preacher

We mustn't move too fast. At the point we've reached in the story, Timothy is not yet a Christian. To lead him through this vital next step, God uses a visiting preacher. So it is with some of today's Timothys. Of course, many children of Christian parents have no unbelieving stage; their faith develops steadily from earliest times, and this seems ideal. But others drift, needing a definite moment to make the Christian faith their own. Mum and gran may lay the foundation; the youngster may have attended junior church and read the Bible for years. But it often takes an evangelist from outside the family to put him or her in living touch with Jesus. It may indeed be a visiting preacher at a guest service, a youth leader at church or at a Christian holiday, a school friend or teacher, or a book that spells out the Good News. For Timothy it was the visiting preacher.

In AD 46 Paul came to Lystra.[17] The circumstances were hardly dignified. He and Barnabas had faced persecution in nearby Antioch; so they moved on to the next main town, Iconium.[18] Here they heard of a plot to stone them, and fled to Lystra. But the Jews from Iconium caught up with them and left Paul for dead.[19] Lystra was a smaller, more obscure place than Antioch or Iconium, not a strategic centre such as Paul usually worked in. He probably went there only as a temporary port in the storm, vainly hoping the Roman citizens would shelter him. If so, Timothy owed a lot to Paul's persecutors: thanks to them, he met Paul, became a Christian and later joined the mission team! God is well able to bring good out of bad human motives.

Space requires Luke to tell the story at great pace and record only the highlights. Read Acts quickly and you may get the impression that Paul's work in Lystra lasted only a couple of days.[20] But one old copy of the book adds two sentences: 'There they preached the Good News . . . And the whole populace was moved at the teaching. And Paul and Barnabas spent some time in Lystra.'[21] The other surviving manuscripts don't include this, but there's no reason to doubt it. Paul and Barnabas must have been there long enough to see a group of believers converted and established as a church.[22]

Evangelized

How can we catch an echo of this teaching that so moved the people, and which Timothy must have heard? Luke doesn't record what Paul preached in Lystra.[23] But we probably get the general flavour from his earlier speech in Antioch;[24] he presumably said much the same in each town, but Luke hasn't the space to repeat it. After an outline of Old Testament history, Paul announces Jesus as the promised Messiah; he tells of his crucifixion, resurrection and appearances to the apostles; he then quotes Old Testament prophecy to justify his concluding appeal: 'We want you to know, my fellow-Israelites, that it is through Jesus that the message about forgiveness of sins is preached to you; and that everyone who believes in him is set free from all the sins from which the Law of Moses could not set you free. Take care, then, so that what the prophets said may not happen to you . . .'

Paul himself also seems to have left us a hint of this stirring preaching in his letter to the Galatians.[25] He reminds his hearers: 'Before your very eyes you had a clear description of the death of Jesus Christ on the cross!'[26] The Greek for 'clear description' is very vivid. It means a large placard or poster on a bill-board. In modern Greece the roads are lined with eye-catching advertisements on hoardings; you can't miss them. Paul's preaching was like that; he painted Jesus' death in words that were public, pictorial, strident and challenging. He spoke, literally, of Jesus 'having been crucified' – the Greek means a once-for-all event in the past with benefits continuing into the present. This view of Jesus' death is the heart of the Christian Good News; the way Paul preached it made Timothy sit up and take notice.

Converted

As Paul goes on to say in Galatians, his preaching won converts: 'You began. You received God's Spirit.'[27] Among them, it seems, were Lois and Eunice: 'I remember the sincere faith you have, the kind of faith that your grandmother Lois and your mother Eunice also had.'[28] There is a word here that GNB virtually smothers. Paul says that sincere faith 'first' lived in Lois and Eunice, before it came to Timothy. It's possible they were Christians before Paul came to Lystra, and that someone from Lystra was in Jerusalem on the day of Pentecost and went back home to start a church. But Luke gives the clear impression that Paul and Barnabas were taking the Good News where it had never been before. So it seems more probable that Lois and Eunice became Christians through Paul's graphic preaching in Lystra.[29] But they did so 'first', before Timothy.

A half-Gentile himself, Timothy must have thrilled as Paul and Barnabas offered the Good News to Gentile as well as Jew.[30] And as a half-Jew in hostile surroundings, he will have tingled to hear of God at work again among his chosen people.[31] Timothy surely also warmed to the idea of Jesus fulfilling the Scriptures he so firmly believed.[32] To hear that Jesus perfectly obeyed God's law on our behalf, and then died under God's curse so that the law might no longer have any claim on us,[33] must have offered unspeakable comfort to a sensitive conscience. But he took longer to decide than his mother and grandmother. This is hardly surprising in an adolescent, bruised and unsure of himself. He was well aware that many Jews disagreed with Paul profoundly. And he could imagine the words of scorn his father would have poured on it all. He needed to make up his mind for himself. His faith, if and when he came to it, would be 'sincere', the real thing – his own, not his mother's.

We can imagine the heartfelt prayers of Lois and Eunice, and the close interest Paul himself took as he visited the household of his new Christian sisters. Isn't it likely he would have worked through the ancient prophecies with Timothy as he did with so many others?[34] When at last Timothy became a Christian, it was certainly (level 1) as a result of what he'd heard from Paul, who repeatedly calls him 'my son', 'my true son in the faith' – his way of describing those he brought to faith himself.[35] Timothy may have come to faith alone as he thought Paul's words over; but this stress on father and son is more meaningful (level 3) if Timothy actually took the great step out of the Old Testament into the New in Paul's presence.

Baptized

Again, Timothy's conversion may have happened privately with Paul. But I get a 'level 4' hunch that it was more public than that, from Paul's emphasis on Timothy's baptism.[36] In apostolic days baptism happened as soon as anyone acknowledged Jesus as Lord;[37] in Timothy's case both may well have been in the same meeting.

There is a verse in Paul's first letter to Timothy which, virtually all scholars agree, looks back to this occasion. Its first two phrases – 'run . . . the race . . . and win' – were perhaps Paul's baptism sermon to Timothy at the time.

> Run your best in the race of faith, and win eternal life
> for yourself; for it was to this life that God called you
> when you firmly professed your faith before many
> witnesses.[38]

As Paul expresses it, God's call to eternal life and Timothy's 'firm profession' were simultaneous. This is very apt, because baptism pictures the double fact that, first, God gives us a completely new start in life, and, secondly, our part is simply to say yes to it. After his delay for thought and prayer, Timothy was now as firmly convinced of Jesus as he was of the Scriptures. He could hear Jesus calling him; he was ready to follow and to 'profess' it.

This meant saying aloud the simple creed, 'Jesus is Lord.'[39] Timothy said it loud and strong, for it was 'before many witnesses'. Baptisms did not have to be public in those early days,[40] but this one was. Lois and Eunice were presumably there, and Barnabas, and perhaps all the other new Christians, at one of the first meetings of the Lystra church. But there were *many* witnesses, so it could have been a more public gathering still. Paul was perhaps placarding Jesus' cross to a mixed audience of Jews and Gentiles, Greeks and Anatolians. And that public commitment to Jesus helped Timothy to stay true to him in the months ahead. Paul was still appealing to it twenty years later in 1 Timothy.

Far fewer scholars agree that he is making the same appeal in 2 Timothy: 'I remind you to keep alive the gift that God gave you when I laid my hands on you.'[41] Most assume he is referring to Timothy's later commissioning to special ministry.[42] But I hear these words as another memory of Timothy's baptism. The verse before is, 'I remember the sincere faith you have, the kind Lois and Eunice had first'; we have already seen that it looks back to Timothy's conversion. And the verse after talks of 'the Spirit that God has given us', in a way that also seems to refer to God's gift to us when we first became Christians.[43]

God gave this gift 'when I laid my hands on you'. Baptism was followed at least sometimes by a 'hands-on' prayer that the Holy Spirit would fill the life of the newly baptized.[44] If this was indeed the occasion, Paul reached out to touch Timothy's head and asked the Holy Spirit to ensure his survival and healthy growth as a Christian. It suggests he baptized Timothy himself, although this was not his usual practice.[45] If so, it adds to our sense of a special closeness between Paul and Timothy from the very start.

Returning to what is certain, Timothy has been baptized, even though he wasn't circumcised. He has become a true Christian, even if he was never fully a Jew. It was a night for celebration and champagne. If you are a Christian, that's the best thing that will ever happen to you. If, like Timothy, you started your Christian journey in your teens, you're one of a large, happy band. Teens are the time for sorting out which way you're going to head your life. What better way could there possibly be than Jesus' way?

Key Bible passages: 2 Timothy 1:5–7; 3:14–15; Acts 14:6–20; Galatians 3:1–3.

Reflect

1. Apart from Jesus, Timothy is the only New Testament character whose childhood we know anything about. Do you think there is a reason for this? If so, what might it be?[46]

2. We all bear scars, or at least inhibitions, from our early life and upbringing. What are you aware of in your own case? How far has God helped you to come to terms with them and overcome them? If you would find it helpful to talk to someone else about them, who might be suitable?

3. Is there a 'Timothy' in your life – a child you pray for and care about? What could you do to help him or her to know the Scriptures and come to believe them?

Share

1. How did Christian faith come alive for you? What aspect of the Good News was especially attractive to you? Who do you look on as spiritual 'parents' or 'midwives' who helped your faith to develop in the early stages? Is there something you could do to encourage them, or honour their memory?

2. Should Christian families need a 'visiting preacher' (or other outside agency) to bring the children to faith? What advice would you give Christian parents (especially lone Christian parents) for bringing children up as Christians?

3. Is it more 'manly' *not* to be a Christian? Why (not)? What can we do – especially for families where only the wife and mother is a Christian – to counter the widespread view that Christian males are 'wet'?

2
Youth

Timothy sat miserably in the corner. His stomach churned with worry and fear. Everything seemed to have gone wrong. Just a few months ago the church had been a happy, united family. But since the Pharisees had arrived from Jerusalem, it was all quarrelling. Christians who used to want to take the love and life of Jesus into every household in Lystra were now fighting each other.

He'd prayed to Jesus to sort things out. But now it looked like happening, he dreaded it. He hated arguments and voices raised in anger. The elders had called a meeting of the whole church for an important announcement. As always it was in his home, because Eunice's house was one of the biggest in town, the only one large enough to take them all.

'At least it's only us and not the Jerusalem Pharisees,' he thought as he looked round the room. He whispered his prayer once again that the elders wouldn't insist on all the things the Pharisees were teaching. Try as he might, he couldn't bring himself to feel happy about them. 'Surely Paul and Barnabas never said I would have to be circumcised.'

The elders arrived together. With them was Gaius, an elder from Derbe. He carried a large scroll. They spoke to Eunice and Lois, and looked anxiously round. One of the elders caught Timothy's eye and instantly turned back to his mother.

'Not being circumcised *in public*, please, Lord,' Timothy breathed.

They called for quiet.

'Brothers and sisters, you know what we are meeting about. But we've had to change our plan. Gaius has brought a letter from Paul.'

Timothy felt a pang in his chest – half excitement, half shame. So did Paul know what was going on? What would he say about it?

'We must hear what Paul has to tell us. It's long! We'd like Timothy to read it to us. He reads so well.'

Timothy wished he could shrink through the wall. He tried to make an excuse, but no voice would come. Gaius forced a smile and handed him the scroll.

Timothy's hands shook as he felt every eye fastened on him. A letter from Paul! He held it tight. He read a little shakily through the greeting, and then stopped as he saw what came next.

> I am surprised at you! In no time at all you are deserting the one who called you by the grace of Christ, and are accepting another gospel.

'Read on, Timothy,' said one of the elders.
'But you're not going to like it.'
'Never mind. We must all hear it.'

> Actually, there is no 'other gospel', but I say this because there are some people who are upsetting you and trying to change the gospel of Christ.

Timothy found his voice coming firmer and stronger. A wave of relief washed through him. Paul was saying the Pharisees were wrong.

> But even if we or an angel from heaven should preach to you a gospel that is different from the one we preached to you, may he be condemned to hell!

There was a gasp of disbelief.

> We have said it before, and now I say it again: if anyone preaches to you a gospel that is different from the one you accepted, may he be condemned to hell![1]

Around the room people stared in dismay. Even Timothy was trembling at the severity of Paul's anger. But he thrilled to it too. It was clearing the muddle and confusion in his mind.

> You foolish Galatians! Who put a spell on you? . . . You began by God's Spirit; do you now want to finish by your own power? Did all your experience mean nothing at all?[2]

Timothy found his heart and mind racing. With half his brain he read Paul's words, caught up in the detailed argument; it explained why the Jerusalem Pharisees were at odds with the Christianity Paul and Barnabas had brought to Galatia. But he still had another half of his mind free to think back to all that had happened since that night when faith first took hold of him.

> Did all your experience mean nothing at all? Surely it meant something!

Yes, yes, yes. It certainly had.

In this chapter we watch Timothy grow, I believe, from the age of sixteen to eighteen. To judge from the fact that 'all the believers in Lystra [his home town] and Iconium [some 35 miles away] spoke well of' him,[3] he was a model Christian adolescent. Imagine a London student still in his teens spreading his reputation as far as Reading. Today's young people can learn a lot from Timothy. And Paul, who in turn sets a model of caring for young Christians, has much to teach today's youth leaders. I know of a church which calls its teens and twenties club 'Timpany – the *Tim*othy com*pany*. This chapter focuses on the slice of Timothy's life which makes him a patron saint of Christian youth work.

Paul's return visit, AD 46/47

In chapter 1 we left Paul limping out of Lystra along the road to Derbe. After such a battering, we might expect him to creep quietly back to base. The quick, direct route was eastwards from Derbe. But he turned west, back to Lystra, and in due course to Iconium and Antioch. He and Barnabas cared enough for their converts to revisit them, at some risk and cost to themselves. Their motive was to strengthen Timothy and the other new believers.[4]

All new Christians need personal 'after-care'. Without it they're not likely to survive as Christians. One powerful form of it is continuing friendship with the person who first helped us to follow Jesus. When she or he is a travelling evangelist, far from home, this calls for discipline and self-sacrifice. But it's worth it. I became a Christian through hero-worship. As a child I had idolized David Sheppard, the England Test cricket captain (now a

Paul	Date	Age	Event
	46–48	16–18	**Grows as Christian, respected in area (Acts 16:2).**
? Writes Galatians. Jerusalem Council (Acts 15).	48	18	Timothy and Lystra church among recipients of Galatians.
48–51, 2nd missionary journey (Acts 15:40 – 18:22).			**Paul at Lystra: circumcises Timothy (Acts 16:3);** commissions him to join team (1 Tim. 1:18; 4:14?).

Church of England bishop). On my first weekend away at college, I had the chance to hear him explain why he'd become a Christian and how I could do the same. I think if he'd told me to leapfrog over the people in front of me, I would have given it a try. When he invited us to ask Christ into our lives to take over as King, wild horses couldn't stop me. I was sincere and genuine; but I was swept along by my feelings for the speaker. Half of me knew that in the cold reality of tomorrow morning I would probably kick myself for a fool. But David Sheppard didn't go home that night, even though his wife was undergoing surgery for cancer. He asked to meet me next day, and gave me advice on how to keep going as a Christian. Just when I was vulnerable, he supported me. He wrote to me later that week; and after a few months he came to the Christian holiday where I was a student helper and invited me to visit his home. We're still in touch after thirty years. This one-to-one friendship with an older Christian would help any new one hang on and grow stronger through the first, rocky weeks and months of discipleship.

A faith to remain true to

Paul and Barnabas did more than just befriend the Lystran Christians. 'They strengthened the believers and encouraged them to remain true to the faith.'[5] 'Encouraged' is too genteel a translation. Luke's word means that they *urged* Timothy and the others to stay true to the faith. We can't drift in and out of

Christianity when we feel like it; we commit ourselves to Jesus for life.

Young people urgently need this teaching. In our fast-moving world, Christianity can seem at first a mere flavour of the month. Last week it was New Age; next week it may be anarchy. The idea that once we're Christians, we're Christians *for ever* is startling, even shocking. It needs driving home. When someone I know becomes a Christian, I say to him or her, 'Just two words of advice: keep going.' And each time I see that person, I repeat it! It's easy enough to bellow, 'I will sing your praises for evermore' in a hyped-up youth meeting, but far harder to stay true to Jesus when you see that Christians have no 'street cred' with your friends at school.[6] Perseverance needs a lot of energetic encouraging. I can still hear one of my first Christian teachers intoning, 'Never, never, never give up.' He said it ever so slowly and emphatically. We loved doing impressions of him. But of course he had the last laugh. The lesson stuck; and we stuck to it. And his words still echo in my head.

Elders to learn from

Timothy was another 'sticker'; he stayed true to the faith. What was the secret in his case? Paul and Barnabas couldn't remain at Lystra for ever, so their next step there, and later in other churches, was to appoint elders to carry on the pastoral care after they left.[7]

The name 'elder' implies not so much old age as long experience and the wisdom it brings. But in Lystra they were almost certainly all recent converts, only a few months old as Christians. Paul and Barnabas had to look for other signs of emerging and potential 'elder-ship'. One is implied in Luke's words: Paul and Barnabas 'commended them to the Lord, *in whom they had put their trust*'. They had genuine faith and looked likely to remain true to it. On top of this, virtually all the elders we meet in the New Testament belonged, as did Timothy himself, to the educated Greek or Jewish population. They were the 'natural leaders', not the native Anatolians, condemned in that society to a lower position. The need for 'educated elders' lies in the one *ability* (as opposed to moral qualities) that Paul came to require of elders: 'able to teach'.[8] It was essential for at least some of the elders to take over the preaching and teaching.[9] For this is how we enable the rest of the church to understand the faith and remain true to it. That is what elders are for.

Every church needs elders. And so does a young people's fellowship or student Christian Union. They must have suitable leaders and teachers. People who will help them learn from the Bible. People who set a mature example of Christian living. People who will not mislead them or abuse their trust and friendship.[10]

We have no idea who the Lystran elders were. But they did a good job with young Timothy. We get a glimpse of their work from Paul's first letter to him; he reminds Timothy to feed himself spiritually 'on the words of faith and of the true teaching *which you have followed*'.[11] The word 'followed' suggests a long process going right back to these earliest years of discipleship, a settled habit developed from the start. And the basic meaning of the word is 'to accompany or live with'; to follow faithfully as a rule of life what you have grasped and understood in your mind. There were certain 'words of faith' Timothy heard and read and made his own; there was a diet of 'true teaching' which he steadily absorbed and based his life on. These words and teaching he heard from the elders. Before that, he and they learnt them from Paul. The words were the beginnings of the New Testament, an outline of the Good News as Paul taught it.

So Paul and the Lystran elders joined Eunice and Lois in the young Timothy's succession of Scripture teachers.[12] Paul refers to them all immediately before his famous 'guarantee' of the Bible in 2 Timothy.

> All Scripture is inspired by God and is useful for teaching the truth, rebuking error, correcting faults, and giving instruction for right living.[13]

You can just make out a faded photo of Timothy, the model Christian teenager, behind the verse.[14] He's learning the Bible from his teachers; he drinks it all in. It's not just ancient history, but alive, *inspired*, breathing with God's vitality, speaking with God's voice. To his intense excitement, it *teaches truth*: it answers his questions and doubts, and gives him a framework to build his life on. It *rebukes error*, sorts out his confusion and muddle-headedness as it shows so much of what 'everybody' says and thinks to be a load of old bull. It stabs his conscience and points out his weaknesses as it *corrects his faults*. Its patient *instruction for right living* unfolds a beautiful ideal for the rest of his life, which stirs his heart and hooks his ambition.

Can anything else help today's Christian teenagers as the Bible can? It is even more important than a good school or job, close friends and wide interests. Help young people to catch a vision of this unique gift from God – a book not to scorn or dispute, but to love and obey – and you've surely given them the best 'coming of age' present imaginable. Some church elders I know of took 2 Timothy 3:14–17 as the 'mission statement' for their entire children's and youth department:

> Continue in the truths that you were taught and firmly believe . . . you remember that ever since you were a child, you have known the Holy Scriptures . . . inspired by God . . . so that the person who serves God may be fully qualified and equipped . . .

Can you think of a better one?

Troubles to pass through

Paul and Barnabas didn't have time for extended Bible teaching. They focused on one stark theme: 'We must pass through many troubles to enter the Kingdom of God.'[15] That was their message to Timothy and the other new Christians. According to Luke, this is *how* they encouraged the believers to stand firm! 'Remain true, folks. It's one trouble after another from now on. Christian discipleship is non-stop pressure till you get to heaven.' No wonder they had to urge and exhort![16]

For Timothy and the others at Lystra, trouble was no vague, distant threat. They knew exactly what Paul meant, for they'd seen it happen to him. He'd been battered to the doors of death.[17] On Timothy's sensitive nature these buffetings made a big impression, and must have contributed to his deep attachment to Paul. 'You know all that happened to me in . . . Lystra,' Paul reminded him. 'You have followed . . . my endurance, my persecutions and my sufferings.'[18] That same word 'followed' again: Paul means that Timothy made a close personal study of it, took in all that it meant, and resolutely adopted it as his lifestyle too. His discipleship was rooted in the understanding that 'everyone who wants to live a godly life in union with Christ Jesus will be persecuted'.[19]

To our modern western minds, especially to teenagers, this is a real shock. It's so unpopular that we shut our minds to it. When trouble comes, we tend either to give Christianity up 'because it doesn't work', or to blame God for letting us down. But the apostles taught that we *must* pass through troubles; they are God's path for us. When we run into opposition or discouragement, it shows that Christianity *does* work. God is simply proving true to his word.

I wonder how many of our 'Now you've become a Christian' booklets and chats for teenagers reflect this emphasis. We easily give the opposite impression. In an attempt to woo them from the world's charms, we stress all the benefits of Christianity. We're not exactly lying; but we're not giving the whole truth. Wouldn't we have much gutsier Christians – tougher, more genuine and more likely to last the course – if we put it to them straight? 'Christians live in a world hostile to God. If you become one, you're in for a fight.' Of course, few young people will be stoned for their faith as Paul was;[20] the world's hate is usually much less physical. The commonest form is for your friends and family to laugh at you; they think you're stupid. And that hurts. To the thin-skinned, uncertain person we all are in our teens, it hurts worse than anything. The old jingle, 'Sticks and stones may break my bones, but words can never harm me', is profoundly untrue. A cutting word, or even the unspoken sneer, can sting worse than any lash. A hail of sticks and stones might seem glamorous or heroic in comparison.

But there's a double consolation. Paul and Timothy learnt it together. Some years later they wrote: 'we show that we are God's servants by patiently enduring troubles, hardships, and difficulties'.[21] The sure sign that we're true Christians is not a little cross round our neck or a fish-badge in our lapel, but hardship – a rough deal of one kind or another. Persecution and other difficulties show that we're the real thing. The second comfort is that Jesus understands from his own experience. He's been through it before; he'll now come through it with us.[22] As Paul and Timothy were to put it, 'Just as we have a share in Christ's many sufferings, so also through Christ we share in God's great help.'[23]

The Letter to the Galatians, AD 48[24]

Eighteen months had passed. Timothy was, on my reconstruction, just eighteen. And there was trouble in the Galatian churches. A group of Bible teachers from Jerusalem descended on them. They were part of a 'traditionalist' faction in the church there, made up of former Pharisees.[25] They believed that Jesus' resurrection showed him to be the Messiah; but otherwise they had made no break from Judaism. They were still completely Jewish in their attitudes. They saw the Gentile Christians as new Jews to replace those who had not recognized Jesus as Messiah. 'The Gentiles must be circumcised and told to obey the Law of Moses.'[26] Paul didn't regard these Pharisees as true Christians, and he resisted them.[27] They must have had a highly persuasive ringleader, for Paul speaks of him 'putting a spell' on the Galatian Christians.[28] They were on the verge of giving in to his teaching; but they hadn't actually undergone that circumcision ritual.[29] This was the moment when Paul sent his white-hot letter to stop the rot.

His outbursts of disappointment at the Galatians – 'I am surprised at you!' 'How can you be so foolish!'[30] – must have stung Timothy. And he was surely shocked by the violence of Paul's indignation at the circumcisers, even if it's tongue-in-cheek: 'I wish that the people who are upsetting you would go all the way; let them go on and castrate themselves!'[31] Timothy could now guess what Paul had been like in the days when he tortured Christians.[32]

But he also heard the anguished tones of a parent's love. 'My dear children! Once again, just like a mother in childbirth, I feel the same kind of pain for you until Christ's nature is formed in you.'[33] Paul compares his anxiety over these immature, unreliable Christians to the pains of labour in an age before anaesthetics. And although all the converts in the four or more Galatian churches were Paul's 'dear children', Timothy would know that, as a specially loved son,[34] he was directly in Paul's mind.

Indeed, there may have been moments when Timothy wondered with a gasp if Paul was singling him out for special mention. Twice in the letter, Paul narrows his focus from all the brothers and sisters down to one man in particular. Timothy must have heard this as Paul speaking personally to him, whether intentionally or not.

> But when the right time finally came, God sent his own Son . . . to redeem those who were under the Law, so that we might become God's sons.
>
> To show that you are his sons, God sent the Spirit of his Son into our hearts, the Spirit who cries out, 'Father, my Father.' So then, *you are no longer a slave but a son. And since you are a son*, God will give you all that he has for his sons.[35]

Few commentators even mention this sudden switch from plural to singular.[36] But there's a message in it especially helpful for Timothy. 'No longer a slave but a son.' As he struggled with the Pharisees' teaching, this was just the reassurance he needed: no slave but God's *son*! There was nothing inferior or incomplete or unliberated about the Christianity he'd embraced from the first. So why go back to being a Jew? He wouldn't and he didn't. We know he didn't, for he was still uncircumcised at Paul's next visit.

There is another strange, disconnected verse.

> The man who is being taught the Christian message should share all the good things he has with his teacher.[37]

'Does he mean any of us learners in particular?' Timothy must have wondered. 'Perhaps he means me.' Timothy was learning the Christian message from the elders and the Scriptures, but his original and closest teacher had been Paul himself. He can't have failed to pause and ponder what 'good things' he could share with Paul. Perhaps all he could offer for now was his loyalty, his determination to stay true to the message Paul had taught, and so to resist the Jerusalem Pharisees. But if ever Paul asked for more – some practical way of helping him – he would love to give it. He can hardly have realized that within a few months Paul would ask him to share everything he had.

The Galatian letter, a mixture of slaps and hugs, must have moved Timothy deeply. It can stir and enlighten us too. It is countering false teaching. Probably not too many Christian males today are under pressure to have their foreskins chopped off! But through the letter Paul helps us to see what *any* false teaching sounds or 'smells' like, and how to build defences against it. All

Christians are exposed to false teaching; it's part of the devil's strategy, as 'the father of all lies' who tries to keep our minds in the dark.[38] Often it is spread by roving teachers (like the Jerusalem Pharisees) or writers who haven't fully grasped the message of the New Testament. New Christians and young ones are especially vulnerable. Student Christian Unions, for example, often have less experience, and so less resistance, than the average church.

Putting it simply, all false teaching results in one (or both) of two opposite errors. We meet Paul fighting both in Galatians.

The first is: *do more than God asks.* Earn bonus points by being a super-Christian. Go over the top. This is sometimes called 'extremism' or 'fanaticism'. It clearly appeals to human pride.

In Galatia it took the form of being Jews as well as Christians, to get into God's extra-specially good books. Today there are other attempts to put some Christians on a pedestal above the rest of us. In some sections of the church, 'ordained ministers' and 'religious' nuns and monks are seen as more fully committed than the normal run of Christians. Others label their heroes 'Spirit-filled' or 'anointed', as if the Holy Spirit left the rest of us empty or untouched. But in fact all Christians are simply sinners who have received God's forgiveness. All God asks of us is humble trust, which leads on to daily obedience.

The second error is: *do less than God asks.* Lapse into a sub-Christian lifestyle. There's no need to be any different from those who aren't Christians. This is sometimes known as 'permissiveness', though another name might be laziness. It clearly appeals to human weakness.

Paul had to warn the Galatians against this low level of living because they were obviously giving in to it.

> What human nature does is quite plain. It shows itself in immoral, filthy and indecent actions; in worship of idols and witchcraft. People become enemies and they fight; they become jealous, angry and ambitious. They separate into parties and groups; they are envious, get drunk, have orgies, and do other things like these. *I warn you now as I have before:* those who do these things will not possess the Kingdom of God . . . *We must not* be proud or irritate one another or be jealous of one another.[39]

43

This sort of behaviour is more common among adolescent Christian groups today than we would like to think. Some church youth groups are just as inward-looking and unwelcoming, just as competitive and materialistic, as any other gathering of teenagers in the town. The only difference is, they're a lot less committed and interesting. They simply haven't taken in God's call to a radically different, Christlike way of life, bearing each other's burdens and sharing each other's blessings;[40] or, if they have, they're saying no to the call. This may not come about through actively false teaching; it could develop through a lack of true teaching, or an unwillingness to obey it.

For the answer to all these ills is a bracing dose of God's truth. That's what Paul sent the Galatians through this letter. And as far as we can tell, it did the job. When Paul returned to the Galatian churches a few months later, there is no hint that they were still under the false teachers' spell.[41]

Paul's second missionary journey, AD 48

Matters came to a head later that year. Paul and Barnabas went to Jerusalem for a major conference. The issue was: could Gentiles become Christians without becoming Jews first? And the answer was: yes! Paul and Barnabas won the day.[42] They returned home with a letter from the Jerusalem apostles and elders disowning the circumcisers.[43]

Several weeks passed; perhaps months. Then Paul felt his missionary instincts urging him out again. He put it to Barnabas that they should revisit the churches they'd planted, to strengthen them and pass on the Jerusalem lettter.[44] The mission almost sank before it set sail. Paul and Barnabas had a row about Mark, Barnabas' cousin, who had deserted them early in the first missionary journey.[45] The argument was so sharp that it split the earlier mission team and field into two. For the second journey, Barnabas and Mark returned to Cyprus; Paul went overland to Galatia.

He had to build a new team. The size and balance of the first-journey team – two more experienced men and one junior apprentice – had apparently worked well; presumably that is part of why he resented its breakup. So for the second journey he now chose a seasoned colleague to replace Barnabas – Silas.[46] But this still left a vacancy for a young trainee, such as Timothy.

Considered

We can't be sure whether Paul set off from Antioch looking for a replacement for Mark, and whether he already had Timothy in mind. All we do know is that Luke sums up the whole Galatian visit in terms of (a) satisfactory progress in general: 'So the churches were made stronger in the faith and grew in numbers every day';[47] and (b) Timothy in particular:

> Paul travelled on to Derbe and Lystra, where a Christian named Timothy lived . . . All the believers . . . spoke well of Timothy. Paul wanted to take Timothy along with him . . .[48]

Timothy is the one significant new development in the whole of Derbe, Lystra, Iconium and Pisidian Antioch.

Indeed, Luke starts the first sentence about Timothy with the Greek word *idou*, 'Look! Lo and behold!' He took the trouble to write it, so it must be more than just an unnecessary word to ignore, as most of the English translations do. But what exactly does it suggest? Is it surprise? Paul was quite resigned to a double act with Silas, when, would you believe it, Timothy appeared out of nowhere and blazed his way into the team! Or does the *idou* speak of hope fulfilled? Paul sped to Lystra praying that Timothy would be ready to step into Mark's shoes, and – yes, yes, here he is, raring to go!

My hunch is this second option. Travelling rabbis tended to have younger disciples with them, undergoing training. Mark had presumably been useful to Paul and Barnabas while with them; Paul's objection was not to bad performance in harness, but to deserting it. He was less likely to say, 'Blow these young people; you can't trust any of them', than to find one he *could* trust.

And if he reflected on Mark's job, he could only be aware that Timothy looked hopeful. Luke describes Mark's role in the first journey as 'to help in the work'.[49] Some of this would have been practical and administrative: making travel arrangements, looking after the money, buying food and medicine, finding accommodation. Timothy came from a business family; he could handle all that OK.[50] But Mark would also have had a hand in preaching the gospel. At the time Luke wrote, his word 'help' had a technical sense of 'document handler'. This could cover Mark's secretarial duties; but it's likely he already had a collection of stories of Jesus' ministry (the beginnings of his gospel), which he read aloud to assist Paul's preaching. Here again, Timothy, to judge from his later ministry of public reading of the Scriptures, preaching and teaching,[51] had natural ability. He was intelligent and well educated; his knowledge and love of the Bible were lifelong. He would be well able to instruct new converts in the faith, especially those of his own age. And Timothy had one big advantage over Mark in Paul's eyes: he was one of Paul's own converts and therefore more likely to stay with him.[52]

The first aim of the journey was to revisit the Galatian churches, where Timothy had the further benefit of being a well-known local lad. But Paul was also looking further afield, wanting to break fresh ground as he had in the first journey[53] – to the Jews first, then on to the Gentiles. Paul's vision of a church uniting Jews and Gentiles was utterly revolutionary. But in Timothy he found someone uniquely suited to it. He virtually embodied Paul's mission. He was not just, like Paul, a Jew brought up in the Greek culture, who then became a Christian. He was genuinely half and half, a Jew through his mother and a Greek through his father. The tensions of his multiracial upbringing now turned into a positive asset for Jesus. The boy they called a misfit proved the perfect fit to assist the Jewish Paul's calling to evangelize foreign Gentiles.[54] Finding out what God wants us to do often makes sense of the background he gave us.

Commended

Whether or not Timothy was in Paul's mind before he reached Lystra, there was no ignoring him once there. 'All the believers in Lystra and Iconium spoke well of Timothy.'[55]

Luke's words mean they went on and on giving him a good report. Timothy was on everyone's lips.[56] He was among Lystra's best. This is how Christian ministers and missionaries should emerge – through good reputation and high praise from those who know them.

Luke doesn't tell us exactly what they were saying. But we can work some of it out at levels 2 and 3. If other believers were enthusing about him, he must have stood out as an exceptional Christian. As he'd been one for only about two years, he must have matured quickly. His faith, understanding and Christlikeness were all growing and deepening. If *all* spoke well of him, he can't have had any major defects or eccentricities. People liked him and valued the part he played in the fellowship. But more than this: he must have done something special to earn such a good reputation. Two possibilities spring to mind. Had he reacted noticeably well to Paul's Galatian letter, by standing out against the heretics when others were wavering? And as Iconium believers joined in giving Timothy this good reference, they must have seen him in action there. Had he taken part in some mission to, with, or from Iconium? If so, the elders had obviously recognized Timothy's potential and given him the chance to prove himself.[57]

A personnel officer studied Timothy and said he would probably not seem strong or forceful enough to get through a modern missionary agency's selection panel. But that wasn't the chief issue that concerned Paul. He more likely asked whether Timothy would make the same mistakes as Mark.[58] Will Timothy give up after a few weeks? Here the answer was surely encouraging. 'No, he is showing every sign of staying true to the faith and sticking to a task.' How dependent is he on mum? 'Deeply attached to her, of course, but he's already stayed away from home in Iconium.' Will he clash with the team's new move to preach the Good News to Gentiles? 'Absolutely not; Timothy is a product of the Gentile mission himself,[59] and he didn't give in to the circumcisers' teachings. We warmly endorse this candidate as a suitable assistant for your team.'

Timothy's good report challenges today's church about all our young people. People recommended Timothy while still very young; on my reckoning he was only eighteen, but on anybody's he could be little over twenty-one. Which of your church's eighteen-year-olds would Paul want to take on a missionary journey? If you're in that age-bracket yourself, how about you? My guess is, we simply don't know, because we don't usually trust teenagers in our churches enough to give them responsibility. Timothy gained his glowing reputation because he had the chance to show he was a genuine Christian and an active church member. Our youth fellowships shouldn't be hived off into their own separate corner, sitting around and being entertained. Their members should be up and doing, alongside the adults – not only in running activities for children or playing music, but in home groups, prayer groups, outreach teams.[60] If you're a teenager with little opportunity to play a part in your church's life, don't give up and go away. Hang on in there and demand (politely!) your rights as a member of the body of Christ.

Chosen

After thought and consultation, Paul made up his mind. He 'wanted to take Timothy along with him'.[61] The word 'wanted' mostly means a reasoned decision; but it also contains a flavour of liking and preferring. Timothy was, after all, one of Paul's own sons in the faith, one who had done him proud. After the bust-up with Barnabas and Mark, Timothy was an emotional investment. 'This one belongs to me, as Mark did to Barnabas. *Timothy* won't let me down.'

Timothy must have known of this pressure on him to come good. He had also known all along that Paul's missionary lifestyle meant suffering – discomfort at the least, probably danger as well. He would be awed and nervous when Paul asked him to join the team. Yet he must also have been flattered and thrilled that Paul – Paul! – wanted him. He would be over the moon.

Here is Timothy, aged eighteen or so, chosen to join the apostolic mission team, partly as a roadie but also as a fledgling evangelist. After a short, local mission to the neighbouring towns, it was to be an expedition into other countries, even another continent, where no-one had even heard of Jesus. This is God's vision for young people, especially young men like Timothy. (I say 'especially' out of no sexist preference for men; simply out of shame that so few of us men are following in Timothy's steps.) Youth is God's time for heroics. So get out there and win the world for Jesus. For the first time in history, it's easy for us to travel as far as Timothy did, and further. You have energy, enthusiasm, guts and bounce; few ties, few barriers. You are the natural missionaries to your own generation; many of them are ready to become Christians, just waiting for someone to show them how. Now's the time to do it.[62]

To begin with, why not give God a full-time year after school or college or training? Use it to assist an older missionary. Don't just go abroad to see the world; go to change it! Offer yourself to Operation Mobilisation, Youth With A Mission or others who make this possible. Or if the part of the world you want to serve is nearer home, try Careforce or Oasis who run similar schemes in

Britain. And if you haven't got a free year just yet, contact the Universities and Colleges Christian Fellowship, Scripture Union and others who will gladly fit you into a mission team in your holiday or vacation.[63]

Circumcised

Luke's next words come as a complete shock. 'Paul wanted to take Timothy along with him, *so he circumcised him.*'[64] Timothy must have reeled. Circumcised! After all Paul had written to the Galatians? After his victory at the Jerusalem conference? Surely Paul couldn't be serious. But yes; Luke explains: 'He did so because all the Jews who lived in those places knew that Timothy's father was Greek.'

At the front of Paul's mind are the unconverted Jews. The Christians may have spoken well of Timothy, but *the Jews* still objected to this half-caste. They wouldn't happily let him into their homes or synagogues. If Timothy was to represent Jesus and preach him to *them*, he must be acceptable to them. In no way was Paul compromising his principles. He wasn't saying Timothy must be circumcised to become a complete Christian; he was that already. But in order to be an effective missionary to the Jews, he must become fully 'one of them'.[65]

We can learn from this. When we bring the Good News to people of different background from our own, we should do all we can to adapt to their way of seeing things and expressing things, even to their scale of values as long as it does not conflict with God's. It's no good, for instance, students using long, technical words with people who've never heard of them; or, if they join a mission team in their holidays, expecting children or older adults to have the same approach to life as they do.[66] The people we live and work among need to be able to say, 'You have taken the trouble to become one with us. We can relate to you. So we can respect and begin to understand what you're saying.' This is simply following the example of Jesus, who, though he was God, became a human being to show us his love and win us with it. It's a simple idea, but never easy to do.

How must Timothy have felt about the plan to circumcise him?[67] At the very least, he must have shuddered. There were more female than male converts to Judaism in the first century because adult circumcision was so painful and embarrassing.

Without modern anaesthetics, it took extraordinary guts to keep still as the surgeon's knife cut in and round. And discomfort remained intense for several days afterwards. I hope Paul gave Timothy time to recover before setting off, otherwise he must have ridden side-saddle!

But beyond the physical pain there was also the emotional cost. It's asking a lot of a sensitive, insecure boy – which we all still are at this sort of age – to lie naked on the operating table in front of his team leader. For very likely Paul performed the incision himself.[68] It was the first big test of their relationship.

Commissioned

We can deduce (level 2) from Paul's later words to Timothy that he had a commissioning service before he left Lystra.

> Do not neglect the spiritual gift that is in you, which was given to you when the prophets spoke and the elders laid their hands on you.[69]

There was a gathering of 'the elders' – certainly those from Lystra, perhaps the other Galatian churches too. Presumably the rest of the Lystra church were there, and maybe a party from Iconium. The elders gathered round, placed their hands on Timothy's head and shoulders, and prayed. They asked God to give his Spirit's strength to equip Timothy for his task. And God gave the moment a divine orchestration. He spoke through human mouthpieces.[70]

When we try to work out what his prophetic words said, we have to go beyond GNB's version, 'the spiritual gift given to you *when the prophets spoke*'. Paul's actual words probably mean 'as the prophecies showed';[71] in other words, they confirmed that Timothy had the spiritual gift needed to do the job Paul had chosen him for. In his letter he is reminding Timothy, 'God spoke more than once that day. He said repeatedly that you were the right person for the team. That's how we knew for sure – despite any natural doubts in me and Silas, in you and your mother, in the church elders and members – that God had equipped you to do the work we wanted.'

The verse's link with the one before it makes clear what Timothy's gifts and role were to be: 'give your time and effort to *the public reading of the Scripture and to preaching and teaching*. Do not neglect the spiritual gift that is in you . . .'[72] 'Preaching' was explaining a passage of Scripture, to help people apply it to themselves. 'Teaching' was probably giving an overall understanding of the Christian faith. In addition to these, Paul notes Timothy's ability to read the Bible aloud. This required some skill; the words were not neatly separated as in modern printing, but ran continuously along the line, one into the next. At his age, Timothy could not have been an *expert* reader, preacher and teacher. But he'd made a start and showed notable promise. He had a vital contribution to offer the team.

Paul's letter gives another echo of what the prophets said: 'I entrust to you this command, which is in accordance with *the words of prophecy spoken in the past about you*.'[73] I now attempt a free translation of the next phrase to get at Paul's meaning. 'I am saying this to make you remember and meditate on those prophetic words so that they help you [and here he presumably quotes the prophecy itself] "to fight the good fight, holding on to your faith and good conscience".' 'You've already got faith,' God was saying to Timothy, 'and an upright Christian lifestyle your conscience can be proud of. Now put them to use – as weapons to fight with! As a member of Paul's team, you're going to meet tough, unrelenting spiritual warfare.'

If that was God's sermon at Timothy's commissioning, it's highly illuminating. It confirms that Timothy had grown fast in faith and Christian character.[74] But why did he need prophets to say it in his own hearing at this moment? Perhaps because, like so many modest people with a low self-image, he was the last to see good in himself. As he stood on the brink of leaving home, he still felt, 'This can't really be me. I'm not up to it . . . except that God says I am!' God knew he needed encouraging and provided it.

God's words were also marching orders: 'fight the good fight'. They closely echo the message at Timothy's baptism, which was, literally, 'struggle the good struggle of the faith'.[75] They also echo the original instruction Paul gave Timothy and the other new Christians at Lystra: 'remain true to the faith . . . through many hardships'.[76] Timothy needs repetition and reminder.[77] Although he has accepted the invitation to go with Paul, we sense a natural shrinking from struggle and suffering.

So natural. So like us, especially when we first leave home. When young people leave their home church, particularly if they are going to join a missionary team, they need commissioning. They should go with the church's encouragements ringing in their ears, assured of continuing love and prayers. Feeling the elders' hands on them reminds them of God's arm round their shoulders.

Like Timothy they set out into the unknown, except that it is slightly less unknown than it was for him. They are benefiting from his achievements. Little though he may have guessed it, with Paul he was about to see Christianity advance and spread till it took root in most of the key cities of the world.

Key Bible passages: Acts 14:21–23; 2 Timothy 3:10–17; Galatians 1:6–9; 3:1, 3–4; 4:4–7, 19; 5:19–21, 26; 6:2, 6, 10; Acts 16:1–3; 1 Timothy 1:18–19; 4:14.

Reflect

1. Which parts of Timothy's story covered in this chapter do you find most (a) relevant, (b) encouraging, (c) challenging?

2. If you are in Timothy's age-group (say, sixteen to twenty-one), which part of this chapter do you think older Christians would most want to draw to your attention? If you are older, which part would the younger ones want to underline for you? Why not check your hunch with someone in the other age-group?

3. What hardships (not necessarily persecution) have you suffered for being a Christian? Do you think this is what God intends for you? How far have you experienced his comfort and help?

Share

1. In his later letters to Timothy, Paul gave instructions which show that Timothy still felt and acted like a young man: 1 Timothy 4:12; 5:1–2; 2 Timothy 2:22. Do you think they have anything to say to Christian teenagers or young adults today? If yes, what exactly? If no, why not?

2. Are you aware of any 'false teaching' or misleading ideas in the Christian circles you belong to? If so, is there anything you can do to correct them?

3. Part of Timothy's work would be to read the Scriptures aloud.

Today we are needing to learn once again to teach the Bible and the Good News to people who either cannot read, or do not choose to do so. What scope is there for gifted reading of the Bible *to* them? Or what other ways are there of bringing it alive without making people read print?

3

Missionary

'Let us prove it to you,' Paul challenged his small group of listeners. Some were Jews at their place of prayer; others were travellers resting where the road passed so close to the river, or townsfolk taking a midday break.

'God said he would raise the Messiah from death,' he went on. 'Hear his words through the prophet Isaiah.'

He turned to Timothy, who stood beside him clutching a scroll. Timothy nodded, breathed in, then read in a clear voice.

'"I will give you the sacred and sure blessings that I promised to David."'

'And what did he promise David?' Paul asked. 'Listen to David's own words.'

Timothy knew his cue. He followed his finger across the page, and picked out the words of the next carefully copied scripture.

'"You will not allow your faithful servant to rot in the grave."'

A shiver of joy ran down his spine. He was 500 miles from home, yet he knew God was with him. You could almost see the Holy Spirit planting the Bible words in people's minds as they listened.

But at that moment the spell was shattered. A strained, high-pitched voice called from up the road, 'Look! There they are.'

'Oh, not her again!' Timothy groaned. 'That's every day this week.'

The wild-eyed slave-girl ran towards them, with her master and mistress following close behind. 'These men are servants of the Most High God,' she shrieked at the listeners and passers-by. 'They announce to you how you can be saved!'

She was a fortune-teller, always popular with the crowd. At first the missionaries had tried to build on the unexpected publicity she was giving them. But now they realized she was a disruption, taking their audience away every time they began to get through to them. She was manipulated by an evil spirit.

Paul had had enough. He rounded on her and commanded the spirit, 'In the name of Jesus Christ I order you to come out of her!'

There was complete stillness, peace after the storm. All the manic frenzy drained out of her. Her movements, her voice, her whole body seemed to subside and shrink. She looked normal for the first time. Timothy suddenly saw a young, frightened girl of his own age. Everyone could see it.

'What have you done to her?' shouted her master. 'Look, you've taken away her powers!'

He advanced on Paul, snarling in his face. 'You can't do this, you know. That's our livelihood.'

Spotting some friends and clients in the rapidly swelling crowd, he called, 'Here! Help me take them to the magistrates.'

Several men closed in on Paul and Silas and jostled them, protesting, up the street towards the market-place. The rest of the crowd swirled behind them. Timothy sat very still and found himself all alone.

Cautiously he got up and followed a short way behind the mob.

When they entered the square, they found the two Roman magistrates hearing cases and complaints. They halted their business and called the disturbance to order.

'What's the meaning of this?'

The girl's mistress had been talking to her husband. He looked slyly at Paul and Silas.

'These men are Jews, causing trouble in *our* city,' he began.

'That's not fair!' thought Timothy. But to his alarm most of the crowd started rumbling, 'Jewish scum!'

'They're teaching us to break the law,' the man went on. 'We're Roman citizens; we're not allowed to follow these foreign customs.'

'That's right!' shouted his supporters. 'We want the law on them.'

Timothy couldn't believe his ears. It was a total distortion of the truth. They'd only been telling people about Jesus. The ugly mood of the crowd frightened him, but he waited for the magistrates to announce a proper hearing of the case.

They turned to the burly officials behind them and pointed to the missionaries. Two strong men climbed down from the platform and grabbed hold of Paul; another two seized Silas. They ripped their shirts off them and roped them to two posts beside the platform.

'But you can't do this,' Timothy found himself quavering in a small voice. 'They're Roman citizens.' Paul and Silas were protesting too. But all were drowned in the howls of the crowd.

Each of the officers picked a birch stick from the bundle on the platform. In pairs they took turns to run and swipe the bare back of their victim. Timothy watched, wide-eyed in horror. Livid red stripes appeared on Paul's back, then blood, then . . . He lost count of the strokes before he turned and ran.

He ran and ran, tears streaming. 'No, no, no, no, no,' he shouted all the way. He wasn't thinking consciously; he just made straight for Lydia's house.

'Why, Timothy, whatever's happened?' she asked, as he flung his arms round her, sobbing uncontrollably. The scroll dropped, twisted and torn, from his hand.

This chapter explores how Paul and Timothy worked together for the next sixteen years, AD 48–64. These are just the main events in Timothy's early adult life, spanning the age-range from, I suggest, eighteen to thirty-four.[1]

As Luke mentions Timothy by name in only six verses of Acts after Timothy joined Paul's team, you may think me rather over-ambitious in writing a whole chapter about this phase of his life.[2] But stay with me; I think you'll find more than you expect. The traditional image of Paul is of a spiritual mountain peak of a man, preaching, making tents and enduring persecution all on his own. This view of Paul has, I believe, spread the damaging idea that Christian discipleship is like being a spiritual 'lone ranger'. But in truth Paul never went alone by choice. On occasions he was forced to deal with crises single-handed;[3] but most of the time he had a team of companions around him.[4] And from this point in the story on, his most consistent companion was Timothy.

This chapter unearths Timothy and restores him to public view. In doing so, it blows a fanfare for fellowship and teamwork. The rediscovery of Timothy (and often other team members) at Paul's side turns teamwork in Christian ministry from an optional extra to an essential. Two or three people working unitedly (sometimes together, sometimes apart but still in touch) make a powerful workforce. The obvious people to gain from this insight are evangelists. Whether they are pioneer missionaries in a foreign country, or leading a special outreach week in a church, or visiting neighbours door to door, they shouldn't have to work alone. They should travel and talk, and, where need be, suffer, in pairs or small groups where they can support and encourage each other. But most other church ministries would be far more effective if they too worked as a team: a pastoral group rather than just a pastor; an eldership in harness with a minister; a music group to reinforce the organist; a finance committee assisting a treasurer. Harmonious teamwork doesn't just add to the effectiveness; it multiplies it. It brings fulfilment and personal growth to each team member. And it's a working model of Christianity in action to the people the team is serving. In this way Paul's mission team is a model for staff teams or other Christian ministry teams in all ages to follow.[5]

And so back to Paul and Timothy in harness. Although there are two intervals of silence, we can reconstruct ten of the sixteen years with fair certainty. They come in three blocks.

Paul's second missionary journey, AD 48–51

Timothy must be part of the 'they' in the two sentences after his call-up and circumcision. He is the third man in the Paul–Silas team.

> As they went through the towns [Iconium and Antioch], they delivered to the believers the rules decided upon by the apostles and elders in Jerusalem, and told them to obey those rules. So the churches were made stronger in the faith and grew in numbers.[6]

This first stage was a teaching mission to fellow-Christians. Timothy was on his home ground of Galatia, and all went well. They saw the churches grow, both in numbers and in their grasp of the faith. Timothy will have felt the exhilaration of all young Christians when they first taste full-time church work, and find they are actually 'paid' and kept to do the most exciting thing in the world!

But then the sky turned darker. They set off to break new ground for the Good News; and they ran into one roadblock after another.

They travelled through the region of Phrygia and Galatia because the Holy Spirit did not let them preach the message in the province of Asia. When they reached the border of Mysia, they tried to go into the province of Bithynia, but the Spirit of Jesus did not allow them. So they travelled right on through Mysia and went to Troas.[7]

There is so much Luke does *not* tell us in this intriguing passage. Why did they aim for the province of Asia? Presumably they were making for Ephesus, the biggest centre of population and culture within reach; it was also on the direct route for Greece and Rome. Why did the Holy Spirit forbid them? It must be because he wanted them somewhere else. *How* did he forbid? Perhaps through circumstances, such as an illness hitting Paul and/or Timothy.[8] Perhaps he spoke directly through prophetic words; but, if so, why did they get it wrong again and wander 150 miles to the north-east, when they should have gone north-west?

God could use these wrong turnings, as he always does, to teach the missionaries to cling close to him and to each other; they wouldn't have learnt it by easy success. But what must Timothy have thought as they zigzagged across empty, unfriendly country, off track and lost? Where on earth would it all end? Had he done the right thing? Wouldn't he be far better off back home? Was Paul hopelessly deluded?[9] These are common worries for beginner missionaries. We can't see what God is up to, and often feel that things have got out of control. We have no clear sense of God leading us anywhere. For Paul and Co., this lasted several weeks as they trudged another 300 miles to Troas.[10]

There at last the mists cleared. 'That night Paul had a vision in which he saw a Macedonian standing and begging him, "Come over to Macedonia and help us!" As soon as Paul had this vision, we got ready to leave . . .'[11] It wasn't to be Ephesus in Asia (yet). God wanted Macedonia, the province of Philippi and Thessalonica. And suddenly 'they' has become 'we'. Luke unobtrusively joined the party; he does not tell us how.[12]

Philippi

All was now energy and advance. 'We left by ship . . . we crossed into Greece . . . we spent several days in Philippi . . . there was no

Timothy's work with Paul

Paul	Date	Age	Event
48–51, 2nd missionary journey (Acts 15:40 – 18:22).			Phrygia, Galatia, Mysia, Troas (Acts 16:4–10).
	49	19	Macedonia: Philippi, Thessalonica, Berea (Acts 16:11 – 17:12). Helps preach and teach in Thessalonica (1 Thes. 3:2, 4). **Stays with Silas in Berea while Paul escapes (Acts 17:13–15).**
Achaia: Athens, Corinth (Acts 17:16 – 18:4).	50	20	**Arrives in Athens with Silas (Acts 17:16; 1 Thes. 3:1). Sent to Thessalonica to encourage persecuted Christians (1 Thes. 3:2–6). Arrives in Corinth with Silas (Acts 18:5).**
18+ months in Corinth (Acts 18:5–18).	50–51	20–21	**Helps preach gospel in Corinth (2 Cor. 1:19).**
Return via Ephesus, Caesarea and Jerusalem to Antioch (Acts 18:18–22).	52–53	21–23	Stays on in Corinth? With Paul? Returns home to Galatia till Paul collects him?
53, 3rd missionary journey begins: Galatia, Phyrgia (Acts 18:23).	53	23	Travelling with Paul.
54–57, Ephesus (Acts 19).	54–56	24–26	Based in Ephesus with Paul.
	56/57	26/27	**Sent with Erastus to Macedonia (Acts 19:21–22).**

Paul	Date	Age	Event
			Sent to teach Corinthians (1 Cor. 4:14–17; 16:10–11).
57–59, Troas, Macedonia, ? Illyricum and Achaia (2 Cor. 2:12–13; Acts 20:1–3; Rom. 15:19).	58	28	Most of the preaching in Troas? (2 Cor. 2:13).
	58–59		**Paul's fellow-worker at Corinth (Rom. 16:21).**
Macedonia, Troas, Miletus, Jerusalem (Acts 20:3 – 21:17).	59	29	**Accompanies Paul on start of journey (Acts 20:4–5).** Goes to Jerusalem (1 Cor. 16:3).
59–61, arrested in Jerusalem, imprisoned in Caesarea (Acts 21:18 – 24:27). 61–62, appeal to Caesar and journey to Rome (Acts 25:1 – 28:15).	59–62	29–32	? Goes on elsewhere from Jerusalem/Caesarea.
House arrest in Rome (Acts 28:16–31).	62–64	32–34	**Accompanies Paul as senior and valued assistant (Phil. 2:20–22).**

Jewish synagogue in the town to form the usual launch pad for the Good News, but *that* didn't stop us . . . we tracked down the few Jews to their riverside place of prayer . . . we saw Lydia converted and baptized and set up her home as the first church in Europe . . . we watched a demonized girl set free.'[13] Timothy is still among the 'we'. He's there, even if not named, in Luke's record: 'She followed Paul and *us*, shouting, "These men are servants of the Most High God! They announce to you how you can be saved!" '[14] Paul and *us . . . they* announce: it wasn't just Paul and Silas preaching, as the children's picture Bibles show it; Luke was doing it too. And so was Timothy. There is no suggestion that 'some of us' did the important work of evangelizing, while the office boy sat in the back room making tea. Timothy was already using his gift of reading, preaching and teaching.[15]

Then disaster struck. Paul and Silas were arrested, whipped and jailed. But not Timothy and Luke. The story is suddenly 'they' again, not 'we'. We don't know where the other two were at the critical moment; perhaps, as I suggested, Timothy was looking on, sick and helpless in the uproar;[16] but perhaps he was with Luke, preaching or teaching elsewhere. Unless they were right out of town, though, we can be pretty sure that by night-time they were back at Lydia's where they were staying, leading the new Christians in urgent prayer: prayer that God answered dramatically. He literally shook Paul and Silas free of their chains, and shook the jailer into Christian faith at the same time.[17]

If Timothy had time to think, he could have little doubt, now, that he was where God wanted him. If he'd been tempted, like Mark, to turn back home, it was temptation no more. After the barren wanderings through Mysia, they had struck gold in Philippi. This was more exciting than Lystra Town Council or Board of Commerce! More dangerous too. He must have wondered how *he* would have stood up to the birch. And *why* did God make them move on so soon?[18] It was such a sudden, violent end to a promising mission. Following Jesus often seems five parts pain and puzzlement to each small spoonful of fierce joy. More pain and puzzlings were to come.

Thessalonica

They stumbled the 80 miles to Thessalonica, as fast as Paul and Silas' lacerated backs would allow.[19] Thessalonica was the York or Edinburgh of Greece, the capital of its northern half. They took a deep breath at the size of the challenge, and God gave them a fresh burst of courage.[20] They went to the synagogue and preached Jesus as the Messiah-king Jews longed for. The results were to become a regular pattern: a good number of Jews and Greeks became Christians; but the Jewish leaders went to the city authorities and accused the missionaries of treason – they were trying to make Jesus emperor![21] Mysteriously, though, Paul, Silas and Timothy disappeared when the crowd came baying at the door. Presumably some of the other Christians hid them in their homes. The variety of God's protection was exhilarating; sometimes he rescued them out of prison as at Philippi; sometimes he saved them from going there at all, as here. Sometimes, they would learn, he wanted them to serve him through a longer spell inside.[22] But whatever happened – and whatever happens to us – he is with us and looks after us.

Written only a few weeks later, 1 Thessalonians refers back to these early days of the church there. The letter's first two chapters give the inside story of the bare facts Luke reports. They offer more of an insight into the methods of Paul's mission team than perhaps any other passage in the New Testament. Preaching was their work, but it was no mere job. They made their whole lives available, as missionaries always should, to the people they had come to tell about Jesus.

> Because of our love for you we were ready to share with you not only the Good News from God but even our own lives. You were so dear to us! . . . We encouraged you, we comforted you, and we kept urging you to live the kind of life that pleases God . . .[23]

Not just evangelism; once the Thessalonians had become Christians, they needed loving, nurturing and teaching.[24] Not just Bible instruction; Timothy and the others lived alongside the new converts to show by example how Christians should live. Not just a church meeting once a week or even once a day; the three missionaries gave personal care and attention.[25] All had to be slotted into the timetable.

On top of this they needed at times to earn their keep.

> Surely you remember, our brothers and sisters, how we worked and toiled! We worked day and night so that we would not be any trouble to you as we preached to you the Good News from God.[26]

They presumably worked in the hours when Thessalonians weren't available for tuition or street preaching. We don't know what job Timothy did. He may have turned his hand to the trade that had made his father prosperous. Or, perhaps more likely from the apparent togetherness of the team, he joined Paul in leather-work.[27] The one thing crystal clear is that, day and night (probably for about six months),[28] it was non-stop work. Front-line mission always is; fulfilling work and varied work, certainly, but let no-one imagine it's a doddle.

It was also work always against the clock; they knew they would soon have to move on again. 'For while we were still with you, we told you beforehand that we were going to be persecuted; and as you well know, that is exactly what happened.'[29] Persecution was a constant theme of their teaching and a recurring pain in their lives. The authorities bound the new Christians over to keep the peace.[30] They could do this only by agreeing to remove the cause of the bad feeling – the missionaries, and supremely the turncoat Paul. They gave their word, probably without consulting him, that he would cause no more trouble. This meant he would have to leave, at least for a time. Presumably to prevent further riots, he went under cover of darkness.[31]

Berea

Berea came as an oasis of encouragement. 'The people there were more open-minded than the people in Thessalonica. They listened to the message with great eagerness, and every day they studied the Scriptures to see if what Paul said was really true. Many of them believed . . .'[32] But this wasn't a main city on the road to anywhere. It was a little summer resort in the hills; it still has the air of a backwater today. It probably reminded Timothy of Lystra. Opposition – and other problems – sometimes close the door on where we would really like to be working. But we can still serve God and tell people about him wherever he takes us. The place may even turn out to have unexpected attractions.

But Paul's eyes were still on Thessalonica. Only 50 miles away, he hoped to return there when things had calmed down.[33] He was to be disappointed. 'When the Jews in Thessalonica heard that Paul had preached the word of God in Berea also, they came there and started exciting and stirring up the mob.'[34] Timothy definitely saw and heard crowd anger, insults and perhaps violence at first hand here, even if he'd missed them in Philippi and Thessalonica. 'At once the believers sent Paul away to the coast.'[35]

Silas and Timothy stayed on; but not for long. 'The men who

were taking Paul went with him as far as Athens and then returned to Berea with instructions from Paul that Silas and Timothy should join him as soon as possible.'[36]

Athens

Luke tells us no more of Timothy and Silas till after Paul has moved again, to Corinth.[37] We might be forgiven for deducing that by the time they reached Athens from Berea, Paul had already left after an extremely short stay – a mere day or two – and that they found a note stuck on the door of his lodgings: 'Didn't like it here. Gone to Corinth. Catch me there.'

But we'd be wrong. Once again 1 Thessalonians gives a fuller version of events. Acts records Paul's physical movements, but 1 Thessalonians shows where his heart was: 'When we were separated from you for a little while . . . how we missed you and how hard we tried to see you again! . . . I myself tried to go back more than once, but Satan would not let us.'[38] Paul saw the agreement barring his return to Thessalonica as a temporary triumph for Satan, the enemy of the Good News. As he trailed, first west to Berea, then south to Athens, he kept trying to head back to the beloved Thessalonian converts. He looked on Athens as no more than a waiting-room till Silas and Timothy reported whether the Thessalonian authorities had relaxed the ban.[39]

They at last reached Athens, and evidently their answer was no once again. And there was worse news: persecution of the young church by their fellow-Thessalonians had not died down, but was still going on.[40]

> Finally, we could not bear it any longer. So we decided to stay on alone in Athens while we sent Timothy . . . to strengthen you and help your faith.[41]

Presumably Timothy hadn't been part of the deal in Thessalonica, and so was free to return. As a junior member of the team, with no past to live down, the Jewish leaders would think him small fry. But it was daring stuff, the tit taunting the hawk. Timothy was barely twenty, and this was his first journey without Paul or Silas.[42] But, as so often with new experiences we dread, God saw him safely through; he made it back to the nest.[43]

Corinth

While Timothy braved Thessalonica, Paul moved on to Corinth alone. It (not Athens) was the capital of southern Greece, matching Thessalonica in the north. But it was bigger – the biggest challenge yet. It was a cosmopolitan commercial centre, exactly fitting the team's strategy for reaching the whole world through its big cities.[44] But it was also a byword for loose living. There were a thousand 'sacred' prostitutes working in the pagan temples. This would be a real test for the Good News.

Paul met a Jewish couple, Aquila and Priscilla. He 'stayed and worked with them, because he earned his living by making tents, just as they did. He held discussions in the synagogue every Sabbath, trying to convince both Jews and Greeks.'[45] It sounds slow going; earning his keep all week, Paul was able to do his missionary preaching only at weekends. Reunion with his beloved team gave him a fresh release of energy. 'When Silas and Timothy arrived at Macedonia, Paul gave his whole time to preaching the message, testifying to the Jews that Jesus is the Messiah.'[46] At last he was able to get on full-time with what he had really come to do, and with the support he needed.

Better still, Timothy brought cheering news from Thessalonica:

> . . . news about your faith and love . . . now we really
> live if you stand firm in your life in union with the Lord
> . . . We thank him for the joy we have in his presence
> because of you.[47]

Through this window in the Thessalonian letter we can hear the whoops of relief and delight as the three friends praised God together. Timothy was just as wrapped up in the welfare of their Thessalonian 'children' as Paul and Silas. With good news from that quarter, they could start living again.[48]

As in Thessalonica, they shared everything. If we had only Luke's words to go on, we might think Paul went full time in the mission work while Silas and Timothy took over the tent-making. But that wasn't how the team worked. They could afford not to earn for a while, because Timothy and Silas had brought a gift of money from Philippi.[49] But when that ran out, they shared the breadwinning to avoid costing the infant church any money: 'we have endured everything in order not to put any obstacle in the way of the Good News'.[50] 'We' – not just Timothy and Silas, but all three working together.

They continued to share the preaching too. There is no doubt that Timothy took part in this. Paul and Silas described him at this time as 'our brother who works with us for God *in preaching the Good News*'.[51] And later Paul reminded the Corinthians about 'Jesus Christ, the Son of God, *who was preached among you by* Silas, *Timothy* and myself'.[52] Timothy's preaching (along with the others') focused on Jesus: 'we preach Jesus Christ as Lord', and especially his death and resurrection: 'we proclaim the crucified Christ' and 'we said that he [God] raised Christ from death'.[53] And it worked – in Corinth! Timothy (as well as the others) had that soul-tingling sight of Corinthians becoming Christians through his words: 'you received . . . the Spirit . . . from us'.[54]

But, although God blessed their efforts, life was no easier here than anywhere else. There was repeated opposition from the Jews; the team wrote to the Thessalonians for prayer 'that God will rescue us from wicked and evil people'.[55] Whenever we tell people the Good News, the devil resists by trying to stop them hearing. At that time it was through malicious attacks, and it sometimes still is. But more often these days, at least in the spoilt and comfortable West, the devil blocks people's ears with the cotton-wool lie that they don't need God. Tragically, millions believe it.

Timothy and the others stayed a year and a half in Corinth.[56] It was their longest mission yet, and the first time they were free to choose when to leave. Paul must have thought that the Corinthians were now secure enough to survive without him. It was three years since he set out on his second journey, and he headed back to base. He called briefly at Ephesus and Jerusalem on the way. He then spent some time at his 'home church' in Antioch, before starting a third journey, revisiting Galatia (including Timothy's home town of Lystra) to strengthen the believers.[57]

Luke tells us nothing of Timothy during these months. Perhaps he stayed on at Corinth; perhaps he left when Paul did, but went straight back to Lystra to see Eunice and Lois.[58] But, in the absence of other information, we should assume he completed the missionary tour with Paul.[59] That would introduce him to Ephesus and the church leaders at Jerusalem and Antioch. All told, they had made a round trip of over 3,000 miles, many of them at sea.

Not a bad first taste of missionary life for the inexperienced lad from the small inland town of Lystra. Not bad? New churches had been planted in a Roman colony (Philippi) and two provincial capitals (Thessalonica and Corinth)! It must have blown his mind. He was now about twenty-one years old.

Paul's third missionary journey, AD 53–59

The third journey had three main strands to it: a three-year ministry in Ephesus (AD 54–57); the ups and downs in Paul's relationship with the church at Corinth; and fund-raising for the poor Christians in Jerusalem. Timothy played a big part in all three.

Ephesus

Paul arrived overland.[60] I assume Timothy was with him. True to form, Luke does not mention him till he is sent away near the end of their time in Ephesus![61] But he describes him there as Paul's *helper* or attendant; we rightly expect him to be with Paul unless other records show him elsewhere.

Now at last they could concentrate on the Ephesus they had had their eyes on for so long. With its population of half a million, and countless visitors from the rest of Asia, it was the big one – far larger even than Corinth. They stayed for three years.[62] It was the longest and most thorough assault with the Good News yet seen anywhere in the world. Luke and Paul's descriptions of it focus almost entirely on Paul, and it's so easy to imagine him working alone. But he suddenly lets slip that his co-workers were helping him: 'You yourselves know that I have worked with these hands of mine to provide everything that *my companions and I* have needed.'[63] Even if this is the only direct mention of him in Ephesus, Timothy was part of the whole campaign, and of the few isolated events recorded in detail. Indeed, this new tactic (Paul taking on all the wage-earning) means that Timothy – by now in his mid-twenties – and the others on the team[64] did more of the front-line teaching and preaching. It was, for all of them, their accustomed mixture of 'hard times' and 'hard work'.[65]

The mission began, as ever, among the Jews; but when some reacted violently, Paul and Timothy moved to a lecture hall belonging to a Gentile called Tyrannus.[66] Some copies of Acts add that they worked there 'from 11 a.m. until 4 p.m.'[67] Tyrannus lectured in the normal working hours, early morning and late afternoon. Then, while the sun was at its hottest and sensible people took a rest,[68] Paul and Timothy pressed the Good News on whoever they could persuade to come in. These five hours in the heat were not their whole working day. They also taught the Ephesians in their homes; it was painstaking, one-to-one, round-the-clock ministry, year after year.[69] And it paid off. By sticking at it in the big city, they saw the Good News take root and spread into the surrounding area.[70]

Alongside this daily routine, Luke records one especially dramatic way the Good News advanced. 'God was performing unusual miracles through Paul. Even handkerchiefs and aprons he had used were taken to those who were ill, and their diseases were driven away, and the evil spirits would go out of them.'[71] Ephesus was a notorious centre of occult power in the ancient world. The worship of Diana,[72] whose temple there was one of the world's 'seven wonders', had an occult tinge to it. Spells cast in her name were supposed to harness special powers, and the city attracted travelling exorcists.[73] When 'many' (not even all) of the new Christians burnt the magic books they had previously used, the value of them came to 50,000 days' wages![74] In this atmosphere God countered 'power' with Power and showed that Jesus is the name to conquer evil. Luke concludes: 'All the Jews and Gentiles who lived in Ephesus . . . were filled with fear, and the name of the Lord Jesus was given greater honour.'[75]

Here's a second form of the devil's opposition to the Good News. It's far less common today than head-in-the-sand apathy. But sometimes, like Paul and Timothy in Ephesus, we hit on something demonically violent. Timothy saw it all happen. My hunch is that he was more than just an onlooker. *Somebody* carried Paul's clothes round on their healing mission (Luke's words make Paul himself sound quite detached from them!); who more likely than Timothy? Like others, he was awestruck to see Jesus at work less than an arm's length away. Jesus is greater and stronger than any other power in the world. He can expel evil spirits from people's lives, and sometimes does so dramatically in answer to prayer. At times he gives to one of his servants a special ability to release people from occult oppression. Timothy couldn't fail to wonder at the extraordinary position God had given Paul. Even the evil spirit said, 'I know Jesus, *and I know about Paul.*'[76] It's good, in the early days of Christian service, to work with someone you can see God is using and blessing; someone you can respect and learn from.

These were heady but highly dangerous days.[77] Paul and Timothy now ran once again into persecution (a third form of the devil's counter-attack). While in Ephesus, Paul described their troubles:

> . . . like people condemned to die in public as a spectacle for the whole world of angels and of humanity . . . To this very moment we go hungry and thirsty; we are clothed in rags; we are beaten; we wander from place to place; we wear ourselves out with hard work. When we are cursed, we bless; when we are persecuted, we endure; when we are insulted, we answer with kind words. We are no more than this world's refuse; we are the scum of the earth to this very moment![78]

The repeated 'to this very moment' shows he is talking about what's happening at the time of writing to him and the rest of his mission team – most notably Timothy. We've already seen Timothy face hard work, cursing, persecution and insult; but the hunger and thirst, the rags and the beating are new to us. The whip-lashes he'd seen and heard biting into Paul[79] have now rained down on his own back.

So much is 'level 2' deduction. But there is a 'level 3' hint of something even worse lurking on the surface. Paul pictures them as the naked prisoners at the end of the procession into the amphitheatre, condemned to die at the teeth of wild animals. This picture would come to mind naturally in Ephesus, where there was just such a theatre. He uses it again later in the same letter:

> And as for us – why would we run the risk of danger every hour? My brothers and sisters, I face death every day . . . I have, as it were, fought 'wild beasts' here in Ephesus . . .[80]

But is his talk of fighting beasts *just* picture language, or was it a real threat?[81]

He says he and Timothy are in permanent danger of death. The next letter goes even further. Looking back on Ephesus a few months later, Paul and Timothy say, 'The burdens laid upon us were so great and so heavy that we gave up all hope of staying alive. We felt that the death sentence had been passed on us.'[82] But then the death sentence was quashed.

> We have been beaten, imprisoned, and mobbed . . . We are treated . . . as though we were dead, but, as you see, we live on. Although punished, we are not killed . . .[83]

We can't be sure exactly what happened, because Luke and Paul don't tell us in so many words. But it sounds as if Paul and Timothy were imprisoned, flogged and sentenced to death in Ephesus, but were then reprieved in the nick of time.

Nero became Emperor in the same year that Paul and Timothy came to Ephesus. Soon after, Nero's mother had the governor of Ephesus' province assassinated. Paul had friends among the provincial officials,[84] and may have been a protégé of the murdered man. This would put him out of favour with the new regime, which may have condemned him and Timothy to be thrown to the lions. Somehow, under God's control of events, the sentence was lifted.[85] But, with Nero still in power when Paul wrote, and perhaps when Luke wrote,[86] it wouldn't be safe to go into details.

And Timothy breathed again. He'd known in theory that following Jesus meant being ready to die at any moment;[87] but the lions' jaws had never come so close before. We too walk a step away from death, even if usually a less grisly one. It's all in Jesus' hands. He often holds us back from the brink, but one day he won't. As for Timothy, his first job in Ephesus looked as if it might be his last. But in fact he was to return for another tour of duty, once if not twice.[88]

Trouble at Corinth

After the end of the second missionary journey, things began to go wrong in Corinth.[89] Perhaps Paul, Silas and Timothy had, after all, left too soon. The Corinthian problems became a running sore for the first four or five years of the third journey. They constantly diverted Paul and Timothy from the positive, new work they wanted to do. Church problems are a fourth form of the devil's warfare. They're desperately common today. We can learn how to approach them from Paul and Timothy's costly care, prayer and dogged persistence. When one idea failed, they simply tried another.

Paul wrote to the Corinthian church from Ephesus and, it seems, paid them a visit.[90] He then heard that things were no better, and received a letter from them with various questions.[91] His reply, written while still in Ephesus, is our 1 Corinthians. He planned to go back as soon as possible: 'I shall come to you after I have gone through Macedonia.'[92]

Meanwhile he sent Timothy ahead of him.[93] He was to give the Corinthians further instruction. 'He will remind you of the principles which I follow in the new life in union with Christ Jesus.'[94] But, despite his visit, some continued to oppose Paul.[95] So Paul changed his mind about going and wrote a severe letter instead; he sent Titus, another of his helpers, with this letter, hoping it would succeed where previous attempts had failed.[96]

Paul then left Ephesus at or before Pentecost (spring) 57.[97] Timothy either was already back with him, or met him *en route*. The first stop on their way to Macedonia was Troas. 'When I arrived in Troas to preach the Good News about Christ, I found that the Lord had opened the way for the work there. But I was deeply worried, because I could not find our brother Titus.'[98] There was mission work to do in Troas, and they probably stayed there through the summer months. But Timothy did most of the preaching and teaching, because Paul was so distracted without news from Corinth.[99] Troas was evidently the planned rendezvous with Titus, but he never turned up. Shipping had to close down for the rough winter months. So when, at the end of autumn, it became clear that Titus had missed the boat and would have to travel the long way round by land, Paul and Timothy moved on to meet him.

First port of call would be Neapolis for Philippi. Then they trailed on to Thessalonica and Berea to cut the distance between them and Titus.[100] The long days of uncertainty dragged on.

> Even after we arrived in Macedonia, we had no rest. There were troubles everywhere, quarrels with others, fears in our hearts.[101]

Timothy shared in the work, the worries, the sleepless nights, the disputes with enemies. He felt the same sickening anxiety about Corinth as Paul did.

Then at last Titus arrived with the news they longed for. 'It was not only his coming that cheered us, but also his report of how you encouraged him. He told us how much you want to see me, how sorry you are, how ready you are to defend me . . .'[102] Joy and relief flooded out into a new letter to the church, our 2 Corinthians. But although Titus is the latest messenger and will return to them with the letter,[103] he doesn't join Paul in writing it. That privilege goes to Timothy,[104] who has shared the peaks and troughs of Corinth virtually from the start. He echoes Paul's burst of praise as they put pen to paper:

> Let us give thanks to . . . God . . .! He helps us in all our troubles, so that we are able to help others . . . using the same help that we ourselves have received from God.[105]

Their joy spilt over into all they did. Paul and Timothy spent the next year encouraging the church members in Philippi, Thessalonica and Berea, and then taking the Good News into virgin territory in Illyricum, the neighbouring province to the north-west (modern Albania and what was Yugoslavia).[106] We can imagine them teaching old and new friends alike how Jesus had helped them through their tussles with Corinth. Perhaps we get a flavour of it through the only description (and a tantalizing one) which Paul and Timothy give us of that year:

> We are often troubled, but not crushed; sometimes in doubt, but never in despair; there are many enemies, but we are never without a friend; and though badly hurt at times, we are not destroyed.[107]

When at last they reached Corinth, they obviously spent much of the three months rebuilding their friendship with the church. But during this time Paul also wrote his letter to the Romans, and sent greetings from those with him. Top of the list is Timothy, 'my fellow-worker'; he had been at Paul's side for ten years, and was now his permanent escort and right-hand man.[108]

The Jerusalem relief fund

The relief fund was one other project Paul and Timothy were working on at Corinth. Paul had been helping to raise funds for the famine-hit Christians in Jerusalem since his early days as a church worker in Antioch.[109] It's easy to get totally wrapped up in our little patch of God's mission-field. But the church of Jesus is a worldwide 'mutual providence society'; the haves look after the have nots.[110]

The relief fund became a major aim of the third missionary journey. Paul told the Galatians and Corinthians to save money for it each week.[111] Then, as his time at Ephesus came to an end, he decided to travel to Jerusalem with the collection himself. He would go via the Greek churches to pick up their contributions and whoever was going to take them.[112] This helps us understand Timothy's special mission at this point. 'So he sent Timothy and Erastus, two of his helpers, to Macedonia, while he spent more time in the province of Asia.'[113] The 'so' shows that their business in Macedonia was to prepare for the Jerusalem collection.[114]

Meanwhile, the project became ensnared in the difficulties at Corinth. By the time of 2 Corinthians, the church there had gone off the idea. They seem to have misinterpreted Paul and Timothy's motives, accusing them of wanting the money for themselves. The missionaries leapt to the defence: 'We have wronged no one; we have ruined no one, nor tried to take advantage of anyone.'[115] And Paul tried a double tactic to shame the Corinthians back into the scheme. He told them he'd boasted to other churches that they would give generously. But at the same time he sent Titus plus two companions to oversee their plans, just as Timothy and Erastus were doing in Macedonia.[116] I get the feel of a heavy mob coming to do a bit of leaning!

It worked. By spring 59 Corinth has become the assembly point for the whole delivery team. They represent the various churches and provinces which have contributed:

> Sopater son of Pyrrhus, from Berea . . . Aristarchus and Secundus, from Thessalonica; Gaius, from Derbe; Tychicus and Trophimus, from the province of Asia; and Timothy.[117]

Timothy alone has no church or district to represent. This is surely because, like Paul, he has been one of the fund managers, helping to organize it throughout this last phase of the third journey.

The purpose of the team was to travel with Paul to Jerusalem.[118] That means that Timothy accompanied him throughout the events of the next chapter and a half in Acts.[119] So he knew how Paul felt at the outset, nervously fearing and then side-stepping Jewish sabotage.[120] He heard Paul's long, impassioned speeches at Troas and Miletus, looking ahead to a threatening future.[121] He saw the shadow of prison and worse fall over Paul, as prophet after prophet foretold it.[122] He felt the pull of the tearful farewells, joining in the hugs and kisses.[123] He cried himself and pleaded with Paul to draw back. He was one of the 'we':

> We and the others there begged Paul not to go to Jerusalem. But he answered, 'What are you doing, crying like this and breaking my heart? I am ready not only to be tied up in Jerusalem but even to die there for the sake of the Lord Jesus.'
>
> We could not convince him, so we gave up and said, 'May the Lord's will be done.'[124]

They all faced the prospect of losing Paul for good; but it must have hit Timothy hardest of all. He was about twenty-nine; he had devoted the last eleven years to serving Paul heart and soul. Within the next few days, Paul might be dead. Where would that leave him?

They reached Jerusalem, and handed over the precious love-gift from the Gentile churches. Then a week later Paul was indeed arrested. He spent at least two years in detention there and at Caesarea.[125] How long Timothy stayed with him we don't know. Luke implies he wasn't on the sea journey to Rome at the end of the two years.[126] So perhaps Paul sent Timothy home to Lystra for a break, or to help lead some other church, or, in his own place, to lead a Gentile mission in some other corner of the world. Timothy must have left sick at heart. Would he ever see Paul again?

Paul under house arrest in Rome, AD 62–64

'For two years Paul lived in a place he rented for himself,' Luke tells us, 'and there he welcomed all who came to see him. He preached about the Kingdom of God and taught about the Lord Jesus Christ, speaking with all boldness and freedom.'[127] Once again, the New Testament letters fill out Luke's picture. Four of them, known as the 'prison letters', seem to date from this time: Philemon, Colossians, Ephesians and Philippians.[128] They speak of other people jailed with Paul: Epaphras and Aristarchus.[129] Onesimus was with him long enough to become a Christian and then serve him.[130] Also in attendance were various fellow-workers: Epaphroditus, Mark, Demas, Luke and Tychicus.[131] The team was bigger than ever before, except for the Jerusalem fund procession. That hired house was a hive of fellowship and mission activity.[132]

And in the company is Timothy. Indeed, he is supreme. He's not among the fellow-workers who send greetings at the end of the letters; his name appears with Paul's at the beginning. Paul calls him the co-author of Philemon, Colossians and Philippians.[133] Fifteen years ago he was number three or four in the second missionary journey team: now he has become Paul's number two.[134] As ever, he helped Paul to preach the Good News. Writing together to the Colossians, they say: 'pray . . . for *us*, so that God will give *us* a good opportunity to preach his message about the secret of Christ.'[135] This time Timothy wasn't a fellow-prisoner; he was free to visit Philippi ahead of Paul's release.[136] How early in the two-year confinement he joined Paul we don't know; but he was there almost to the end, because by the time of Philippians, Paul's release sounds imminent.[137]

In a later imprisonment Paul was to lament to Timothy, 'No one stood by me . . . all deserted me.'[138] But, as Paul faces trial this time, we can be quite sure Timothy stands by him. In Philippians Paul gives him a top-grade testimonial:

> I hope that I will be able to send Timothy to you soon
> . . . He is the only one who shares my feelings and who
> really cares about you. All the others are concerned only
> with their own affairs, not with the cause of Jesus

Christ. And you yourselves know how he has proved
his worth . . .[139]

Beside Jesus' affairs, his own are unimportant; he will stay with
Paul or go to Philippi, wherever Jesus wants him. Beyond this, he
shares Paul's feelings; he has developed a pastor's heart, and
really loves the Philippians.

They can endorse all Paul says: 'you yourselves know how he
has proved his worth'. They've known Timothy for fifteen years;
they've seen him develop. They remember the raw youth who
helped Paul and Silas plant the church at the beginning. They next
saw him in his mid- to late twenties organizing the relief fund; he
was back soon after, in the agonized hunt for Titus and news of
Corinth. They've heard of Timothy's steadfast steadiness under
every kind of buffeting.

Now they will see him again in his mid-thirties. He has become
a mature Christian. That is the effect mission work should have on
us. But Paul says more. He chooses his words deliberately: 'He is
the only one who cares about you. Everyone else is concerned only
with his own affairs.' Paul is echoing what he said only a couple of
paragraphs back:

Look out for one another's interests, not just for your
own. The attitude you should have is *the one that Christ
Jesus had* . . .[140]

Timothy has become not just any old Christian minister; he has
grown like Jesus.

*Key Bible passages: Acts 16:4 – 17:15; 18:1–23; 19:1–22; 20:1 – 21:17;
28:30–31. 1 Thessalonians 2:1 – 3:10; 1 Corinthians 4:9–13; 15:30–32;
2 Corinthians 6:5–9.*

Reflect

1. What did you learn from your early experiences of serving
Jesus?

2. As you review the outline of Timothy's early adult life in this
chapter, can you pick up any sense of God leading and controlling

what happened to him? Which phase or mood of Timothy's story mirrors your current experiences?

3. Review your workload: include your main daytime occupation and any church or other voluntary responsibilities. Is there anything you are doing alone which would be better shared with others? If so, how could you set it up?

Share

1. Retell one incident from this chapter through Timothy's eyes. You could follow the approach of the episode at the start of the chapter, or write it as Timothy might have done in his diary. What new insights do you gain from looking at it this way?

2. What new things have you learnt about Timothy from this chapter? And what about Paul?

3. Look again at the direct references to Timothy in Acts after his call: 17:14–15; 18:5; 19:22; 20:4. If Timothy was such an important member of Paul's circle, what might be some of the reasons Luke says so little about him? In today's church and in mission work, who will and who won't get recorded in the history books? Does it matter?

4

Son

How might Timothy have meditated on Psalm 23?[1]

The LORD is my shepherd . . .

'Yes, but Paul too is my pastor; I shall not miss out.'

. . . green grass . . . fresh water . . .

'Paul keeps me studying and learning from Scripture; food and drink for my spirit.'

. . . new strength . . . right paths . . .

'He's helping me to grow into a stronger, more whole person, following the way that Jesus taught and lived.'

. . . deepest darkness . . .

'We've faced the threat of death together, but I've never had to go it alone. Jesus was there as the unseen Lord, but Paul was there too as friend and guide.'

. . . a banquet . . . an honoured guest . . .

'Paul helps me come out on top even when I'm scared out of my wits; he calms me, cheers me, reminds me that Jesus always has the last word.'

. . . your goodness and love . . . all my life . . .

'Paul may die and go to heaven, but his example and love for me will never be out of my mind. And with Jesus' help, I will do what Paul would want of me always.'

This chapter covers the same period of Timothy's life as chapter 3. But we now look beyond what Timothy and Paul did, to explore the relationship between them.

We shall keep coming back to Paul's remarkable tribute to Timothy in Philippians:

> He is the only one who shares my feelings ... you yourself know how he has proved his worth, how he and I, like a son and his father, have worked together for the sake of the gospel.[2]

Paul looked on all the people he had led to Christian faith as his spiritual children. But no-one was a more complete 'son' to Paul than Timothy.

Apprentice

Timothy was more than just a convert to the faith. He was an apprentice learning Paul's ministry. This was true to the culture of the ancient world. Among the Jews and Greeks, it was a father's duty to apprentice his son in his trade; and among the Romans a father was his son's teacher.[3] To Paul, a son should quickly grow into a workmate. We've seen that he may have taught Timothy his sideline of leather-work.[4] But in Philippians Paul is speaking of the most important business of all: 'he and I, like a son and his father, have worked together for the sake of the gospel'. You can almost picture the sign outside the shop: 'Paul and Son, gospel-preachers'. Our glimpses of their travels have confirmed it: Timothy was Paul's assistant preacher and teacher. His apprenticeship was in planting and tending churches. We read of Paul's achievements at Thessalonica, Corinth and Ephesus, and we marvel from a distance; but Timothy was actually there with him, learning it all at first hand.

Apprenticeship is an excellent form of training – probably the best – but sadly neglected today. Rather than studying a job in a book or at college, you go out with people actually engaged in it. You watch them in action, picking it up as they talk through what they're doing. And you soon have a go yourself, under their guidance and supervision. Together you analyse how you got on, and learn from your successes and mistakes. Gradually your 'tutor' or 'master-craftsman' allows you more and more freedom, until you're confident and skilled enough to do it all on your own.[5] It is learning by experience – but not being tipped into the deep end and left to sink or swim, as happens in many churches. The expert is there, or at least available, throughout the apprenticeship to direct, explain, advise and correct.

It would be an ideal pattern of training for full-time pastors today, but not only for them. All sorts of tasks in churches – leading children's and youth groups, adult home groups or Sunday services, visiting door to door, organizing a church's administration – would be better done if novices learnt the trade in one-to-one partnership with a gifted 'old hand'. Some churches have begun to make it standard practice that people should not retire from any post or ministry without 'training up their successor', or at least a period of overlap in which they show how they do the job and pass on their accumulated wisdom.[6]

Paul gave Timothy exactly this blend of detailed instruction and hands-on practical experience. Come back to a passage where Paul sums up their many years of partnership:

> You have followed my teaching, my conduct, and my purpose in life; you have observed my faith, my patience, my love, my endurance . . .[7]

We've already noticed the word translated 'followed' and 'observed'; it's the Greek term for an apprentice learning from an expert. It's not just watching from the sidelines; it means copying and making your own. As William Barclay explains, 'it includes the unwavering loyalty of the true comrade, the full understanding of the true scholar and the complete obedience of the dedicated servant'.[8] Timothy's apprenticeship course, outlined in this verse, subdivides into two main strands: teaching and conduct.

Teaching

Paul trained Timothy to teach by the way he himself taught. He reminds Timothy of this several times in his letters to him:

> . . . the words of faith and of the true teaching which you have followed . . .

 . . . the true words that I taught you, as the example for you to follow . . .

 . . . the teachings that you heard me proclaim in the presence of many witnesses . . .

 . . . the truths that you were taught and firmly believe . . .[9]

Timothy heard thousands of Paul's sermons and teaching sessions. He knew better than anyone else the way Paul thought and taught. Paul's example was his model to follow and copy. It was the grounding for his own ministry of 'public reading of the Scriptures . . . preaching and teaching'.[10] When he took over from Paul at Troas and elsewhere,[11] he was quite literally the 'understudy'.

Not that he need feel cramped by Paul imposing his style on him. All beginners, whether artists, athletes, technicians or teachers, need an example or 'hero' to base their early efforts on; they develop their own technique on that foundation. And Paul's example was far from restricting. He felt himself bound, as every Christian teacher should, by the content of the Bible and the Good News. But within that territory he roamed widely. His approach at Ephesus is particularly instructive. As we've seen, he held daily discussions in Tyrannus' hall as well as teaching the new converts in their homes.[12] This taught Timothy variety of method. Public debate and private instruction are quite different approaches suited to different people on different occasions. And both are more varied, flexible and demanding than the lecture method that usually passes for 'preaching' today.[13]

But Paul says more: '*I did not hold back* anything that would be of help . . . as I preached and taught . . . *I have not held back* from announcing . . . the whole purpose of God.'[14] This double denial maps out the content of his teaching: in one direction, anything that would help the new converts; in the other, everything God has said. That seems to me a matchless syllabus for any church. But the first to learn and follow the example was Timothy. One writer betrayed his lack of insight by commenting on Timothy's place in Paul's team, 'I wonder if he took the children's meetings?'[15] In fact, from as early as Thessalonica he was teaching (adults!) alongside Paul: 'Hold on to those truths which *we* taught you . . . in *our* preaching . . . keep away from all believers who do not follow the instructions that *we* gave them.'[16] Apprenticed by Paul, Timothy must have been on his way to becoming one of the best-equipped preachers and teachers in the early church.[17]

Conduct

Paul apprenticed Timothy not only in teaching but in an entire way of living. This was essential, for the Christian faith is taught even more by our lives than by our words.[18] Christians need to be apprenticed in the daily disciplines of *following* Jesus as well as the practical skills of *serving* him. If the latter was apprenticeship in ministry, the former is apprenticeship in being a Christian disciple. Timothy learnt to live as a Christian every second of every day by watching and copying Paul; master and apprentice shared their lives together.

In Timothy's syllabus,[19] Paul spells out more of what it meant to apprentice him in Christian conduct.

'*You have followed . . . my purpose in life.*' Think how Paul stated his life's purpose. 'I have no right to boast just because I preach the gospel. After all, I am under orders to do so.' 'I have an obligation to all peoples, to the civilized and to the savage, to the educated and to the ignorant.' 'The one thing I do . . . is to forget what is behind me and do my best to reach what is ahead. So I run straight towards the goal in order to win the prize, which is God's call through Christ Jesus to the life above.'[20] 'You have followed . . . my purpose in life.' Timothy was learning to be equally single-minded.

'*You have observed my faith.*' 'Faith' is a rich term in the New Testament. Here Paul seems to mean both his daily, dependent trust in Jesus, and the quality of faithfulness or reliability that God's Spirit develops in our characters as a result. Timothy is growing in this direction too, for Paul calls him 'my true son in the faith'.[21] 'Son-in-faith' was a technical term for a disciple-apprentice; but Paul put in the word 'true' to show it was no courtesy title. Timothy was the genuine article, a son (a growing reproduction) in the area of faith and faithfulness.

'*You have observed . . . my patience, my love.*' 2 Corinthians shows us Paul's patience and love perhaps more powerfully and poignantly than anywhere else. But the letter, written in the name of both of them, speaks of Timothy sharing these qualities with Paul. 'By *our* purity, knowledge, *patience*, and kindness we have shown ourselves to be God's servants – by the Holy Spirit, by *our* true *love*, by our message of truth, and by the power of God . . . Dear friends in Corinth! We have spoken frankly to you; we have opened our hearts wide.'[22] Timothy has come to reflect to the Corinthians (and to all the other churches they served) the pastoral care he himself received from Paul.

'You have observed . . . my endurance, my persecutions, and my sufferings.' One of Timothy's earliest memories of Paul was under the hail of stones at Lystra. Since joining Paul's team, he suffered more and more hardship and opposition himself. Foot-slogging across Mysia, dodging mob violence in Thessalonica and facing it in Berea, worrying himself sick over Corinth, working all hours in Ephesus, then bracing himself for the lash and the chain of the condemned cell . . . It was no cushy number being the apostle's apprentice. I don't think suffering was an easy piece of heroism for 'Tiger Tim'. He would have to steel himself for each fresh blow. It took all the guts and commitment he had.

Yet he rose to the challenge. Timothy is the patron saint of all Christian apprentices. A missionary society called the Navigators describes disciple-apprenticeship as 'the Timothy principle'. They base the title on Paul's 'deathbed' instruction to Timothy: 'Take the teachings that you heard me proclaim . . . and entrust them to reliable people, who will be able to teach others also.'[23] In this 'four-generation' ripple effect (Paul to Timothy to reliable people to others) they see the seed of church growth. Each Christian shows a new apprentice how to live for Jesus, by meeting regularly to keep him or her up to the mark. They share news, help each other with problems, read the Bible and pray together. Then when the apprentice is ready, she or he swaps roles and takes on a new Christian to teach. This is the secret to make sure discipleship survives and multiplies from one generation to the next. One reason Christianity is such poor quality in the West today is the lack of this kind of apprenticeship. Many churches have rediscovered the value of small groups, but not yet the smallest of all – the twosome! We should all be in a Paul–Timothy pairing with one other person – perhaps as a subdivision within a home group – learning the faith or passing it on.[24] As a student, I was one partner in several of these two-person teams, first receiving encouragement and advice, later giving them. The excellence of apprenticeship as a way to learn has helped ensure that almost all of us are still going strong as Christians thirty years later.

Timothy's apprenticeship was thorough and productive. It was also long term. He and Paul worked together for nearly twenty years. This was not unusual in its time;[25] the Roman ideal was for a young man to attach himself to a role model, often for the rest of the older man's life. But the idea of long-term apprenticeship and continuous training is unusual today, especially in Christian circles. Most church training courses are relatively short. Assistant pastors often serve only three years with a senior partner; five years at most.[26] Everyone expects them then to move on to 'get their own church'. This may be appropriate for some people; but Timothy stands as a New Testament question mark over this automatic progress, and any similar ideas of promotion up a career structure. There should rightly be increasing responsibility and 'personal development' *within* apprenticeship (and Paul clearly gave Timothy that);[27] but not necessarily a rapid advance *from* apprenticeship. Depending on how complex the job is and how quickly the apprentice picks it up, the stage where learning remains the main activity may be long indeed. In the past, artists were pupils of their master for many years; and even now few people become lasting bestsellers or market-leaders without serving a long apprenticeship.

Many in their twenties or thirties are tempted to feel they're not 'getting on in life' as they'd hoped; their long years of work and experience aren't valued as they should be; it's surely time for them to have their own project or department or team. Timothy can perhaps help them to learn patience, and to see that apprentices aren't just passive receivers; they give as well. Happy the church or missionary society today where junior, assistant ministers are happy to stay 'junior assistants' for seven years, ten or more; the benefits all round can be immense. They stay long enough to get on top of the job, do really effective work and build lasting relationships, while their managers are saved from for ever training yet another new assistant soon after the last one started.[28]

Colleague

Timothy came, of course, to be much more to Paul than just an apprentice. Paul's mission team, usually of one, two or three assistants, was an ideal size for giving the personal attention and extended time that apprentices in training need. But he didn't keep them in an inferior, learner role. He moulded them into a team of co-workers. In his Philippians character-reference for Timothy, Paul uses an unexpected phrase. It was the custom for the son-apprentice to serve his father;[29] and this could have led Paul to say, 'As a son with his father, he has served me in the gospel.' But he doesn't; he says, 'He has served *with* me.' Or, as GNB puts it, 'he and I have worked together'.[30] Far from keeping Timothy aware of his junior status, Paul regards him as a true collaborator.

Paul uses two other words throughout his letters which show Timothy as a full colleague, not a permanent novice. They're the titles he gives to all his team members: 'fellow-worker' and 'brother'. Three times he calls Timothy a 'fellow-worker'; on one of them, dizzily, *'God's* fellow-worker', to remind his readers whose work Timothy and the others were doing.[31]

Paul and Silas also speak of Timothy as 'our brother'.[32] (This gives us the seeming paradox of Timothy as both brother and son to Paul!) 'Brother' was, of course, a general name for all other Christians in God's family; Paul often speaks to his readers as 'my brothers'.[33] But it also became a technical term for church leaders and members of the apostles' mission teams, especially Paul's own.[34] Timothy appears in three New Testament letter-headings as 'the brother'.[35] The title can't just mean Timothy the Christian – obviously he was that! It must refer to his job or 'rank', which was 'brother', a member of Paul's team.[36] And as the name 'brother' clearly implies, he was a member on a par with the others, not a minor skivvy.

Paul never calls himself a 'brother' in this sense. He was the boss. But, as a fellow-servant, he let his team members become colleagues he could share with. They grew and developed together. Paul was humble enough to learn new things himself, even through younger colleagues such as Timothy. There are several incidents along the Paul–Timothy journey which show Paul growing spiritually. Timothy was present in each case, and was surely more than a passive onlooker.[37] He was part of the dynamic or chemistry which helped Paul to change. You can't rate a colleague as highly as Paul rates Timothy in Philippians without him having an effect on you.

Just before Timothy joins the team in Acts, we see Paul in a self-assertive phase. He has fallen out with Mark, and now falls out with Barnabas. Although he chooses Silas to go with him, the start of the second missionary journey sounds as if Paul is in sole charge: 'He went through Syria and Cilicia, strengthening the churches.'[38] Ten verses later there is an extraordinary shift in the team's centre of gravity.

> That night Paul had a vision in which he saw a Macedonian standing and begging him, 'Come over to Macedonia and help us!' As soon as Paul had this vision, *we* got ready to leave for Macedonia, because *we* decided that God had called *us* to preach the Good News to the people there.[39]

'He' has become 'we'. It was Paul's vision, but the team's decision. He consulted them about what it meant, and they agreed together on what God was saying. This is no flash in the pan. Once they reach Philippi, the team members continue to act together in joint planning and deciding.

> On the Sabbath we went out of the city to the river-side, where *we thought* there would be a place where Jews gathered for prayer . . . After she [Lydia] and the people of her house had been baptized, she invited us, 'Come and stay in my house if *you [plural] have decided* that I am a true believer in the Lord.' And she *persuaded us* to go.[40]

More than one factor helped this growth into mature team leadership and guidance. They'd been welded together through the humbling series of 'No entries' into Asia and Bithynia.[41] And Paul found himself able to trust the others' judgment, because they were trustworthy. Silas and Luke were more experienced than the young Timothy. But he was there too and must have played some part in the process.

Moving on to Thessalonica, we find a description of pastoral teamwork that has been a textbook of care for new converts ever since. The whole approach was radically new; the historian H. V. Morton commented, 'Nothing like St Paul and his Christian communities had been seen in the world' before.[42]

We were gentle when we were with you, like a mother taking care of her children . . . You were so dear to us! . . . we treated each one of you just as a father treats his own children. We encouraged you, we comforted you, and we kept urging you to live the kind of life that pleases God.[43]

The contrast with Galatians is striking. There was parent-love there too, but it was a single parent.[44] Here we see the shift from 'I' to 'we' again. With the team working together, they give the Thessalonians the love of a 'father' *and* a 'mother'. And their love is less autocratic than Paul's in Galatians. The change is partly due to the Thessalonians' ready response to the Good News, no doubt; but the team determined from the outset not to insist on apostolic rights and authority.[45] I can't help feeling that Paul has mellowed. To quote H. V. Morton again, 'The gentleness, the tenderness, and the charm which Paul, a man capable of so much nervous temper, expended on these simple converts is one of the most beautiful things in ancient literature.'[46] I would need a lot of convincing that the team member who'd been on the receiving end in Galatia had no hand in moulding this softer touch.

By the time of 2 Corinthians Paul and Timothy are running the Jerusalem relief fund together. They have to react on the hoof to Corinthian cussedness. 'We are taking care not to stir up any complaints about the way we handle this generous gift. Our purpose is to do what is right, not only in the sight of the Lord, but also in the sight of others.'[47] Paul is usually credited with defining his team's policies and refining any changes to them; very likely he was the dominant thinker. But clearly he and Timothy prayed and planned together. How many of the great ideas emerged through this process? We can't know whether Timothy was an original, creative thinker. But even if he made only *one* suggestion that worked itself into *one* of the plans of campaign, or came up with *one* idea that stimulated Paul's mind, that would have been intensely valuable. And surely, as a valued, long-serving colleague, he contributed a great deal more than once! One way and another, Timothy made his mark on the team's development simply by being an active part of it.

So we've found another set of people with Timothy as their patron saint: members of Christian ministry teams. Timothy became the linchpin of Paul's team, presumably because he was an ideal team member. Where there's a team leader (in this case, Paul), the others by definition are not the leader. If they seek the limelight they will disrupt everything. Many teams are upset by members who are selfish or abrasive or loners. Timothy must have been the opposite of all this to fit in so well, to last so long and to gain so much of Paul's respect. But that doesn't mean he was a doormat. When teams work well, the members value each other and help them to play their own full part. It becomes impossible to say that one person is the 'star'; every contribution is vital. Paul may have been the leading preacher in Corinth and Ephesus; but his preaching achieved practically nothing when he had no team with him.[48] Timothy's willingness and hard work were a vital component of this extraordinary partnership which, as even its enemies conceded, 'turned the world upside down'.[49]

Assistant

Timothy grew into a very special team member. He became Paul's colleague *par excellence*. He started as the team's general 'gofer' but came to be Paul's personal 'gaffer' or foreman.

And so Timothy's banner also covers assistants. I've had a succession of seven wonderful assistants in my work. I've never called them secretaries because they've been so much more than that to me. Esther, Anne, Katherine, Marion, Alison, Yvonne and Yasmin are all quite different. Each has brought different qualities and skills to the formidable task of getting me through each day, and keeping my big heapum work in some sort of order. But they've all lightened my load by being there and helping; by taking an interest in what interests me; and by making sure things *get done*. My rooms are littered with accusing lists of things I haven't done over the last *n* years. But thanks to my assistants, I haven't disappeared without trace under hundreds more lists! They've made me able to do much more than I could without them. They've been real Timothys (or Timotheas?!) to me.

That's what Timothy was: Paul's PA. For sixteen years he remained Paul's second, giving hidden, background support. Some emerge through apprenticeship to be the next generation of leaders. But not Timothy. He wasn't a pushy, flashy, natural leader, moving out to set up his own evangelistic agency after a three-year assistant pastorate. He was a natural assistant. And so are plenty of people today. God has designed them to be lifelong assistants, not overall leaders. They're happier, more secure and more effective following someone else's instructions rather than issuing them themselves. They should resist the misguided pressure to become top dog, because that's not the kind of person they are. By temperament and inclination, they're seconds. That doesn't make them *second best*. They're first best at what they do best.[50]

And as with Timothy, that may often be behind-the-scenes, back-up work. Every church or missionary society needs at least one person with an assistant, enabling function. Their aim is less to pursue their own ministry than to set everyone else free to fulfil theirs. They save stacks of (God's) time and energy by looking after things which are important, but not essential, to the other members. A growing number of churches have the blessing of an administrator or secretary eager to serve the others by co-ordinating their efforts and looking after the details. They're content to be in the background; it's vital to the success of the whole enterprise that they should be. The very key to Timothy's value is his apparent invisibility. He was Paul's shadow; from our vantage-point, usually in the shadows. That's where he could be most use. Without him as right-hand colleague, Paul would have achieved far, far less. The New Testament and the Christian church would be smaller than they are today.

I think Paul knew this. Although history has minimized Timothy's contribution, Paul did not. On more than one occasion he links his name with Timothy's in exactly equal partnership. Timothy's function was assisting, but that didn't make him any less vital than Paul. Twice their names appear jointly as servants of Jesus and of God.[51] Elsewhere Paul commends Timothy 'because he is working for the Lord, *just as I am*'.[52] Countless passages in the letters show the two of them working in closest possible harness. To take just one example of how they shoulder the burden of Corinth together, there is a twenty-six-verse passage where they discuss the challenges they face; but four times they stress that they're resisting discouragement:

> God in his mercy has given us this work to do, and so
> *we are not discouraged* . . . as God's grace reaches more
> and more people, they will offer to the glory of God

more prayers of thanksgiving. For this reason *we never become discouraged* . . . God . . . gave us his Spirit as the guarantee of all that he has in store for us. So *we are always full of courage* . . . our life is a matter of faith, not of sight. *We are full of courage* . . .[53]

The two voices speak as one. You can almost hear the bracing effect of working together on the letter. They build each other up in faith: 'not discouraged', 'never discouraged', 'full of courage', 'always'. Timothy was a uniquely helpful companion and partner to Paul.

Friend

Once again, Timothy was more than just a colleague or PA. In a set of 'Bible pairs' – David and Jonathan, James and John, Mary and Martha, and so on – whose name would you link with Paul? Barnabas for a while, certainly; Silas perhaps. But the name that would rightly spring to mind and stay there is Timothy. 'Paul and Timothy' is the team we know best from the letters, and it was the team most of 'Paul's churches' knew best. Timothy was the colleague above all others; Paul's closest, longest-serving, and most usual travelling companion. Paul couldn't have written that 'you have followed my teaching, my conduct . . .'[54] to anyone else, because no-one knew him as well as Timothy.

He knew the answers to the questions that intrigue and puzzle us about Paul. He knew what the 'thorn in the flesh'[55] was, and the exact balance of Paul's attitude to women. He must often have been Paul's mental sparring partner, the first to hear and react to Paul's growing insights into Christianity. They went down to the depths together, where you come to know what someone's really like. They discovered some of Christianity's deepest secrets together there: 'although saddened, we are always glad; we seem poor, but we make many people rich; we seem to have nothing, yet we really possess everything'.[56] Timothy may have been nervous of Paul at the start of their travels, but the relationship clearly blossomed into exceptional warmth.[57] Among the ancient Jews, Greeks and Romans, a son-apprentice looked after his 'father' as a personal attendant.[58] In Timothy's case, this included dressing Paul's wounds after beatings; perhaps other medical care as well.[59] Time and again he must have kept Paul going despite the superhuman pressures and discouragements they faced. It's easy to see how a strong bond would form between them.

Paul never uses the word 'friend' as such to describe Timothy, but he glows at the special closeness between them. My predecessor in a job I once did had an astonishing talent for making and keeping friends. Unmarried for much of his life, he devoted most of his spare time to visiting dozens, if not hundreds, of lonely Christians dotted round the country. When he died, the text at his crowded memorial service was part of Paul's toast to Timothy: 'He is the only one who shares my feelings and who really cares about you'.[60] This is the only time the word for 'share my feelings' appears in the New Testament. It echoes the one use of it in the Old Testament: 'you, my companion, my colleague and close friend'.[61] That's what Timothy was to Paul. One translation catches Paul's words well: 'I have no-one else who is heart and soul with me.'[62] Timothy was a kindred spirit and natural confidant.

This friendship between Paul and Timothy is quite surprising. It survived and grew despite – or perhaps because of – big differences in their characters.[63] Paul must be one of the strongest characters who ever lived. He still arouses strong emotions now! His strength is what made him such a good choice as a pioneer missionary.[64] But he would have found it impossible to work with a carbon copy of himself. The fallout would have been radioactive! The fact that Timothy stayed with him so long and inspired such confidence argues that he must have been a quieter, gentler, more accommodating character altogether. He was ready and happy to fit in with Paul's needs and Paul's initiative. They were hand and glove. However much they enjoyed real teamwork and partnership, their basic relationship remained that of Paul the leader and Timothy the follower. But it was devoted following, not forced. Paul reminds me in many ways of the leader of the youth work where I served my Christian apprenticeship. He was utterly single-minded, and could at times be sharp and overbearing in applying the standards he set. But he inspired enormous affection from a succession of younger 'Timothys'. Paul too drew deep love from his friends, and felt deep love in return; to none more than his young friend and confidant Timothy. John was 'the disciple Jesus loved',[65] but Timothy the disciple Paul loved.

The difference in their ages is another striking feature of their friendship. On the usual reckoning of Paul's age, Timothy was about thirty years younger.[66] One Bible teacher commented that 'Paul's friendship with Timothy was a model of friendship between an older and a younger man'.[67] A model too for a mix of ages on church staffs, or mission teams and committees. Young and old need and help each other. There's no hint in Paul or Timothy of the lack of sympathy which creates today's 'generation gap'. This hostility between the generations is no new phenomenon; it was there in the ancient world. Take the eighth-century BC Greek poet Hesiod: 'I see no hope for the future of our people if they are dependent on the frivolous youth of today, for certainly all youth are reckless beyond words . . . When I was young we were taught to be discreet and respectful of elders, but the present youth are exceedingly impatient of restraint.'[68] There was none of this intolerant harking back to the 'good old days' in Paul's attitude to Timothy, though it could have developed from his state of mind in Galatians. Equally there can have been no prejudiced impatience with older people in Timothy, although we might expect him to find it difficult to relate to older men, after losing his father in early years. In Paul he found an elder he could respect; he saw how much he could learn from him. He presumably had the wisdom to see that Paul had been through the early, learning years of Christian ministry he was now experiencing; and also through young adulthood, with all the tensions and trials it brings.

They were two adult friends, single and of the same sex. It was a partnership that would be highly suspect today, when two friends cannot share a house without raised eyebrows and lowered whispers. Indeed, some have claimed that Paul's friendship with Timothy must have been gay.[69] They reach this partly from the modern insistence that 'friendship' is impossible without sexual attraction and, usually, sexual activity, and partly from Paul's emotional language to Timothy, which they read as affection to the point of intimacy.

> I give thanks to God, whom I serve with a clear conscience . . . as I remember you always in my prayers night and day. I remember your tears, and I want to see you very much, so that I may be filled with joy.[70]

It obviously needs a fertile imagination to stretch that into proof of a gay liaison! But it's no good flinging up horrified hands and closing our minds with a Pauline 'Perish the thought!'[71] It's a sincere theory deserving a reasoned answer. And recent talk of Paul's repressed gay sexuality has buttressed it to some extent.[72] Mere silence on the subject in the New Testament isn't conclusive denial. So let's review the known facts and the likely fancies.

It's clear (level 2) that Timothy was deeply attached to Paul; other separations, or threats of it, led to tears.[73] And it's true (level 1) that Paul had no wife, or at least one who lived with him.[74] We also gain the impression (level 3) that Timothy was unmarried throughout the years he appears in the New Testament. There's no mention of any wife or children. He seems to have embodied Paul's teaching on the subject.

> An unmarried man concerns himself with the Lord's work, because he is trying to please the Lord . . . I am not trying to put restrictions on you. Instead, I want you to do what is right and proper, and to give yourselves completely to the Lord's service without any reservation.[75]

Timothy's loyalty to Paul probably meant he never seriously considered marriage while he was on the mission team. He would seldom have had a moment free even to dream of a home and family.

It's also clear (level 2) that neither of them would have considered sex with each other a course open to them as Christians. Paul shared the Old Testament's horror at homosexual acts.[76] He and Timothy (together with Silas) gave Christian sex education to the Thessalonians. It firmly sets out sex within marriage and self-control outside it as God's will. 'God wants you to be holy and completely free from sexual immorality. Each of you men should know how to live with his wife in a holy and honourable way . . .' In strong language they go on to confirm and extend this, warning that stealing another man's wife or daughter, or forcing a man to have gay sex, will run into God's opposition: 'No man should do wrong to his fellow-Christian or take advantage of him . . . we strongly warned you that the Lord will punish those who do that . . . whoever rejects this teaching is not rejecting a human being, but God.'[77]

In the light of this, it's inconceivable that Paul and Timothy would deliberately embark on a gay relationship. And if they had once been swept off their feet in an unguarded moment, Paul would have felt deep shame. Yet he insists, with Timothy and to Timothy, on the purity of his life. To the Thessalonians they say: 'You are our witnesses, and so is God, that our conduct towards you who believe was *pure, right, and without fault.*' And to Timothy Paul says, in the very verses some have read as evidence of a gay friendship, 'I give thanks to God, *whom I serve with a clear conscience . . .*'[78] We can be confident the Paul–Timothy relationship was a clear demonstration – perhaps even, in the openly homosexual climate of the times,[79] a deliberately aggressive demonstration – of how to be friends without being gay.

Timothy is a patron saint of good, straight friendship, which seems an endangered species in the late twentieth century. Friendship is affection based on a shared interest, not attraction indulged in a shared bed. Single people – all people, come to that – need *friends* more than sex-partners.

Child

Timothy wasn't homosexually active; but it's quite possible (level 4) that he felt more drawn to other men than to women, perhaps without fully realizing it. Modern research shows this is likely in someone whose relationship with their same-sex parent is damaged in early life, as Timothy's seems to have been.[80] Losing normal father–son love in childhood can lead a boy to search for it in adolescence or early adulthood. As this is the time when sexual feelings awaken, the search for parent-love can be confused with them. And the attraction towards other men stunts the development of normal, mature relationships with girls. This could be a further reason why Timothy was unmarried in his middle to late thirties.

There may be a hint (level 3) of Timothy's immaturity in Paul's one word of sexual advice to him.

> Treat the younger men as your brothers, the older women as mothers, and the younger women as sisters, with all purity.[81]

Paul stresses to Timothy that he needs to treat the younger women 'with all purity'. Towards the other sex, the word means 'chastity' – the friendship and respect we would give to our sister or brother, as opposed to the nudge-nudge innuendoes reeled out on TV as the normal way for men and women to treat each other today. And Paul asks for '*all* chastity', mind as well as body. Technical virginity that stops a few inches short of going the whole way isn't good enough for Christians; we need a self-controlled resolution that sexual arousal and fulfilment belong to marriage alone, and we won't even consider them outside it.

By the time of this letter Timothy was in his mid-thirties, and it's surprising to hear Paul talk like this to him. But he wouldn't do the heavy 'with all purity' bit unless he felt he needed to. A paragraph earlier he was telling Timothy to work at setting an example in this chaste purity.[82] Most commentators read this as Paul reminding Timothy not to play fast and loose with the women's hopes of landing a dishy young curate. But Paul may have an equal concern for Timothy's own stability. He's inexperienced and untested in this part of his life. He no longer has the constant comradeship of the mission team, but is trying to sort out a church's problems alone: a church, what's more, containing younger widows more eager to remarry than to stick to Christian principles.[83] Paul cautions him to tread warily. He could easily be swept off his feet.

One thing is clear, though (level 2): Paul knows Timothy has eyes for younger women, not for older men! If this signals a change in Timothy's sexuality, what has brought it about? The answer may be Paul's fatherliness to him. The very sentence which tells him to keep his hands and thoughts off the girls also contains a sensitive hint of Timothy's relationship with Paul.

> Do not rebuke an older man, but appeal to him as if he were your father.[84]

Paul knew it was twenty years or more since Timothy had known his real father. The man Timothy would think of when working out how to appeal to a father was Paul himself. He was to treat older men in the church as gently, modestly, reverently as if they were Paul; if they had faults and errors, he should exhort and encourage them kindly as he did with his own spiritual father. This brings us back to Philippians: 'he and I, like a son and his father . . .'[85] It's more than just an image for apprenticeship; and they were more than mere friends. There was a real father–son dimension to their relationship.

Paul's 'fatherhood' may have healed Timothy and helped him to mature. He increasingly took it in that Paul had spotted his potential and chosen him as a companion and friend in his life-work, seen him through early misfortunes and mistakes and stuck with him without giving him the sack. For twenty-one years Paul remained the stable, dominant influence in his life, the supporting stake he grew up beside. Paul liked him, respected him, trusted him, wanted him, said nice things about him to the Philippians, and needed him! Timothy came to trust Paul in return. He felt great love and fondness for him, but family love, not sexual. If he'd been unsure how to get on with older men, because he'd not known one at close quarters before, Paul now filled the gap.

It can be the same today. If the arrested development of people who've lost the love of their same-sex parent is to pick up and come good, they need to find replacement parent-love later in life. It may be through a counsellor, or, quite unconsciously, in a good friendship with a same-sex parent-figure. This is an important insight for our times, when lone-parent families spawn an increasing number of 'psychological orphans', especially boys who don't know their fathers. Churches can stretch out a healing hand if they train their mature adults to be 'parent-figures', especially father-figures, to the younger generation. This doesn't have to be a daunting specialist 'ministry', just people willing to be wholesome, positive examples of a Christian adult, taking a kind and friendly interest in a younger person.[86] To grow up whole, we all need not just a hero to look up to, but a parent who approves of us and encourages us. That's exactly what Paul seems to have done for Timothy. Far from leading him into gay sex, he provided the father-love which made marriage and straight sex more possible in the long run.[87]

Some writers claim that Paul virtually adopted Timothy as his son. The New Testament doesn't quite say this (level 1). In Philippians Timothy is *like* a son. In his letters, Paul addresses him as 'my son' and 'my son-in-faith'. But these were standard names for a teacher to call his spiritual child.[88] There's no denying the special warmth he felt for Timothy; he twice calls him 'my dear' son.[89] Yet even this isn't conclusive, as Paul calls the whole

Corinthian church 'dear children' too.[90]

So the 'son' references don't *prove* that Paul and Timothy were adopted parent and child to each other. But it surely pulsates through the rest of what we know. When Timothy parts from Paul or contemplates his death, there are tears; and Paul longs to see him again.[91] Timothy has supported him through exertions and torments that would have broken a lesser man. He writes about Timothy not just with paternal pride, but with poignant tenderness and vulnerability.

> If Timothy comes your way, be sure to make him feel welcome . . . No one should look down on him, but you must help him to continue his trip in peace, so that he will come back to me.[92]

> If it is the Lord's will, I hope that I will be able to send Timothy to you soon . . . He is the only one who shares my feelings and who really cares about you . . . you yourselves know how he has proved his worth . . .[93]

We're almost reminded of the parable of the tenants in the vineyard: 'I am sure they will respect my son.'[94]

When Paul pleaded for mercy for Onesimus, the runaway slave, he used an extraordinarily strong idea to express his love: 'with him goes my heart', or literally, 'he *is* my bowels, or guts, or heart'![95] He could have said it even more feelingly of Timothy. For Timothy was more to Paul than Onesimus. He was his loyal apprentice and hard-working colleague; the indispensable PA; always at his side; his best friend. Above all, he was the Christian son he never had.[96] Paul chose to invest a large part of his life in bringing him up to be a mature Christian minister and missionary. Looking at it the other way, Paul became the Christian father Timothy must often have missed.[97] They refined each other; Timothy mellowed Paul, and Paul strengthened Timothy. He was never to be so strong on his own.

Key Bible passages: Philippians 2:19–22; 2 Timothy 3:10–11; Acts 16:10, 15; 1 Thessalonians 2:7–8, 11–12; 1 Corinthians 7:32, 35; 16:10–11; 1 Timothy 5:1–2.

Reflect

1. Write your own adaptation of Psalm 23 to record what you gained from the person (or people) who has helped you most as a Christian. (You could perhaps give it to him or her as a thank-you present.)

2. Paul and Timothy aren't the only case of one-to-one disciple-apprenticeship in the New Testament. Look at Barnabas with Saul (Paul's original name) (Acts 9:27; 11:25–26, 30) or Priscilla and Aquila with Apollos (Acts 18:24–28). What do you owe to any similar relationships in your life? If you're not apprenticing or being apprenticed at the moment, is there someone you could ask to join you?

3. How would you complete the following sentences? A friend is ... Three close friends of mine are ... One obstacle to developing my friendships is ... To build up my friendships I need to ...

Share

1. Read Philippians 2:20–22 again. What does it tell you about Timothy? And what about Paul? And how does it inspire or challenge you to follow their example?

2. What different teams or groups do you belong to? (Think of 'work' or daytime occupations, church, social interests, *etc.* Include the group you're discussing these questions with.) What part do you play or contribution do you make in each? How could you strengthen it further?

3. In 1 Corinthians 12:28 Paul includes 'the power to help others' among a list of spiritual gifts. His Greek word means 'acts of assisting'. Timothy clearly demonstrated this gift (even if it's not the one Paul singled out for mention; 1 Timothy 4:13–14). Whom do you know who has this gift of helping? It's a self-effacing gift, easily buried and lost. How can you encourage that person and show you appreciate him or her?

5
Letter-writer

Timothy laid the single sheet of papyrus in front of him. He dipped his reed pen in the ink and looked at Paul.

'The usual heading?' he asked.

'No need to call me apostle,' Paul answered.

Timothy began to write.

> From Paul, a prisoner for the sake of Christ Jesus . . .

He looked up. 'Just from you?'

Paul thought for a moment. 'No. It needs both of us.'

Timothy wrote on.

> . . . and from our brother Timothy –

'In fact,' said Paul, 'show that we're all in this together. Not just Epaphras – the whole team.'

Timothy made a mental note of how the letter would end.

> Epaphras, who is in prison with me for the sake of Christ Jesus, sends you his greetings . . .

Philemon would expect that; Epaphras was founder of the church at Colossae, after all. But the other team members had never been there. Let him know they supported the letter too; that should add a bit of weight.

> . . . and so do my fellow-workers Mark, Aristarchus, Demas, and Luke.

'Another thought,' said Paul. 'Include the church and his family in the address.'

Timothy smiled and nodded. 'Nice.'

> To our friend and fellow-worker Philemon, and the

church that meets in your house, and our sister Apphia, and our fellow-soldier Archippus . . .

'How shall I do the introduction?'
'Stress his love and his faith,' said Paul. 'That's what we need to appeal to.'

I hear of your love for all God's people and the faith you have in the Lord Jesus . . . Your love, dear brother, has brought me great joy and much encouragement!

'Not just me,' said Paul, as Timothy read out what he'd written. 'Show him he's got a wide reputation to live up to.'

You have cheered the hearts of all God's people.

Timothy laid down the pen and waited while Paul thought, 'This is the hard part,' he muttered at last.
'Why not just tell him he must do what you want?'
'It would be asking too much all at once. This is the biggest test of his Christian calling. We need to help him think it through slowly. Like this.' Paul began dictating.

I could be bold enough . . . to order you . . . But because I love you, I make a request instead . . . on behalf of Onesimus . . .

Timothy looked down at the terrified slave-boy kneeling at Paul's feet. He felt a great surge of thanks to God for the way he himself had spotted the boy in a Roman back street . . . recognized him as Philemon's slave . . . persuaded him to come to Paul's house even though he was a runaway . . . seen him put his hope in Jesus as Paul explained the Good News. He guessed that Onesimus looked very like he did when he became a Christian seventeen years ago.

He took more ink as Paul spoke again.

I am sending him back to you now, and with him goes my heart.

Onesimus threw his arms round Paul's legs. 'Let me stay, let me stay,' he moaned.

Paul placed a hand on his head, and turned back to Timothy.

> I would like to keep him here with me . . . so that he could help me in your place. However, I do not want to force you . . . I would like you to do it of your own free will. So I will not do anything unless you agree.

Timothy shook his head. Surely that was risking *too* much. Into his mind came the scene facing Onesimus if he'd belonged to any other slave-owner in Colossae: a merciless flogging was the very least a runaway could expect. The law permitted torture or even execution. Could they really leave it to Philemon to see that a Christian should stand out against the customs of a whole city – in fact, a whole empire?

Paul cut into his thoughts.

> How much he means to me! And how much more he will mean to you, both as a slave and as a brother in the Lord! So, if you think of me as your partner, welcome him back just as you would welcome me.

Timothy felt his heart pounding. *That* was better. It was brilliant. Philemon would give *Paul* the best food, the best bed . . . how could he give Onesimus the whip or the rack after that appeal?

But Onesimus was crying again. 'He'll never forgive me. What about the food and clothes I stole? I can't take them back; they've gone.'

'*We* could pay for them,' Timothy burst out.

Paul nodded.

> If he has done you any wrong or owes you anything, charge it to my account.

'Yes,' said Timothy, excitement mounting. 'Sign it, make it official.' He took the paper across to Paul, and watched as he wrote.

> I, Paul, will pay you back.

'Will it be enough to persuade Philemon?' Timothy asked himself. 'Oh please, Lord, bless this letter. Make it work.' He looked down to see that Paul had gone on writing.

> (I should not have to remind you, of course, that you owe your very self to me.) . . . I am sure, as I write this, that you will do what I ask – in fact I know that you will do even more.[1]

Timothy knelt down beside Onesimus and put an arm round him. 'It's going to be all right,' he said quietly. 'I feel sure of it.'

Like the two before it, this chapter stays in the sixteen-year period when Paul and Timothy worked together. One vitally important product of these years is the set of nine New Testament letters, from Thessalonians to Philemon.[2] In earlier chapters we've only glanced at them in passing. It's now time to look at them directly, and see what part Timothy played in them.

Thessalonians, AD 50–51

There's a lot of Timothy in these letters. For a start, 1 Thessalonians is a reply to the news Timothy brought back from his visit to Thessalonica.[3] Chapters 1 – 3 defend the team's behaviour against criticisms Timothy picked up; chapters 4 and 5 set about making good the shortcomings Timothy saw in the Thessalonians' faith.[4] Without Timothy's visit and report, the letter simply wouldn't exist. But his contribution is much bigger than that.

When we read the Thessalonian letters straight after the only earlier Pauline letter, Galatians, we instantly notice two big changes.[5] The first is their positive tone. 'We always thank God for you all . . . you became an example to all believers in Macedonia and Achaia.' 'Our brothers and sisters, we must thank God at all times for you . . . because your faith is growing so much and the love each of you has for the others is becoming greater. That is why we ourselves boast about you in the churches of God.'[6] It's a far cry from the opening notes of Galatians: 'I am surprised at you! In no time at all you are deserting the one who called you by the grace of Christ, and are accepting another gospel.'[7]

Timothy the letter-writer

Paul	Date	Age	Event
18+ months in Corinth (Acts 18:5–18).	50–51	20–21	**Helps write 1 and 2 Thessalonians (1 Thes. 1:1; 2 Thes. 1:1).**
57–59, Troas, Macedonia, ? Illyricum and Achaia (2 Cor. 2:12–13; Acts 20:1–3; Rom. 15:19).	58	28	**Helps write 2 Corinthians (1:1).**
House arrest in Rome – Acts 28:16–31).	62–64	32–34	**Helps write Colossians (1:1), Philemon (1:1), Philippians (1:1).**

Obviously Paul's relations with the Thessalonians were better; they'd caused less anxiety than the Galatians. But don't imagine that everything at Thessalonica was as rosy as the opening words suggest. Among other problems, Timothy found at least a pocket of resentment towards the missionaries. And some of the Thessalonians were contradicting their teaching about sex.

But look how tactfully and gradually the first letter deals with the dispute. 'You learnt from us how you should live in order to please God. This is, of course, how you have been living.' Before even naming the bone of contention, it congratulates those who have stayed true to their foundations. 'God wants you to be holy and completely free from sexual immorality.' The letter gently reminds the readers that the original teaching was what God wanted, and only then packs its punch. 'So then, whoever rejects this teaching is not rejecting a human being, but God.'[8]

It's a very different approach from the frontal assault on the Galatians, all guns blazing: 'You foolish Galatians! Who put a spell on you? ... How can you be so foolish!'[9] The threat to the Thessalonians was less deadly than the attack on the Good News itself in Galatia. But it's still a clear change of tactic. Timothy had a part in both sets of letters. He was on the receiving end of the Galatian bombshell; he was on the sending end of the Thessalonian billets-doux. Junior though he was, I can't believe he had no say in the softer approach; he must have at least approved it, probably asked for it. After all, he was with the Thessalonians only a few days ago. If a phrase sounded too strong, he'd be bound to say, 'Ouch! Please don't put it like that. That'll hurt them. Remember, I know what it's like to get one of Paul's rockets.'[10]

The other big difference between Galatians and Thessalonians is even more obvious and fundamental. It's the words 'we', 'our', 'us'. In Galatians 'we' and its partners come fifty-two times; 'I' and its partners 123. In the Thessalonian letters the score is: 'we', 152; 'I' eleven. Some of these Thessalonian 'we's' are, like the vast majority in Galatians, 'inclusive'; that is, the writer includes the readers in a statement that's true of 'us' all. 'God did not choose *us* to suffer his anger, but to possess salvation through *our* Lord Jesus Christ, who died for *us* in order that *we* might live together with him, whether *we* are alive or dead when he comes.'[11] But most of the Thessalonian 'we's' are not inclusive like this. They clearly refer to the person (or people) writing the letter.

> We always thank God for *you all* and always mention *you* in *our* prayers.[12]

For years I read them as a sort of 'royal we', as in Queen Victoria's 'We are not amused'. Most commentators treat them like this. Their comments refer only to Paul, as if he were talking for himself alone. But this must be wrong, because five times in the two letters Paul *does* speak for himself for a moment.[13] These show that when he means 'I', he says it. He makes a clear distinction between 'us' and 'me'. So much so that two of the passages simply repeat what has just been said about 'us'; this makes them awkward to read.

> As for *us*, brothers and sisters, when we were separated from you for a little while – not in *our* thoughts, of course, but only in body – how *we* missed you and how hard *we* tried to see you again! We wanted to return to you. *I myself tried to go back more than once*, but Satan would not let us . . .
> *We* could not bear it any longer. So *we* decided to stay on alone in Athens while *we* sent Timothy . . . *We* sent

him to strengthen you and help your faith . . . That is
why *I had to send Timothy.* I could not bear it any longer,
so *I* sent him to find out about your faith.[14]

If 'we' is just a pompous way of saying 'I', there would be no need
to say 'I' at all.

There's a simple explanation if we take in (rather than gloss
over) what the headings of both letters clearly state: 'From Paul,
Silas, and Timothy.'[15] Their natural meaning is that Paul didn't
write them on his own at all. The letters are joint compositions.
From time to time, Paul felt it important to identify himself and
butted into a 'we' sentence with an 'I' of his own.[16] But the rest of
the letter was from all three of them.

This idea of joint authorship sounds strange only because of the
way we've been brought up to think of Paul. For centuries he's
been presented as the only person in the mission team who
matters. The GNB gives clear examples of this in its section
headings. It calls 1 Thessalonians 2:1–16 'Paul's Work in
Thessalonica', yet the passage contains no 'I' at all and speaks
entirely of what the team did together. It heads 2:17 – 3:13 'Paul's
Desire to Visit Them Again', a topic specified in only half a verse;
four verses tell how the *whole team* desire to visit, and eight verses
dwell on the fact that Timothy actually did visit,[17] but this is
apparently unimportant to the Bible editors. It's a typical example
of how most readings of the New Testament marginalize Timothy.

In the same way, all Bible translations continue to treat Paul as
the sole author of his letters, and head these as *Paul*'s letters to the
Thessalonians. But that's just what they say they aren't. They
claim to be the letters of Paul, Silas and Timothy. There are other
surviving first-century letters from two or more writers; in each
case they talk as 'we', and are genuine co-authors, taking shared
responsibility for the contents of the letter.[18] But a letter claiming
to be from three people, when in fact it was really only from one of
them, would have no parallel at all. When pressed to explain why
the letters say 'we', some commentators say that Paul is
courteously speaking on behalf of Silas and Timothy (who had
worked with him in Thessalonica and were still with him in
Corinth at the time of writing). This would be perfectly possible in
a letter from Paul alone; but not in a letter from Paul and the
others. Quite apart from not being a first-century custom, it's

unthinkable that Paul would present the other two with a document of his own, in effect saying, 'I have put the following words into your mouths; kindly sign on the dotted line at the top.' And even if he *might* have done it to the still very young Timothy, he surely wouldn't to the highly regarded and experienced Silas.[19] The 'we's' weren't Paul speaking on behalf of the other two, but the three of them speaking together.[20]

Anyway, the Thessalonian letters do more than just claim joint authorship. They breathe it in almost every verse. After the formal heading, they come to the introductory thanksgiving, which is the key indicator in 'Paul's' letters. '*We* always thank God for you all and always mention you in *our* prayers.'[21] With 'we', 'our', 'us' coming immediately after the greeting from Paul, Silas and Timothy, how else could the Thessalonians read it? It was a letter from the team who had introduced them to Christianity. Those first readers hadn't had RE teachers drumming into them that the New Testament epistles are 'by St Paul' alone!

As we read the letters carefully, much of the process of writing becomes clear. The starting-point was prayer. Each letter opens by listing the team's thanksgivings for the Thessalonians. And each returns more than once to petitions obviously taken direct from the three's regular praying for the church.

> Day and night we ask him with all our heart to let us see you personally and supply what is needed in your faith.
> May our God and Father himself and our Lord Jesus prepare the way for us to come to you! May the Lord make your love for one another and for all people grow more and more and become as great as our love for you.[22]

Naturally, these weren't just the prayers of Paul or Silas; some of the words were Timothy's.

Part of their prayer reflected on the past. 'We remember before our God and Father how you put your faith into practice, how your love made you work so hard, and how your hope in our Lord Jesus Christ is firm.'[23] There is much loving dwelling on the details of their original mission.[24] The three must often have revived each other amid difficulties in Corinth with bracing memories of Thessalonica. Here again, Timothy will have joined in the conversation as much as the other two.

But this wasn't just to cheer them up; they were planning how to reply to the news and needs from Timothy's visit. And here we can hear Timothy's own words quoted.

> He has told us that you always think well of us and that
> you want to see us . . .[25]

Several times the letter talks of what the Thessalonians are doing now; for instance, '. . . encourage one another and help one another, *just as you are now doing*'.[26] How did Paul and Silas know what they were doing? Because Timothy told them. These words too must be echoing his report.[27]

They then worked together on how to reply. For instance, Timothy said some of the Thessalonians were questioning whether Paul and Silas really cared about them, since they had not run the risk and defied the ban. So they retorted: 'We wanted to return to you . . . After all, it is you – you no less than others! – who are our hope, our joy, and our reason for boasting of our victory in the presence of our Lord Jesus when he comes.' Again, Timothy reported that the Thessalonians were worried about some of their number who had died. 'We want you to know the truth about those who have died, so that you will not be sad . . .'[28]

Timothy was obviously not the chief authority in framing these replies; he was the junior member and had come back for the others' wisdom. But he's bound to have influenced the final wording: 'No, no, they know that. What they're saying is . . .' His thoughts and words are as much part of the fabric of 1 Thessalonians as those of Paul and Silas.

And so to the actual writing. We can't be sure who did what; we can only deduce from the evidence (level 2) and from parallel experience (level 3). It's tempting to imagine them all scribbling their own messages at the same time, or haggling over each phrase, but I doubt whether that's how it was. I used to belong to a group of three partners running a small business. When we had an important and sensitive letter to write, we discussed it together. We decided what to say, and even summarized it in the minutes. We appointed one of us to draft it. He then showed it to the others for comments and revisions. When we were all happy, we signed.

Something of the kind seems to have happened here (except

presumably for the minutes!). Timothy clearly didn't do the drafting, because the others refer to him as a third party: 'We decided to stay on alone in Athens while we sent Timothy . . . Now Timothy has come back, and he has brought us the welcome news . . .'[29] We've also seen evidence to suggest that Paul wasn't the draftsman.[30] That leaves us with Silas. This seems very likely, as Peter also acknowledges Silas' help in writing *his* first letter. As a prophet and Roman citizen, Silas was well suited to the task.[31]

But did Silas write the Thessalonian letters longhand, or did he dictate them? The first-century custom was to leave the actual writing to a secretary, and Paul did this with the church letters that are in his name alone. If they used a secretary here, did they employ a professional scribe, or did they keep it within the team? Several commentators have suggested Timothy as the secretary for 1 and 2 Thessalonians; the original manuscripts would then be in his handwriting. It's a 'level 4' suggestion, with no evidence, but it's perfectly likely. If so, it would simply underline the fact, already so clear, that the Thessalonians received letters which Timothy had a big hand in composing.

1 Corinthians, AD 56/57

The tone of 1 Corinthians is closer to Galatians than Thessalonians is. 'Which do you prefer? Shall I come to you with a whip, or in a spirit of love and gentleness?' 'What do you expect me to say to you about this? Shall I praise you? Of course I don't!'[32]

And, as is already clear, it's largely an 'I' letter.[33] The opening thanksgiving is Paul speaking alone: '*I* always give thanks to *my* God for you . . .'[34] From then on we hear the unmistakable tones of Paul over and over. 'While I was with you, I made up my mind to forget everything except Jesus Christ and especially his death on the cross.' 'I may be able to speak the languages of human beings and even of angels, but if I have no love, my speech is no more than a noisy gong or a clanging bell.' 'I am the least of all the apostles – I do not even deserve to be called an apostle, because I persecuted God's church. But by God's grace I am what I am, and the grace that he gave me was not without effect.'[35]

But it's not quite so simple as that. For one thing, there's a co-writer mentioned in the letter-heading – 'our brother Sosthenes'. For another, there are some 'we' passages in the letter, but not all of them seem to be Paul and Sosthenes speaking together.

Most commentators have understood the 'we' passages as an 'apostolic we'; Paul is, they say, speaking on behalf of the other apostles. In one or two places they're right, but not all. Most times the 'we' refers to Paul's mission team.[36]

> We have sown spiritual seed among you. Is it too much if we reap material benefits from you? If others have the right to expect this from you, haven't we an even greater right?
> But we haven't made use of this right.[37]

The first sentence looks back to the original gospel-preachers in Corinth – Paul, Silas and Timothy. Then Paul slides forward to his companions at the time of writing – Timothy, Sosthenes, Erastus and perhaps others. He regards his team as an ongoing 'we' on whose behalf he can speak. Here is the 'courteous we', speaking *for* them, instead of the collective 'we' that speaks *with* them. Rather than the thoroughgoing joint authorship of Thessalonians, in 1 Corinthians Paul refers incidentally to his companions from time to time.

So why does he announce Sosthenes as co-writer? Paul writes 1 Corinthians in highly personal terms. Some of the church wanted to replace him with Apollos as 'their' apostle. He meets the attack head on. But he places alongside himself Sosthenes, one of their own number; someone they respected, whose support for Paul would carry weight with them. Sosthenes was a prize recruit during Paul's first visit to Corinth, the second leader of the Jewish synagogue in succession to become a Christian.[38] But why announce him as *co-writer*, if he did little more than nod in agreement every two or three chapters? The answer is, he did a lot more. By putting his name to the whole letter he shows his complete agreement with all Paul says.[39]

But if there *is* a co-writer, why not Timothy? If he was one of the founders of the Corinthian church, why didn't he give *his* name in support of this important letter? The answer seems to be that he did, but in a different way. Each Pauline letter was quite an industry. There was usually a secretary and a co-writer, sometimes but not always the same person. There were other team members who appear in the 'we' sections and to some extent influence the contents. There are other local Christians who know about the letter and ask to be remembered to the recipients.[40]

Then there's one other vitally important person – the courier. In the first century every letter needed a personal messenger to deliver it. In Paul's letters he usually introduces the courier with the words, 'I am sending X.' For 1 Corinthians, this postman seems to have been Timothy.

> I am sending to you Timothy . . . He will remind you of the principles . . . which I teach in all the churches everywhere.[41]

Six or seven years older and more experienced than when he helped write Thessalonians, he now had the intensely challenging task of backing the letter up, and filling out all that Paul would have said in addition to it if he had come in person. If he was with Paul while the letter was being written, and had the delicate job of delivering it and explaining it, he must have known intimately what it said. As co-founder of the church as well, he's bound to have given advice, comments and suggestions as the letter took shape. His contribution was probably more weighty (though less direct and less visible) than in Thessalonians, because in the meantime he'd become Paul's senior assistant.[42]

But Paul is clearly nervous that, in their present rebellious mood, the Corinthians will not take kindly to him: 'Be sure to make him feel welcome among you . . . No one should look down on him . . .'[43] It may help Timothy's position when he arrives if he's not too closely connected with the exact wording of the letter. That will set him free to find other ways of explaining and justifying what Paul (and Sosthenes) were getting at.

2 Corinthians, AD 58

2 Corinthians claims to be by Paul and Timothy.[44] The opening thanksgiving confirms this at once by talking of 'we'. 'He helps *us* in all *our* troubles, so that *we* are able to help others . . . if *we* are helped, then you too are helped and given the strength to endure . . .'[45]

Many of 'Paul's' most famous passages in the letter turn out to be 'we', not 'I'.

But thanks be to God! For in union with Christ we are always led by God as prisoners in Christ's victory procession. God uses us to make the knowledge about Christ spread everywhere like a sweet fragrance . . .

For it is not ourselves that we preach; we preach Jesus Christ as Lord, and ourselves as your servants for Jesus' sake . . . Yet we who have this spiritual treasure are like common clay pots, in order to show that the supreme power belongs to God, not to us . . .

We are ruled by the love of Christ, now that we recognize that one man died for everyone, which means that all share in his death.[46]

As in 1 Corinthians, such passages about how 'we' carry out 'our' missionary work apply to Paul's mission team. At this stage, Titus has just rejoined the team from Corinth, and some other unidentified 'brothers' are with them temporarily. But the permanent core of the team was just Paul and Timothy, the two named authors of the letter. So the 'we' passages are spoken in their name, and primarily refer to them.[47]

The difference from 1 Corinthians is striking and significant. There it was mostly 'I' with occasional 'we'; here the majority is 'we' with patches of 'I'. This can't be chance; it must reflect the difference in who the writers are. There it was Paul (with Sosthenes alongside); here it is Paul and Timothy. We're back to the 'joint we' of two people speaking together.

Yet the fabric of 2 Corinthians is a little more complex. The sprinkling of Paul's 'I's is uneven. In about one third of the letter, it's actually dominant, with more 'I' than 'we'. In these passages, Paul directly answers the attacks the Corinthians are still levelling at him personally.[48] A second third is more mixed; sometimes 'we' dominates, sometimes 'I'.[49] Meanwhile, the opening thanksgiving and the central description of the team's ministry are entirely 'we', with just three 'I's.[50] As in Thessalonians, these 'I's read as if Paul added them as insertions to strengthen the point when he checked the letter before despatch: for instance, 'We know what it means to fear the Lord, and so we try to persuade others. God knows us completely, *and I hope that in your hearts you know me as well.*'[51]

111

Readers have always found 2 Corinthians disjointed and difficult to follow.[52] Paul and Timothy wrote it on the move, during the Macedonian follow-up visit Luke summarizes in the words: 'He went through those regions and encouraged the people with many messages.'[53] It was also a troubled time for them. 'Even after we arrived in Macedonia, we had no rest. There were troubles everywhere, quarrels with others, fears in our hearts.'[54] They had other things on their minds, other problems to deal with, pressing in on them each day. There was no question of taking a leisurely weekend off in the hills to give their uninterrupted concentration to the Corinthian letter! Almost certainly they had to write such a long one in snatches.

And it looks as if they shared out the letter between them. Paul must have taken the initiative with the long 'I' sections. He presumably dictated them to a secretary as usual; and that secretary may have been Timothy, although it could have been Titus or one of the other brothers. But just as Paul seems not to have been the primary draftsman of Thessalonians, the same is true of the major 'we' sections here. He read them through and authorized them, certainly. He surely also discussed their content before they were written down; they reflect his thinking and teaching, and his authority as an apostle.[55] But he didn't actually write them himself; he can't have done if the repeated 'I' inserts are a postscript.[56] Somebody else was the prime writer of these passages. And it certainly looks as though that 'somebody' was Timothy. Not only does the letter-heading say it was him; but there was no-one else it could have been. Silas wasn't with them on this journey; and those who *were* with them were the postmen, deliberately kept distinct from the writers.[57]

My suggestion is novel but simple.[58] It is that Timothy composed nearly half of 2 Corinthians.[59] In that half the thoughts chime with the thoughts of Paul, but the voice is the voice of Timothy.[60] If this is right, it inks in the tentative history of the last two chapters. If it was Timothy who wrote, 'We felt that the death sentence had been passed on us',[61] there can be no doubt that he was in the condemned cell with Paul. Similarly, if he listed the catalogue of suffering in 6:5–10 – 'We have been beaten, imprisoned, and mobbed; we have been overworked and have gone without sleep or food . . .' – it helps to explain the otherwise rather puzzling overlap with 11:23–27 which is obviously by Paul.

Again, if Timothy wrote these words, we get our clearest echo of how he preached the Good News:

> Our message is that God was making the whole human race his friends through Christ. God did not keep an account of their sins, and he has given us the message which tells how he makes them his friends. Here we are, then, speaking for Christ, as though God himself were making his appeal through us. We plead on Christ's behalf: let God change you from enemies into his friends![62]

This same image – enemies into friends – unfolds what may be part of Timothy's spiritual history as well as Paul's (as people have always taken it).

> No longer, then, do we judge anyone by human standards. Even if at one time we judged Christ according to human standards, we no longer do so. Anyone who is joined to Christ is a new being; the old is gone, the new has come. All this is done by God, who through Christ changed us from enemies into his friends and gave us the task of making others his friends also.[63]

Even if Timothy didn't write these 'we' passages in 2 Corinthians on his own, he's the named co-author with Paul. On any normal first-century understanding of the letter, this would include him in all the 'we' messages to the Corinthians. In this letter, seen in this light, his collaboration in Paul's 'epistles' becomes substantial and open to view.

Romans, AD 58–59

Romans is a different matter. Paul writes and gives thanks in his own name alone.[64] He's writing, unusually, to a church he didn't found and which he hasn't yet visited.[65] He's hoping for their help in the next stage of his missionary plans: 'Now that I have finished my work in these regions and since I have been wanting for so many years to come to see you, I hope to do so now. I would like to see you on my way to Spain, and be helped by you to go there, after I have enjoyed visiting you for a while.'[66] For Paul, this is an unusually tentative and sensitive tone. It sounds as if he's unsure of their support, and so takes utmost pains over the letter.[67] The long, theological essay in the first three quarters of the letter may well be, in effect, his credentials to persuade them that he's a missionary worth supporting.[68]

Timothy appears in the letter only to send greetings; as Paul's senior fellow-worker, he is top of the list.[69] But although he plays no visible part in composing the letter, he was there at the time. As Paul's closest companion, he must at least have heard about what Paul was saying. Paul didn't go into an isolation hospital to write it! Timothy was probably the first reader to thrill to the glories of what we know as Romans 3, 5, 8 and 12.

And he was surely more than a passive onlooker. It's more than likely, after the previous letters, that Paul consulted him closely. Without the original manuscript we can't tell whether 1:12 is an insertion in Paul's own hand, but it reads like a careful addition in case verse 11 sounds too patronizing:

[11] For I want very much to see you, in order to share a spiritual blessing with you to make you strong.
[12] What I mean is that both you and I will be helped at the same time, you by my faith and I by yours.

Was it Timothy who suggested this tactful clarification?

And what about the new style in Romans? Paul writes parts of it in the form of a debate, directly addressing an imaginary opponent: 'Do you, my friend, pass judgement on others? You have no excuse at all, whoever you are. For when you judge others and then do the same things which they do, you condemn yourself . . . What about you? You call yourself a Jew; you depend on the Law and boast about God . . . You teach others – why don't you teach yourself?'[70] This may be how Paul *spoke* in the cut and thrust of dialogue in Athens or Ephesus. But it's not how he usually *wrote*. Did Timothy perhaps 'talk him through' the questions and answers, the different stages of the argument, playing the part of a potential hostile reader? We can't know.

Nor can we know what invisible part he played, both at the time and earlier, in helping Paul forge the letter's magnificent statement of the Good News – one of the highest peaks of the whole Bible.[71] But we can be sure that, as Paul's fellow-preacher for the last ten years, he had *some* influence.

Colossians and Ephesians, AD 63–64

Colossians, like Romans, is a letter to a church Paul didn't found himself. Like Romans, it has less 'I' and 'we' than some of the others, because it isn't answering a direct charge or request from the church. But Paul's relationship with the church at Colossae is much closer than at Rome; the founder was one of his own team members, Epaphras, himself a Colossian.[72] The letter comes from Paul and Timothy,[73] and has the marks of a joint composition. The opening thanksgiving is in the 'we' form. '*We* always give thanks to God, the Father of our Lord Jesus Christ, when *we* pray for you. For *we* have heard of your faith in Christ Jesus and of your love for all God's people . . . For this reason *we* have always prayed for you, ever since *we* heard about you.'[74]

The letter is much shorter than 2 Corinthians; it would have been natural to write it at a sitting, or two at most. And the conditions for writing were much more settled.[75] Paul and his companions in the Roman hired house had visitors to talk to; but they had plenty of time, and they could share out the talking. Paul wasn't going anywhere; he was rooted to the spot. He and Timothy could move into a back room to write the letter any time. So there's no need to look for bits Paul wrote and bits Timothy wrote. And there's no sign of more than one mind working on the written draft. On the face of it that mind was Paul's. For as well as the 'we' passages, there are substantial 'I' passages.[76]

Yet the letter has two strange features suggesting all is not what it seems. One is several turns of phrase quite different from the other 'definitely Paul' letters.[77] This has led some scholars to believe it can't be Paul writing.

The other puzzle in Colossians is its connection with Ephesians. There are some obvious, basic differences between the two letters. Colossians is from Paul and Timothy, with some 'we' passages; Ephesians is from Paul alone and is all 'I'. Colossians is addressed to one church, with many greetings and references to its members and problems; Ephesians has no such local colour at all. It looks like a more general, circular letter to all the churches in the Ephesus region.[78]

Yet despite these differences, there's more overlap between them than in any other two of 'Paul's' letters. The second half of each follows the same outline: (1) live the life of the new self; (2) detailed instructions for wives, husbands, children, parents, slaves and masters; (3) pray, especially for us/me as we/I speak about Jesus.[79] And although the first halves of the letters deal with different topics, they too have several identical phrases. It's these word-for-word echoes jostling next to quite distinct treatments of them that many scholars find so unsettling.

Within the detailed instructions for members of households, for instance, the slaves–masters section in both letters says exactly the same thing.[80] But just a few verses away, the wives–husbands sections receive totally different treatment. Colossians has two terse sentences: 'Wives, submit to your husbands, for that is what you should do as Christians. Husbands, love your wives and do not be harsh with them.' In Ephesians this becomes a twelve-verse paragraph exploring a parallel between marriage of man and woman and the marriage of Christ and the church.[81]

Then again, both letters speak of singing to God with thanksgiving.[82] But Ephesians puts this in the setting of the instruction: 'Do not get drunk with wine, which will only ruin you; instead, *be filled with the Spirit*'; whereas Colossians says: '*Christ's message* in all its richness must live in your hearts.' There's no *contradiction* between the two ideas. Indeed, people have often pointed out that the rich indwelling of Christ's word (Colossians) is precisely one of the main ways the Holy Spirit fills us (Ephesians). But this different emphasis runs throughout the letters: Ephesians talks of the Holy Spirit twelve times, Colossians only once – and even that may mean the human spirit.[83]

The build-up of all this makes many scholars who think Colossians is by Paul lose their nerve with Ephesians. They say it's the work of a later imitator, using Colossians as his model. But their idea creates more problems than it solves. It's hard indeed to imagine someone stolidly copying Colossians word after word for half a sentence, half a verse, and then suddenly sweeping aloft into what others have rightly called 'the divinest composition of man' or 'God's highest and best',[84] only to fall back to earth for another fix of Colossians a paragraph later.

116

Despite the squeamish scholars, it's perfectly possible that Paul wrote both, one after the other; one directly engaged with the false teaching at Colossae, the other in more uplifted, reflective mood. But that still leaves us asking why Colossians comes from Paul *and Timothy*, and why parts of it aren't in Paul's style.[85]

My own suggestion is only a 'level 4' hunch, but it follows the drift and development we've seen all through this chapter. Tychicus was ready to set off as courier to both churches.[86] Onesimus was also ready to take the letter to Philemon.[87] All that remained was to write the two letters, Colossians and the 'round robin' Ephesians. And there was the team of two experienced letter-writers: Paul and Timothy. As ever, they prayed and talked over the contents together. What did the Colossians need to hear in response to the invasion of false teaching?[88] And what more general message would be helpful for Ephesus and the surrounding churches? Presumably they made rough notes of their ideas. And then – perhaps for speed's sake – they divided the two letters between them. Paul took Ephesians as the bigger challenge; Timothy took Colossians and wrote it himself in the name of them both. He had just planned it with Paul, so the words are often the same or very close to Paul's Ephesians. But the un-Pauline way of putting things is Timothy's.[89]

At times the letter says 'I, Paul'; perhaps Timothy broke off at that moment and asked for a direct quote, or perhaps he wrote the words himself for Paul to authorize when he added his autograph at the end.[90] This is perfectly standard practice in letter-writing, where many secretaries or juniors draft 'I' letters over their boss's name and signature. A friend of mine, as a church administrator, used to write letters in this way for his vicar. After two or three years the vicar said the letters were *exactly* how he would have expressed them himself, both in what they said and in how they said it. Timothy had now been with Paul for about fifteen years and knew his mind intimately; Paul in his turn trusted him totally as his spokesman.[91]

On this reconstruction, Timothy shared in the thinking behind Paul's Ephesians, as he must have done with Paul's Romans and 1 Corinthians. But Colossians is the most 'Timothean' of all the letters. This is only a theory to explain the facts, but in its favour is the outstandingly Christ-centred flavour of the letter. It fits the man who, Paul said, was uniquely concerned with the cause of Christ and truly shared the attitude of Christ.[92]

Philemon and Philippians, AD 63–64

Two more letters from this Roman imprisonment survive. Both name Paul and Timothy as authors. After the sequence so far, with Timothy appearing to take an ever-increasing hand, it's a surprise to find two 'jokers' at the end of the pack.[93]

For although they claim at the top to be joint letters, Philemon and Philippians don't look like it once you read on. Both move straight to 'I' thanksgivings. 'Brother Philemon, every time I pray, I mention you and give thanks to my God.' 'To all God's people in Philippi . . . I thank my God for you every time I think of you . . .'[94] They both remain overwhelmingly 'I' letters throughout. In Philippians 'I/me/my' appear 162 times; 'we/us/our' only fourteen times, and all but two of those are inclusive (meaning the readers as well as the authors). These are, with 2 Timothy, the most personal letters we have from Paul. Unlike Colossians, they were written to people he knew personally, and his warm friendship pours out of almost every verse.

So why does Paul address them from himself *and Timothy*? The traditional explanation is that Timothy was the secretary for these two letters. That may be true; but it can't on its own be a full explanation. After all, Tertius was the secretary for Romans; but Paul doesn't say Romans is from him and Tertius.[95] Indeed, it's hard to imagine Timothy as the secretary for Philippians, because it includes the glowing tribute to him we've already looked at several times.[96] How can the letter be *from* Paul and Timothy, when in it Paul writes *about* Timothy?

In Philemon, one of the reasons for naming Timothy as co-author may be the same as for Sosthenes in 1 Corinthians – to add a bit of pressure to Paul's words.[97] For although Philemon is a personal letter, friend to friend, Paul is at great pains, as in the episode at the start of this chapter, to ask a favour he fears Philemon may not grant.[98] It's not totally clear to us what the favour was. At the very least Paul asks Philemon to welcome Onesimus back as a now Christian slave, and so presumably not to punish him for desertion.[99]

But that will be a searching test of Philemon's Christianity. It will mean stepping out of line with all the pagan slave-owners in Colossae. It may cost him insult, ostracism, persecution. So, to broaden his appeal, Paul makes it an open letter. He addresses it

not just to Philemon, but to Apphia and Archippus (presumably
two of his family, perhaps his wife and son) and the church who
meet in their house.[100] Philemon can't just bin the letter; he must
discuss it with his Christian family and friends. And it comes not
only from Paul, with his natural fatherly love for Onesimus.
Timothy joins in the appeal with him. Paul *and* his assistant leader,
representing the whole team,[101] stand together in this momentous
request. The voice speaking in it is Paul's, but the hand firmly
supporting him (as well as perhaps penning the words) is
Timothy's.

There may be a second reason for Timothy as co-author, which
comes more into focus when we turn to Philippians. By now it has
become second nature to Paul to name Timothy as at least a
'passive' fellow-writer. After all, the Philippians know Timothy
too; they've known him as long as they've known Paul. Paul is
saying to them, in effect, 'This is me speaking, but Timothy – who,
of course, shares every part of my mission – has discussed it with
me; he's seen what I've written and agrees with it.' The process
here seems to be the reverse of what I suggested for Colossians.
There it looks as if Timothy may have composed the finished
wording, to which Paul was happy to sign his name. Here, in
Philemon and Philippians, it looks as if Paul decided the final
wording, with Timothy happy to add his name.[102] This would
simply confirm the conclusion of chapters 3 and 4 that Paul now
treats Timothy as a very senior colleague indeed, virtually on a par
with himself.[103]

Philippians gives a revealing hint of what Timothy has come to
mean to Paul. The letter sounds like a missionary writing to a
church pledged to provide his financial support.[104] Philippi was
the first church he and the team founded in Europe; he probably
looked to them as 'base camp' for all stations to the west: Greece
and Illyricum, and on towards Rome and Spain.[105] He has now
reached Rome, in less than ideal circumstances but still joyful, and
he reports back to his support group.[106] He faces trial but is
confident he'll be acquitted and released.[107] Yet he and they must
face the possibility that the trial might go against him.[108]

This is the immediate lead-in to the pregnant paragraph about
Timothy we keep coming back to. 'It's possible I'm about to die,'
Paul tells this key supporting church. 'In that case, this is my last
letter to you, and these my last words:'

> I hope that I will be able to send Timothy to you soon
> . . . He is the only one who shares my feelings . . . you
> yourselves know how he has proved his worth, how he
> and I, like a son and his father, have worked
> together . . .[109]

It's just beneath the surface, but isn't there an undercurrent of 'This is my son and heir; in the event of my death, he is my successor'? Paul continues: 'So I hope to send him to you as soon as I know how things are going to turn out for me.'[110] In the event, it seems Timothy was able to announce the happy outcome they were all praying for. But if he *had* arrived with news of Paul's death, how would the Philippians have read the paragraph? Surely as Paul's last will and testament, bequeathing his mission to Timothy. They would have known to direct all their resources of love, prayer and giving to Timothy as warm-heartedly as they had to Paul. So the whole letter comes to them from Paul *and* his designated successor. The next letter may be from Timothy alone.

The letters of St Timothy?

Now to review the findings of this chapter. Paul is most famous and most important to us today for his letters. Most ordinary readers assume he's the sole author of the thirteen surviving letters that bear his name. In fact he claims to be sole author of only five of them: Romans, Ephesians, Titus and 1 and 2 Timothy.[111] And of those, Romans seems likely to carry at least the indirect influence of Timothy as Paul's closest assistant at the time of writing. In Ephesians the influence appears more direct than indirect, as the comparison with Colossians shows.

Of the remaining eight letters, six claim to be joint compositions with Timothy. Exactly what and how much Timothy contributed seems to vary from background input (1 and 2 Thessalonians, Philemon and Philippians) to writing part (2 Corinthians) or perhaps even all (Colossians) of the finished copy. It looks as if he also had some say in the final content of 1 Corinthians, if he was the courier charged to deliver it, explain it and carry home its difficult and many-sided message. In addition he may have been the actual penman of any or all of these letters except Romans and, probably, 1 Corinthians; we don't know how many. Of the letters to churches, the only one he had no hand in fashioning was Galatians, if I'm right to date it before he joined the team. But in that case he was one of the people who received it; and I've suggested that his experience then almost certainly shaped his contribution to all the other Pauline letters.

So on this understanding of the evidence, Timothy helped to write or had some impact on 69% of these letters (9 out of 13), or 81% of the total verses (1,640 out of 2,031). And if we accept that of the four letters he did *not* help to write, three were addressed to him (1 and 2 Timothy to him personally, and Galatians to him among others), the percentages for the Timothy factor rise to 92% of the letters and 98% of the verses. And even the remaining 2% of the verses (the letter to Titus) have considerable overlap with 1 Timothy.[112] If Timothy hadn't existed, the 'Epistles of St Paul' would have been unimaginably different from what they are.

The burden of this chapter is less to find Timothy's fingerprints on particular chapters and verses – an impossible task – than to rediscover his constant presence in Paul's mind (and usually at his side as well). My suggestions for the exact part Timothy played in the writing are 'level 4' hunches, or at best 'level 3' inferences. But the case that Timothy as Paul's colleague and friend must have had *some* influence climbs to 'level 2' deduction. And it's simply a 'level 1' fact that six of the letters *say* that Timothy was co-author.[113] Here's another case of people *thinking* for centuries that Paul did it all on his own, and unconsciously assuming that one-man bands are the normal way for Christians to behave. But all along Paul has been telling us that, even in this bastion of his supposed solo activity, he actually worked with his team – above all, with Timothy. Important letters – and *certainly* books – are better as a duet or team effort.

From this we must conclude that Timothy is a crying example of someone history has simply effaced. Not that *he* would cry or complain about it. He was not the sort to want publicity. But if you feel you haven't received the credit due for work you've done or influence you've exerted, you have a friend in Timothy. And as it's never too late to right an injustice, perhaps you will feel moved to join my Rehabilitate Timothy Campaign!

At the very least, let's credit the 'we' passages to Paul *and* whoever he says wrote them with him, not just to Paul alone. In church services we could use two or more voices to read them.

And I think the evidence of the letters themselves demands that we should refer to the authors of Thessalonians as Paul, Silas and Timothy; and of 2 Corinthians and Colossians as Paul and Timothy.[114] If that seems a pedantic mouthful, it's only because we aren't used to it (yet!). Scholars have no difficulty in calling their Greek-English dictionary, compiled by Messrs Arndt and Gingrich, 'Arndt-Gingrich'; and Church of England church-wardens know their standard manual, quite correctly, as Mac-Morran, Elphinstone and Moore! We honour working partnerships in other fields: Victoria and Albert; Gilbert and Sullivan, Rice and Lloyd Webber; Laurel and Hardy, Astaire and Rogers (or Fred 'n' Ginger), Torvill and Dean; Rolls-Royce. How much more should we acknowledge those joint authors of six world-changing letters – Paul and Timothy![115]

Key Bible passages: 1 Thessalonians 1:1–3; 2:17–19; 3:1–2, 5–6, 10–12; 4:13; 5:11; 1 Corinthians 1:4; 2:2; 4:17, 21; 9:11–12; 11:22; 13:1; 15:9–10; 2 Corinthians 1:1, 3–4, 6, 9; 2:14; 4:5, 7; 5:11, 14, 16–20; 6:5; 7:5; Romans 1:11–12; 2:1, 17, 21; 15:23–24; 16:21; Colossians 1:1, 3–4, 9; 3:16, 18–19; Ephesians 5:18, 22–33; Philemon 1, 4; Philippians 1:1, 3; 2:19–20, 22–23.

Reflect

1. Read the letters through in the order they were written. Or, if that would take too long, compare a 'we' letter (like 1 or 2 Thessalonians) with an 'I' letter (like Galatians or Philippians). What new insights do you gain from looking at them in this light?

2. Does the idea of Timothy as joint writer of Paul's letters – and the main writer of some passages – threaten your belief in their value and authority? Why (or why not)?

3. When might there be value today in Christian leaders or missionaries writing joint letters or books? What would be the advantages and disadvantages?

Share

1. Read one of the 'we' letters (Thessalonians, 2 Corinthians or Colossians) aloud straight through. Use a different voice for each of the named authors. Work out as you go along when they should read together, and when 'Paul' should read on his own. What insights does this give you into how the letter was written, and how it sounded to the first hearers?

2. Write a joint letter as a group (to 'absent friends' – former members or occasional attenders, or missionaries you are supporting; or to some body you want to influence – your church's leadership or your MP, a managing director or government organization). How will you set about it?

3. 'Rehabilitate Timothy Campaign'. Have you spotted any other ways Timothy's contribution to Paul's mission has been overlooked? Do they matter? What about people who get ignored or slighted today?

6

Go-between

From Timothy, to Paul – Grace and peace from Jesus our Lord.[1]

I thank God for you in every prayer. I ask the Lord Jesus to continue his great work through you at Ephesus – especially among all the Diana-worshippers at Pentecost-time. May he keep you safe from all our opponents!

Wonderful news from Macedonia. I felt sick on the boat again, but it was worth it! I told Erastus we shouldn't press them too hard at Philippi, as they've always supported us so generously. I didn't see how they could give any more to Jerusalem as well.

But of their own free will they begged us and pleaded for the privilege of having a part. It was more than we ever dreamed! I kept telling them not to overdo it. But they said they'd given themselves to the Lord, so all their money was his. They brought us everything they had and laid it at our feet. It was all I could do to get them to keep it till you come.

It was the same at Thessalonica and Berea. Their troubles have continued; it's been a severe test for them. But as soon as I told them more about Jesus, you could see the joy overflowing out of them. They're only poor, but they're being extremely generous to Jerusalem. Erastus has the details for you. But I can assure you they gave as much as they could – and even more.

Erastus has given me every help and encouragement. I'm sending him with this letter, as you said. But oh, father, I wish I was coming with him. I know you think I'm well equipped to deliver and explain your letter to Corinth. But I'm sure they'll look down on me. I dread the quarrels and harsh words. I wish you were here too, or would let Erastus come with me.

I confess I prayed there would be no boat to take him; but there was. I even prayed that I'll have an accident on the road to Corinth, to stop me getting there. Forgive me. I know I must really do what you want – and what Jesus wants.

Pray for me. Grace be with you.

Chapters 3–5 have traced Timothy's career as Paul's assistant; they've charted the work they did together between AD 48 and 64. But they weren't together all of that time. There are some gaps we know nothing about. But there were also at least five occasions when Paul left or sent Timothy as his representative.

Timothy the go-between

Paul	Date	Age	Event
(48–51, 2nd missionary journey (Acts 15:40 – 18:22).	49	19	**Stays with Silas in Berea while Paul escapes (Acts 17:13–15).**
Achaia: Athens, Corinth (Acts 17:16 – 18:4).	50	20	**Sent to Thessalonica to encourage persecuted Christians (1 Thes. 3:2–6).**
53, 3rd missionary journey begins: Galatia, Phrygia (Acts 18:23)			
54–57, Ephesus (Acts 19).	56/57	26/27	**Sent with Erastus to Macedonia (Acts 19:21–22).** **Sent to teach Corinthians (1 Cor. 4:14–17; 16:10–11);** apparently unsuccessful.
House arrest in Rome (Acts 28:16–31).	63/64	33/34	Goes to Philippi for news? (Phil. 2:19, 23).

Paul didn't always keep his team of co-workers alongside him. At times he sent them in ones or twos, to work elsewhere. Their job was to carry messages, preach the Good News, encourage Christians in distress or sort out disputes.[2] This doubled Paul's impact and kept several projects moving forward at once.

For Timothy and the others, it was first-class experience, all part of the training. We can't grow into complete preachers, teachers or pastors (or complete anythings) if we're always under the inspection of a team leader. We need our own spheres of responsibility, sometimes in harness with others, sometimes alone. That's exactly what Timothy gained from Paul. Some he took in his stride, others less so. Chapter 3 noted that these tours of duty happened; let's now look at them more closely.[3]

With others
Berea, AD *49*

Back in Timothy's first year of travelling with Paul, they had only a few weeks' or months' refuge in Berea before the Thessalonian Jews tracked them down.

> At once the believers sent Paul away to the coast; but both Silas and Timothy stayed in Berea.[4]

This wasn't a carefully planned piece of delegation; Silas and Timothy got left behind in the crisis. And it didn't last long; once he reached Athens, Paul sent for Silas and Timothy to join him as soon as possible.[5] Paul's 300-mile journey from Berea to Athens by boat would have taken three or four days, so Silas and Timothy kept working in Berea for something between a week and a fortnight, perhaps ten days.

Silas was obviously the senior partner, making any ultimate decisions; but now that there were only two of them, Timothy will have felt that much more involved and responsible. He must also have felt alarmed; he was probably still a teenager, and as far as we know this is the first time on the journey that he wasn't at least in the same town as Paul. His nervousness would drive him to urgent prayer, and to draw on everything he'd learnt during his first three years as a Christian. The experience can only have left him stronger, more battle-hardened, as a front-line missionary. God gradually pushes us out of our sheltered upbringing to stand on our own two feet.

Luke doesn't tell us *what* they did during those ten days, but it's not hard to infer. Task no. 1 in Berea was to preach the Good News about Jesus to Jews and Greeks;[6] they would keep doing this as long as possible. But the Jews may have been able to stop them.[7] If so, Silas and Timothy would do all they could to stick with task no. 2, to stabilize the new Christians. They would pass on exactly the early teaching Timothy had himself received from Paul in Galatia: 'We must pass through many troubles to enter the Kingdom of God.'[8] It was no small task for the two of them, for the infant church at Berea numbered *many* of the Jews, *many* Greek women of high social standing and *many* Greek men.[9] Silas and Timothy left 'as soon as possible', but not, we may be sure, before they were confident that the Bereans had understood that Jesus would continue to teach them and sustain them through the Scriptures and some form of eldership.[10]

Macedonia, AD 56/57

Seven or eight years later Timothy went back to the Berea area.

> Paul . . . sent Timothy and Erastus, two of his helpers, to Macedonia, while he spent more time in the province of Asia.[11]

The province of Macedonia included Berea, Thessalonica and Philippi. Timothy and Erastus visited the churches there, and perhaps others in the neighbourhood that had been planted through their outreach. Timothy is now, on my calculation, in his mid- to late twenties. On this trip he appears as the senior partner; last time it was 'Silas and Timothy', now it's 'Timothy and Erastus'.

We've seen that Paul's ambition was to take money from the Macedonian and other Gentile churches to help the famine-stricken Christians in Judaea.[12] Timothy and Erastus' job was to prepare for his visit. Perhaps they went to make final arrangements or plead for another round of generous giving. Or this might be the first proposal that Macedonia should contribute to the fund. The Christians at Philippi in particular regarded themselves as pledged to supporting Paul's expenses,[13] and may have needed some persuading to transfer meagre resources to Jewish strangers. But whatever precise part Timothy played among his old friends in Macedonia, it was outstandingly successful. He and Paul described the results like this: 'they gave . . . even more than they could . . . they begged us and pleaded for the privilege . . . they gave themselves to us'.[14] When all missionary societies are struggling to balance their budgets, I wish more fund-raisers today had the Timothy touch!

We know little about Erastus,[15] but the good results suggest Timothy worked well with him. It's another slight indication that Timothy was an ideal team member, playing his part and enabling others to play theirs. The record of his 'go-between' missions with others, although briefer than brief, is spotlessly impressive. The assignments he took on alone he found harder.

Alone

Thessalonica, AD 50

Timothy's first solo mission was conceived in heartache. Following their exile from Thessalonica, Paul and Silas longed to give first aid to the persecuted church, which was only a few months old; but the city gates were closed to them.

> Finally, we could not bear it any longer. So we decided to stay on alone in Athens while we sent Timothy . . .[16]

Imagine his feelings. The others have set him a hugely daunting task. It's partly fact-finding; are the Thessalonians still Christians? 'I sent him to find out about your faith. Surely it could not be that the Devil had tempted you and all our work had been for nothing!'[17] That task on its own would be highly dangerous. If persecution has been severe enough to kill their faith, Timothy runs the risk of attack or prison himself.

But Paul and Silas want more than just facts.

> We sent him to strengthen you and help your faith, so that none of you should turn back because of these persecutions.[18]

He must teach them, exhort them, convince them, fill them with iron and backbone and faith. All depends on him! He knows how much is at stake for Paul and Silas; he *must not* let them down. But he's only twenty, or very little older. What can *he* do against the devil? He prays like stink. Every moment of the journey he prays and prepares. He feels sick with stress. And perhaps seasick too. Once again he finds himself tossed and jostled in a small boat – he who till two years ago had never strayed far from Lystra, 100 miles from the sea.

This idea of Timothy feeling sick isn't just guesswork. In his major solo responsibility fourteen or fifteen years later at Ephesus, Paul advised him to 'take a little wine to help your digestion, *since you are ill so often*'.[19] The Greek phrase is, literally, 'because of your stomach and your frequent weaknesses or illnesses'. The letter seems to have come early in Timothy's time at Ephesus,[20] so Paul can hardly be talking of a sudden string of tummy upsets all at that time; he must be looking back over a more chronic condition, prone to flare up when Timothy was especially vulnerable. It may have been a physical infection, such as dysentery, set off by impure water; or a more nervous disorder, triggered by stress – very likely, a bit of both.[21] Being left on his own to cope with heavy burdens would cause just this sort of stress; his first such mission, all the more so. Flinging all modesty aside, I confess I had constant diarrhoea for the first six weeks of my first full-time job when I was twenty-two! This is normal experience for people with a certain temperament. Timothy's temperament looks as if it was this same kind.

How did he get on at Thessalonica? At first glance, all looks well. He was able to bring the report Paul and Silas so wanted to hear: 'the welcome news about your faith and love'. The Thessalonian church has survived. Task no. 1 satisfactorily accomplished. More than satisfactorily! The church members are still basically well disposed towards Paul and Silas. 'He has told us that you always think well of us and that you want to see us just as much as we want to see you.'[22]

And yet all is not quite right. How far has Timothy succeeded in task no. 2, to 'strengthen them and help their faith, so that none should turn back because of persecutions'? Not totally. Their faith has survived, but not in full working order. 'Day and night we ask [God] with all our heart to let us see you personally and supply what is needed [literally, 'adjust the shortcomings'] in your faith.'[23] Timothy's visit alone was not enough; the young church needed 1 Thessalonians (*and* 2 Thessalonians!) as well. The basic short-coming Timothy hadn't been able to make good was the way they handled the belief that Jesus will come back to earth.[24] It led some of the Thessalonians to worry about the fate of Christians who die before the great day; but others to reckon that, with the world due to end so soon, it didn't matter how they behaved – in bed, at work or in church.[25]

It was unrealistic to expect Timothy to cope with all this alone. We wouldn't today want to reproach one so young for his limitations. He was younger than many modern missionary students. But it seems the Thessalonians did blame him; or Timothy felt they did. Paul and Silas insert an extraordinary phrase when they refer to Timothy's visit. They say they sent Timothy, 'our brother who works with us for God in preaching the Good News about Christ'.[26] There would be nothing odd about this introduction and recommendation if the Thessalonians had never met Timothy before. But he'd been part of the original mission team there; *of course* the Thessalonians knew he worked in preaching the Good News; they knew him as well as they knew Paul and Silas. The phrase would also be understandable in a letter of authorization before Timothy's visit or which he carried with him: 'You remember Timothy – he's our colleague and doing good work.' But this was written *after* Timothy's visit, probably just a week or so after he'd said goodbye to them all. So why do Paul and Silas stress that he is 'our *brother* – a full colleague; a *fellow*-worker in the Good News'? Presumably because some at least of the Thessalonians had looked down on him. They weren't impressed with his performance. In their dissatisfaction they misunderstood exactly why he'd come. This is clearly a source of some bad feeling, because Paul has added one of his 'I' repetitions to clarify his motives. 'That is why I had to send Timothy. I could not bear it any longer, so I sent him to find out about your faith.'[27]

There are important lessons here. On the one side, people shouldn't take on too much responsibility too young, however promising they are. Paul and Silas acted in desperation, and it's hard to see what else they could have done. But they made Timothy bite off more than he could really chew, and then had to cope with the problems of indigestion! Ideally, all Christian ministry (and indeed any form of responsible work) should progress gradually and smoothly from working under supervision to working alone. Ideally also, much of it is best done in a team rather than alone.[28] Without Paul and Silas to guide him, Timothy may have bluffed and blustered. He probably tried to sound like them, copying their teaching material (perhaps even their tone and mannerisms!) to look more authoritative than he was or felt. He may have offered simplistic answers to the Thessalonians' questions and fears. There are few things more galling than having to take instruction from someone still wet behind the ears.

But on the other side, the Thessalonians (those of them who did this) were wrong to look down their noses at Timothy. While young and inexperienced adults have their limitations, and can seem inept or brash, they still have a lot to give. We 'older and wiser' Christians need the challenge of their enthusiasm, commitment and impatience. God often wants to speak to us through them. Their very inexperience can make them depend on him much more purely and fully than us old hacks who 'know what we're doing'. That makes them fit mouthpieces for God's words and fine tools for his work.

But if Timothy was the sensitive person I think he was, this expedition will have knocked dents in his confidence. It was good that he now had eighteen months of settled work with Paul and Silas in Corinth. It gave him the chance to rebuild and develop, to lay a surer foundation for the next time he would journey out as Paul's go-between. Things would surely go better then – wouldn't they?

Corinth, AD 56/57

As it turned out, Timothy's next journey as Paul's lone spokesman was *to* Corinth six or seven years later. By now Paul was in sharp dispute with the church. The job at Thessalonica had been to shore up a mainly friendly church against persecution from outside; here at Corinth there was open hostility against Paul from inside. His words introducing Timothy as the courier of 1 Corinthians are very angry. He first tries to bring his haughty, headstrong children to their senses with withering sarcasm, then threatens a further verbal lashing when he next sees them.[29] Hardly the atmosphere Timothy would have chosen for his entrance.

Yet he was older and more experienced now; he'd just had the successful fund-raising visit to Macedonia. All his work since he'd last seen the Corinthians equipped him for the purpose of this mission: to remind them of Paul's way of living and teaching.

> I beg you, then, to follow my example. For this purpose
> I am sending to you Timothy, who is my own dear and
> faithful son in the Christian life. He will remind you of
> the principles which I follow in the new life in union

with Christ Jesus and which I teach in all the churches everywhere.[30]

Who better than Timothy, by now Paul's PA in church after church? If anyone could repeat Paul's teachings and explain what he meant, Timothy could. If anyone shared Paul's love for the Corinthians and anxiety to clear up the mess, it was Timothy. If anyone could speak for Paul, almost *as if he was Paul*, Timothy was the man. Indeed, the quieter Timothy must have seemed cut out to resolve the problem more easily than the dominant Paul. He was well qualified to mediate and show Paul's more acceptable, human face.

But there are ominous signs. Timothy's difficulties in Thessalonica keep haunting this project before he even starts it. Paul again feels he has to reinforce Timothy's position by reminding the Corinthians of what they already know perfectly well: 'Timothy, who is my own dear and faithful son in the Christian life'.[31] Timothy is struggling under a double disadvantage: on the one hand, he's *Paul's* go-between and so as unpopular as Paul; but on the other, he's *only* Paul's go-between and so an insult. In the very next verse Paul acknowledges that the Corinthians regard a substitute visitor as a sign of weakness.[32] He foresees they're most unlikely to respect Timothy's authority.

He can't leave the letter without returning to these fears. Two sentences at the end judder with foreboding.[33] 'If Timothy comes your way' – Paul sounds in two minds, already half-hoping Timothy won't get there.[34] 'Make him feel welcome': literally, 'see to it that he has nothing to fear while he is with you', because that's the state of mind he's coming in. 'He is working for the Lord, just as I am': again comes this reminder, which ought to be unnecessary, of Timothy's true worth. 'No one should look down on him', yet the very need for Paul to say it shows that he fears it will happen. 'You must help him to continue his trip in peace, so that he will come back to me': in other words, 'don't send him packing with a flea in his ear, because I shall be the first to hear about it.'

With such a bleak forecast, Timothy must have been tempted, like Jonah, to run in the opposite direction. However much the Corinthians were to blame for their arrogance, they still had a point; Timothy didn't seem an adequate stand-in for Paul. Poor

Timothy must have approached Corinth with dread; he knew they thought he was inferior, and he felt inferior. He may have pleaded with Paul that he wasn't the best person for the job. But his loyalty to Paul and Jesus kept him going – just!

And how did the Corinthians receive him? We hear of no joyful reporting back, as there was after Thessalonica. Only a pregnant silence. Paul's words in 2 Corinthians help us to read between the lines.[35] He tells how he wrote again, another letter between our 1 and 2 Corinthians. 'I wrote to you with a greatly troubled and distressed heart and with many tears: my purpose was not to make you sad, but to make you realize how much I love you all.'[36] Trouble, distress, tears – Timothy and 1 Corinthians had totally failed; Paul was back at square one. He shows no anger with Timothy, but shares in his anguish and shame. We're left to guess at what had happened. Did the Corinthians flatly refuse to let Timothy read the letter to them at all? Did some boycott or even picket the meeting? Or did they listen with a mixture of stony silence and stormy heckling?[37]

At all events, in rejecting Timothy, the Corinthians also rejected Paul.[38] So Paul wrote his troubled letter. And *this* letter got through to their consciences at last. They repented and changed their attitude.[39] But it wasn't just the letter; there was another force at work as well. Paul sent a different messenger this time, Titus; and he succeeded where Timothy had failed. 'Not only were we encouraged; how happy Titus made us with his happiness over the way in which all of you helped to cheer him up!'[40] Titus was clearly the right person for this moment in a way that Timothy wasn't. He'd been an associate of Paul's since before the first missionary journey,[41] so he was older and more experienced than Timothy. 'He remembers how all of you were ready to obey his instructions, how you welcomed him with fear and trembling.'[42] He could make the Corinthians jump to it and obey him! He must have been a more forceful character. He was the sergeant-major they needed, where Timothy had been a soft touch.

Timothy handled this outcome well. It's doubly humiliating to make a mess of something and then see someone else put it right. He must have been tempted to be jealous or bitter. But as the 'we's' in 2 Corinthians show, he joined in Paul's delight at Titus' success.[43]

Nor is the failure itself a reproach to Timothy; we can't change our age or personality. But it contains vital lessons, if he (and we) can absorb them. Different courses suit different horses. God uses different people – different blends of background, character and experience – to meet different needs. No Christian is a super-hero, able to do *everything*. There are some openings and some invitations Timothy must learn to say no to. It may flatter his ego to feel wanted, but there's a double failure if he says yes. He won't do the job well because he's not suited to it, and he'll get in the way of Titus who could do it better. Sadly, we don't enter the world with a finely tuned awareness of our strengths and weaknesses. Some of them we discover only by trying – and failing. We need the chance to experiment. It's painful, but positive. The blessing is, we can then concentrate on what we *are* good at, and avoid further pain by letting someone else do what we're not good at.

There are other blessings in failure too. It makes us humbler about ourselves, and gentler towards others. I remember hearing a gifted young evangelist smugly criticizing someone who had been doing the job ten years longer than him, and I realized that until then he himself had known nothing but unbroken success. I thought, 'Only when his way of doing things has let him down once or twice will he recognize the pressures on the older man.'

That's the easier layer of failure to accept; but there's a tougher side. We can't walk away from *everything* we aren't instantly good at. Some skills and qualities we simply have to develop; some difficult relationships we have to repair and improve. And it may be quite a struggle. For instance, if Timothy was to remain Paul's PA, he couldn't avoid the Corinthians for ever. Titus may be the right person to see this project through, but Timothy would need to visit them again at some stage, and rebuild damaged relationships. That may be another reason Paul included him in writing the next letter to them, our 2 Corinthians.[44]

A few months later they returned to Corinth together for the outset of the Jerusalem relief trip. It must have taken a great effort of will for Timothy to look again at faces and places with such bitter memories. But he will have found healing and strength from facing the past and putting it behind him. We mustn't let our weaknesses and failures make us sign off at God's job centre and run away.

134

Philippi, AD *63/64*

Seven years have passed since Timothy's deputation to Corinth. Paul is under arrest in Rome. Now he plans to send Timothy to 'go between' again, back in Macedonia. At first sight all looks set fair. By this time Timothy is into his thirties, at the height of his partnership with Paul. The Philippian Christians are old friends and supporters.[45] And on the surface the purpose of Timothy's visit looks like a mere exchange of news.

> I hope that I will be able to send Timothy to you soon, so that I may be encouraged by news about you . . . So I hope to send him to you as soon as I know how things are going to turn out for me.[46]

Timothy is to tell the Philippians the news of Paul's trial, and to bring back the church's news for Paul.

But Paul is not after any old news about who's had babies and who's had 'flu. His enquiry into their well-being is a great deal more pointed. The first thing he says when he gets down to the 'business' of the letter is this. 'Now, the important thing is that your way of life should be as the gospel of Christ requires, so that, whether or not I am able to go and see you, I will hear that you are standing firm with one common purpose and that with only one desire you are fighting together for the faith of the gospel.'[47] Timothy's tour of inspection is to ensure that the Philippians are resisting opposition. Like the young churches everywhere, they're under attack for their faith. It comes from 'enemies of Christ's death on the cross' who 'think only of things that belong to this world', and from false teachers who 'insist on cutting the body'.[48] It's the old enemies – 'less than God asks' (this world only) and 'more than God asks' (keep the Jewish law and get circumcised) – which Paul was fighting way back in Galatians.[49] The problem in Thessalonica was persecution; in Corinth it was division and opposition to Paul; now in Philippi it's false teaching.

Paul's central word to the Philippians is, 'As you always obeyed me when I was with you, it is even more important that you obey me now while I am away from you.'[50] And in Paul's absence, who has to see to it that they're obeying him? Timothy, of course. But it won't be an easy task, for there are signs that some in the church are beginning to drift away from Paul's lead. 'If some of you have a different attitude, God will make this clear to you . . . Keep on imitating me, my brothers and sisters. Pay attention to those who follow the right example that we have set for you.'[51] He deliberately refers to Timothy's past work at Philippi: the example that *we* have set'. That's exactly what Timothy will have to repeat and reassert.

There are too many echoes of Thessalonica and Corinth for Paul or Timothy to be over-confident. Seen at the end of this sequence of Timothy's 'go-between' missions, Paul's glowing character reference for him appears in a less happy light.[52] It doesn't take away one speck of Timothy's value to Paul; but it adds an uneasy undertone to the words 'you yourselves know how he has proved his worth'. If they already know, why does he need to say it? Because the Thessalonians had known that Timothy 'works with us for God in preaching the Good News', but they had not given him the credit due. And the Corinthians had known that 'he is working for the Lord, just as I am', but that didn't stop them slighting him. No wonder Paul works hard to give him a solid platform: 'He is the only one who shares my feelings and who really cares about you.' And, Paul hastens to reassure them, sending Timothy isn't a way of crossing them off his own visiting list. 'I trust in the Lord that I myself will be able to come to you soon.'[53]

It seems Paul *was* able to revisit them in person.[54] Did he follow Timothy to Philippi, or perhaps accompany him? We don't know. Tantalizingly, we don't even know for sure that Timothy himself made this planned trip to Philippi; and if he did, whether this time he succeeded.

My 'level 4' hunch is that if he went, all turned out well. For one thing, he would be carrying the bracing news of Paul's release. And for another, he wouldn't be representing Paul alone. The courier with the Philippians letter was Epaphroditus, who'd been with Paul and Timothy in Rome.[55] There's a clear hint that he was to stay in Philippi once he arrived, and begin the process of sorting things out. 'Receive him, then, with joy, as a brother in the Lord. Show respect to all such people as he.'[56] On top of this, Paul addresses part of the letter to his 'faithful partner' in Philippi.[57] Very possibly this is Luke, one of Paul's closest associates, who has also been with him and Timothy in Rome. So Timothy would have strong assistance as he rallied the troops at Philippi. It would feel less like a lone operation than a joint effort with others.

Debriefing

What are the lessons to learn from Timothy's go-between missions? In this chapter, for the first time, we've seen Timothy wrong-footed. Suddenly the record of outstanding success is tarnished. It had to be, eventually. We all have weaknesses and flaws. It would be an incomplete picture of Timothy if we didn't discover his. Only when we see how people deal with problems and mistakes do we see them in the round.

The position he liked best was at Paul's right hand: number two, follower, interpreter. It suggests he was quiet and reserved, even shy and diffident by nature. He found fulfilment in serving someone else. The 'trouble' was that Paul valued his service so highly. He made him his 'permanent secretary'; not just one of his assistants, but his chief assistant. And this meant he couldn't hide in the background for ever. While the job was usually at Paul's side, it had to include trips away from base as Paul's go-between. And this he found much harder.[58] His efforts at Thessalonica and Corinth show that he didn't command respect when thrust into the overall lead. There's a huge difference between the sheltered consultant giving advice, and the lonely leader making the final decision. Under this exposure Timothy no longer looked such a prodigy, advanced beyond his years; he suddenly revealed his youth and vulnerability. He was less good at leading than at following.

This is the temperamental difference between Timothy and Paul. It worked to great advantage on the mission team. Any team needs both sorts: the pioneer and the partner, the extrovert and the introvert, the upfront star and the background assistant. The unfairness is that the Timothys suffer by comparison. The front person steals the limelight and attracts all the applause. The backer-up is grossly underestimated, often thought to be a nonentity. This may not matter while he or she is working as assistant to a Paul. But when pushed to step forward and take a front-stage role, the backstage people have a right to be heard and respected for their true worth. It's deeply wounding to be ignored or scorned simply for lack of glitter or 'charisma' or dynamism.

Those who flock to Christian conferences and road shows could help themselves by judging speakers on what they say, rather than on their exciting or powerful personalities. Committee members too would do well to remember this; they should seek truth, wisdom, and God's will wherever they come from, not just nod passively when 'the leader' or the most eloquent holds forth.

But the fact remains that this was an area of weakness, not strength, for Timothy. He was given the chance for solo responsibility, but didn't thrive on it. His results were better when he was with at least one colleague. He gritted his teeth and did his best when forced to work on his own, but that wasn't his natural habitat. He was a team man, not a lonely genius. He found encouragement and support in having a team-mate to share the load and the responsibility. Many of us are like this. Our ideas flow better with someone else to bounce them off. We perform more strongly, knowing a colleague is backing us up. We can concentrate on our own specialities. And if we discover that God has made us this kind of person, it can help us to know what sort of job will suit us – and what sort to avoid. It should also help our employer or manager to know what sort of tasks to pass our way.

I wonder how good a manager Paul really was in this department. No-one's perfect, even major Bible heroes like Paul! It seems he and Silas had to send Timothy alone to Thessalonica. But Corinth was a different matter. Ideally Paul should have gone himself. But if that was really impossible, couldn't he have sent Erastus along with Timothy? Or summoned Titus to join the expedition at that stage? Perhaps then Timothy would have got on better. And 2 Corinthians could have been written sooner, with much less pain!

It seems there was a mistake in Paul's ambitions for Timothy. We've seen how the proposed mission to Philippi had a flavour of parading the heir apparent.[59] As Timothy's 'father', Paul probably tried to groom his son to stand alone without him. This gave him two problems. One was to convince Timothy: naturally cautious, he lacked self-belief. That led to the second problem: convincing the churches. They obviously didn't see leadership qualities in Timothy. He didn't come over as another Paul. He didn't go out and grab them. To them he seemed weak, insecure, uncommanding. He needed a warm, loving support-base to help him give his best. If he scented hostility or lack of appreciation, he retreated into his shell.

To Paul he must have seemed self-effacing to a fault. If he wouldn't sell himself, Paul would have to do it for him. Hence the increasingly strident testimonials to his virtues. There's almost a feeling of Paul tipping him out of the nest before he's fully fledged. What's the matter with him? Is he just an incredibly slow developer – so advanced in some directions, but unnaturally stunted in others? Or (and perhaps Paul never thought to ask this question) was Timothy actually designed to fly from the nest on his own? Was he a bird at all?

Key Bible passages: Acts 17:14–15; 19:21–22; 1 Thessalonians 3:1–10; 1 Corinthians 4:16–17; 16:10–11; 2 Corinthians 2:4; 7:15; Philippians 2:19–23.

Reflect

1. What do you see as your strengths and weaknesses, in both personality and ability? Review all the jobs you do and the responsibilities you carry. Are there any you're not suited to? Is there anyone else who could do them instead? (You may need other people to help you judge this.)

2. Draw a diagram or chart of the people you look to for a lead, and of the people who look to you for it. This may be at work and/or at church and/or in other parts of daily life. How good is the relationship and understanding between you? Are there any changes or improvements you would like to suggest?

3. What have you learnt from failure? How can you help yourself remember the positive lessons the next time you fail at something? If you are responsible for helping other people to develop and grow, how can you reassure them it's all right to fail, and help them to make it a learning experience?

Share

1. Use this chapter and the list of Bible quotes above to take a closer look at one of Timothy's 'go-between' trips. Draw up a job description for it (list the tasks involved), then a person

specification (describe the character and abilities needed to do the tasks). How well suited do you think Timothy was to do it? How far is the outcome a surprise or 'just what you'd expect'?

2. Taking the same 'go-between' trip or one of the others, write Timothy's diary of it and the church's letter to Paul reporting on it. Then appoint two people to act Paul and Timothy, and hold the conversation they would have when Timothy got back to base. What can you learn from it for yourselves and any church or mission work you're involved in?

3. Most people have problems in some area of self-esteem, self-belief or self-confidence. How would you encourage each other (a) from your own experience; (b) from a Bible truth or passage?

Wimp?

'I don't remember it ever being this hard,' moaned Timothy as they walked back to their lodgings.

'Oh, come on!' Titus tried to summon up a little late-night enthusiasm. 'It was worse at Corinth. And Ephesus was hardly a rest-cure.'

'Yes, but that was red-blooded opposition. Satan must have thought we were worth fighting. But here, we're not getting anywhere. We haven't found *anyone* to make an elder yet. They're all so unreliable.'

Paul nodded. 'It looks as if we're here for a long stint.' Then he tried out the idea he had been chewing over. 'You know what they say, "Cretans are always liars, wicked beasts, and lazy gluttons."'

Titus chuckled. 'Well, that certainly fits most of the ones we've met.'

Timothy didn't like the direction this line of thought was taking. 'But they shouldn't be like that if they're Christians. I'd like to . . .'

He stopped as a familiar figure stepped out of the shadow of the lodging's door.

'Tychicus?' asked Paul, only half-believing it. 'What brings you here?' But suddenly he knew. 'Something's wrong in Ephesus.'

Tychicus nodded. He thrust a piece of paper into Paul's hand. They went indoors to read it in candlelight.

Secret Knowledge

Hymenaeus and Alexander's Academy offers your house-church a course of instruction in Higher Christianity.

1 *Higher-life forerunners:* the real meaning of Old Testament genealogy
2 *Higher-life morality:* keeping the whole law
3 *Higher-life sexuality:* avoiding the shackles of marriage and children
4 *Higher-life diet:* getting wise to the perils of meat and alcohol

5 *Higher-life finance:* finding God's blessing in riches
6 *Higher-life spirituality:* experiencing the resurrection
   now

Fee includes kosher meals
Household and whole-church discounts negotiable
Applications to Philetus the Registrar[1]

Paul sat in silence for a long time. His face looked tired and painfully sad. 'How many of them have fallen for it?' he asked at last.

Tychicus' answer was a sigh. 'Most.'

Paul turned to Timothy. 'We leave for Ephesus in the morning. At least it's the right direction for Macedonia; they need me there too.'

'But . . .' called Titus.

'You must stay here, my son. Things need putting in order.'

Timothy in Ephesus

Paul	Date	Age	Event
64 ? Released; further travels (1 Tim. 1:3, *etc.*).	64/65	34/35	**Left in Ephesus as Paul's delegate (1 Tim. 1:3).**
	65/66	35/36	**Receives 1 Timothy: instructions for dealing with crisis.**
Traditional date for re-arrest and martyrdom in Rome.	66/67	36/37	Probably still at Ephesus, **receives 2 Timothy: final instructions, including summons to Rome.**

---

1 Timothy

This is how a widely used Bible dictionary describes Paul's first letter to Timothy.

He is given instructions about the requirements for bishops, deacons, elders. He is warned against false teachers. But most of the letter consists only of general exhortations to endure suffering, seek righteousness, shun controversies, fulfil his ministry. Timothy emerges as a much more real person in the indirect references to him in 2 Corinthians than he does in this letter which purports to have been addressed to him. The Pastorals [a common term for Paul's letters to Timothy and Titus] are of no help, therefore, in reconstructing the portrait of Paul's youthful associate, Timothy.[2]

This is a common view among those who think that the letter is not genuine. They dismiss it as addressed from a 'pretend' Paul to a 'pretend' Timothy, written much later than the AD 60s.[3] This blinds them to all the blushes and aches and stammers of the real Timothy which stare at us from every section of 1 Timothy – and 2 Timothy, for that matter.

Unfortunately, this school of thought has also dimmed the sight of those who do accept that these letters are from the real Paul.[4] It's common to talk of them as if they were a sort of handbook which Paul gave to his assistant for running the affairs in any church: a cool, calm collection of handy hints.[5] In fact they're raw and sore from the crisis in Ephesus in 64 or 65. They make sense only when we look back through them at the crisis, and what happened to Timothy when Paul left him to handle it.

The Ephesus crisis

What crisis? And why Timothy? Paul's opening words in 1 Timothy[6] help us to reassemble the story, piece by piece.

I was on my way to Macedonia.

Paul's confidence that he would soon be released from his house arrest in Rome was well placed.[7] He set off on a fourth missionary journey, which included plans to visit Macedonia. The journey is not recorded in Acts, but we can re-create some of it from the pastoral letters.[8] The letter to Titus shows that he visited Crete. 'I left you in Crete, so that you could put in order the things that still needed doing and appoint church elders in every town.'[9]

As usual, Paul wasn't alone. Titus was with him (and, as the next extract will show, probably Timothy too). They were in Crete long enough to preach the Good News in each town (a few months, perhaps), but not long enough to consolidate the infant churches and appoint elders. Paul wanted to move on to Macedonia.[10]

> . . . just as I urged you when I was on my way to Macedonia.

Whether Timothy made his 'go-between' visit to Philippi or not,[11] he evidently rejoined Paul at or after his release from Rome. They certainly made part of the trip to Macedonia together. It's natural to infer (level 3) that they evangelized in Crete together before setting sail.

> . . . in Ephesus, just as I urged you . . . on my way.

It would be normal to put in at Ephesus on the voyage from Crete to Macedonia. In the opening episode of this chapter I've followed my hunch that Paul and Timothy got word of Ephesus in Crete, and had this further, urgent reason for calling there. But they may not have done. They may have been rejoicing at the prospect of seeing again the Ephesian elders they had worked so hard with.[12] If so, they had a bitter shock.

> Some people there are teaching false doctrines.

Once again a young church had gone down to wrong teaching. Many have assumed that these false teachers were travelling missionaries from outside, as at Galatia and Corinth. But there's no hint of this in 1 Timothy. The 'some people' teaching untruth at Ephesus were from their own number, some of the elders themselves. It was exactly as Paul had feared and foreseen on their last visit. 'The time will come when some men from your own group will tell lies to lead the believers away after them.'[13]

But so soon – and despite Paul's warnings! In just half a decade – the time it took Timothy to grow from twenty-nine to thirty-four – some of the Ephesian leaders drifted right away from the moorings of the Good News and the Bible to which Paul had roped them as hard as he knew how.[14] Firm grounding in the faith and high position in the church are no automatic safeguard from creeping error.

And it was more than just one or two of the elders. Paul excommunicated Hymenaeus and Alexander,[15] presumably the ringleaders. But as he leaves Ephesus for Macedonia, 'some people are teaching false doctrines' still!

It's almost certainly wrong to picture a single congregation meeting in 'Ephesus Central Hall'. A huge city like Ephesus would have several small churches in different homes; one met in the house of Aquila and Priscilla, for example.[16] The elders were the leaders of these different churches. When the elders of a house-church started teaching untruth, that whole church went downhill. That's the crisis facing Timothy: several – perhaps most – of the little congregations rolling away off the rails.

It helps to explain why some of their wrong ideas contradict each other.[17] Some people were carried away with their new authority as Bible teachers, but got sidetracked into irrelevant details of the Old Testament.[18] Others showed off their new spiritual freedom without thinking, in ways that upset the conventions of the Ephesian citizens, and made them less likely to become Christians.[19] Some made a virtue (more Greek than Christian) of abstaining from meat, alcohol and marriage.[20] Others thought they'd found a nice way to feather their nest by charging fees or demanding donations for their teaching 'ministry'.[21] Probably some of the churches majored on one idea and some on another. In one form or other, they are still with us today.[22]

Timothy's job

Now the last two phrases of Paul's opening instruction fall into place. '*I want you to stay* in Ephesus, just as I urged you when I was on my way to Macedonia. Some people there are teaching false doctrines, *and you must order them to stop.*'[23] He gives Timothy three tasks.

1. *Stop the false teachers.* They're leading their church members astray. And their un-Christian behaviour is bringing the name of Jesus into disrepute. So they must be stopped. How? Paul gives Timothy two crisp instructions.

(a) 'Order them to stop.' Timothy is Paul's go-between, carrying his apostolic authority. So he can take a firm stand when he confronts the elders. The word 'order' is a soldier's term for giving commands. 'By the right; stop all this rot; *halt!*' No argument, no discussion, no compromise. All being well, they will return to living and teaching the true word of God. This will make their peace with Paul, and restore the churches to good health.[24]

But if they pay no attention? Then turn to the second instruction; (b) 'Rebuke publicly all those who commit sins, *so that the rest may be afraid.*'[25] This is no whispered finger-wagging in the corner. Timothy is to explain their error in front of their church and their fellow-elders, and then remove them from eldership. Paul hopes the others will take fright at such drastic steps and mend their ways.

False teaching isn't a misfortune we can do nothing about; still less an interesting variation on the truth! It's a noxious weed which must be uprooted. No-one who deliberately persists in contradicting the Bible should expect to remain a church leader.

2. *Replace those who won't stop, with true teachers.* Timothy is to commission some replacement elders. He is 'to lay hands on [them] in dedication to the Lord's service'.[26]

But there's no rush. Paul is learning that his earlier policy of appointing elders within a few months of founding a church has dangers. It's easy to choose people not mature enough to handle it. Too much haste was the root of the problem at Ephesus. So now Paul cautions Timothy to weigh up the candidates' qualifications carefully before selecting them. 'The sins of some people are plain to see, and their sins go ahead of them to judgement; but the sins of others are seen only later. In the same way good deeds are plainly seen, and even those that are not so plain cannot be hidden.'[27] The right people to choose will become obvious in due time.

In the same way today we need to beware of appointing people to church leadership or senior posts in missionary societies too soon or too young. It's very rare for people to be ready to share in a church's eldership in their twenties. Paul gave Timothy a list of the qualities to look for. They're exactly the qualities the erring elders in Ephesus lacked; Paul drew this character-sketch from bitter experience. There's a high premium on virtues that will prevent the disaster happening again: tried and tested maturity, and respect from those outside the church who will therefore be more likely to take Christianity seriously. 'A church leader must be without fault . . . sober, self-controlled, and orderly; he must welcome strangers in his own home . . . he must not be a drunkard or a violent man, but gentle and peaceful; he must not love money; he must be able to manage his own family well and make his children obey him with all respect. For if a man does not know how to manage his own family, how can he take care of the church of God? He must be mature in the faith . . . respected by the people outside the church . . .'[28]

Once in place, these elders should encourage prayer in church meetings, rather than the bad-tempered arguing the false teaching has generated.[29] Above all they should preach and teach the truth.[30] The one skill they must have is to 'be able to teach'.[31] That's how to build the churches up to resist any further attacks from erring teachers. And that's what Paul wants his letter to achieve in Ephesus: 'This letter will let you know how we should conduct ourselves in God's household, which is the church of the living God, *the pillar and support of the truth*.'[32] It's not general tips on Christian conduct, as casual readers have often supposed, but a strategy to make each house-church a pillar and buttress propping up the true faith, so that it won't cave in again.

And that demands a third key task of Timothy. Our need is just the same; we should look for this from our church and mission leaders too.

3. *Set the example of true teaching and living yourself.* Timothy isn't to be a mere supervisor, firing one set of teachers and hiring another. He's to get into the thick of it himself, both teaching the Christian way and showing how to live it.

(a) First, Paul's command to him to teach repeats like a recorded jingle through the letter. He's to do it and keep doing it.

> Give these instructions to the believers . . . Give them these instructions and these teachings. Give them these instructions . . . You must teach and preach these things. Command those who are rich . . . Command them . . . Watch yourself and watch your teaching. Keep on doing these things, because if you do, you will save both yourself and those who hear you.[33]

'Save yourself and those who hear': that's the rich dividend Paul expects from Timothy's teaching. It's hard to imagine any stronger way to say how vital teaching is in church life, now as well as then.

(b) Secondly, Paul says: 'Watch *yourself* and your teaching.' It won't do to issue instructions from the armchair. Timothy's own life must match his teaching. He's to be the model Christian for others to learn from: 'Be an example for the believers.' In each part of life where the false teachers went wrong, he is to show the right way: 'in your speech, your conduct, your love, faith and purity'.[34] As Paul closes the letter, he urges Timothy again to keep up the highest standards of Christian living: 'Strive for righteousness, godliness, faith, love, endurance, and gentleness. Run your best in the race of faith.'[35] He would surely make the same repeated appeal to our leaders in our struggle against false teaching.

That's what 1 Timothy is about. It isn't, in the first instance, a handbook on church government. It's an urgent plea from Paul to Timothy to stop the rot in Ephesus, to appoint new elders and to show them what to do. Together with 2 Timothy, it can guide us in resisting false teaching today, and in preventing it in the first place.

So much is clear and on the surface. But there's a great deal more going on between the lines. I don't know about you, but I read these instructions to Timothy with a sense of doom. After his difficulties in Thessalonica and Corinth, I wonder how on earth he'll cope with openly rebellious elders at Ephesus. And you don't have to look far to see that Paul obviously had the same misgivings. He knows he's asking a lot of Timothy, probably too much. He has learnt from experience that Timothy needs a huge amount of encouraging to exert authority; perhaps all the more after those earlier troubles. So Paul isn't just telling Timothy what to do; he also has to battle to persuade Timothy that he *can* and *must* do it! This becomes the constant undercurrent and subtext of the letter.

Is Timothy up to the job?

The best way to scent Paul's worries about Timothy is to compare this letter with the one he wrote to Titus. Paul had left Titus in Crete; he wrote to him there, apparently at the same time as he wrote to Timothy. The outline of what he says, shorn of the detail, is remarkably similar to 1 Timothy.

> I left you in Crete, so that you could put in order the things that still needed doing and appoint church elders . . . Remember my instructions: an elder must be blameless . . . For there are many . . . who rebel and deceive others with their nonsense. It is necessary to stop their talk, because they are upsetting whole families . . . For this reason you must rebuke them sharply, so that they may have a healthy faith . . . you must teach what agrees with sound doctrine. Instruct the older men . . . the older women . . . the young men . . . In all things you yourself must be an example of good behaviour. Be sincere and serious in your teaching. Use sound words that cannot be criticized, so that your enemies may be put to shame by not having anything bad to say about us . . . use your full authority as you encourage and rebuke your hearers. Let none of them look down on you . . . But avoid stupid arguments, long lists of ancestors, quarrels, and fights about the Law . . . Give at least two warnings to those who cause divisions, and then have nothing more to do with them.[36]

That is, if you like, Paul's standard job description for his envoys in AD 64. There's no unnecessary repetition; it's a straightforward set of marching orders.

1 Timothy issues much the same orders. But it's got the volume turned up and the echo chamber on! Paul repeats himself, and uses extraordinarily strong language compared with the simple statement to Titus. This will stand up off the page at us if we take a fresh look at the six main passages where Paul speaks personally to Timothy.

1 Timothy 1:1–3

> From Paul, an apostle of Christ Jesus by order of God our Saviour and Christ Jesus our hope –
>
> To Timothy, my true son in the faith:
>
> May God the Father and Christ Jesus our Lord give you grace, mercy and peace.
>
> I want you to stay in Ephesus, just as I urged you . . . you must order them to stop.

It's an unusual greeting in several ways.[37] But the most striking is that, unlike every other letter except Galatians,[38] there are no words of thanksgiving. Paul has nothing to give thanks for, either in the Ephesian elders, or in Timothy himself. He plunges straight into business. The abrupt tone reflects his difficulty in getting Timothy to agree to the job. 'I want you to *stay* in Ephesus, just as I *urged* you' – a clear hint that Timothy wanted to get out and had pleaded with Paul to let him go. He needed a lot of persuading to see it through.

1 Timothy 1:18–19

> Timothy, my child, I entrust to you this command, which is in accordance with the words of prophecy spoken in the past about you . . .

Paul begins, 'Timothy, my child.' He talks intimately, father to son, because these important, delicate words will be hard for Timothy to take. He then repeats the instruction he began the letter with. 'I entrust to you *this command*' refers back to the 'order them to stop' of verse 3.[39] He can only need to repeat himself because he's not sure that Timothy will act on the first instruction.[40] And he adds further pressure by saying, 'I *entrust* to you this command.' It's the word for the most sacred request in ancient society. It means leaving your dearest possession in the safe keeping of someone you trust to guard it well. How could Timothy let Paul down after language like this?

Unfortunately, Paul seems to think that Timothy might indeed let him down, because he lays it on even more thickly. He reminds Timothy of his commissioning when he joined the team in Lystra sixteen years earlier.[41] Paul is making no new, unreasonable demand of him; it's 'in accordance with the words of prophecy spoken in the past about you'. God has clearly stamped him as a gifted teacher and one of Paul's team responsible for these Asian and European churches. But sometimes we need someone else to bring these obvious truths back to our memory. So Paul lingers a little longer on what the prophecies said.

> Use those words as weapons in order to fight well, and keep your faith and a clear conscience.

The words after 'in order to' seem to be a direct quote of the prophecies.[42] 'Fight well'; literally, war the good warfare. The Good News of Jesus is at stake; it's in danger of being distorted and lost, and the churches along with it. This calls for a battle royal; fight this good fight against untruth with all your might.

But fight fair. 'Keep your faith and a clear conscience,' urges verse 19 – even more revealing and shattering than 18. If verse 18 was saying, 'Do your duty as an apostolic missionary', 19 is saying, 'Don't give in to the false teaching, and so stop being a Christian.'[43] Surely *Timothy* doesn't need such a basic reminder? But yes, he evidently does, because Paul goes on to give a dire warning. 'Some people have not listened to their conscience and have made a ruin of their faith.' Oh, Timothy, make sure it doesn't happen to you too. Paul fears Timothy isn't immune to the lure of false teaching.

1 Timothy 4:6–16

These two paragraphs are very poignant when we hear what they really are: a sustained effort to encourage and reinforce the diffident, reluctant Timothy. We too may quail at the daunting task of resisting and reforming wrong ideas in the church; it *is* lonely, even frightening, to stand up against people who don't base their ideas on the Bible, especially when they're in senior positions. Paul would want to boost our resolve with much the same words.

The first paragraph is sandwiched between two repetitions of task 3a, 'Teach the truth.'[44]

> If you give these instructions to the believers, you will be a good servant of Christ Jesus, as you feed yourself spiritually on the words of faith and of the true teaching which you have followed. But keep away from those godless legends, which are not worth telling. Keep yourself in training for a godly life . . . We struggle and work hard, because we have placed our hope in the living God, who is the Saviour of all and especially of those who believe.
>
> Give them these instructions and these teachings.

If Paul thought Timothy would find task 3 easy to do, he wouldn't keep repeating it. And to show that this is what's on his mind, he has crammed several other strong hints about it inside the sandwich. 'If you give these instructions, you will be a good servant of Christ'; it's your job as a Christian minister to teach the truth and warn of error. 'Feed yourself on the words of faith and true teaching . . . Keep yourself in training'; don't forget or give up the essentials of spiritual food and exercise yourself. 'We struggle and work hard, because we have placed our hope in the living God'; it's tough going for all of us in this job, but *God is with us*, so don't give up! *And don't give in*: 'keep away from those godless legends'. Literally, 'refuse the godless old wives' tales'. Paul feared that Timothy would visit the widows' houses that were one centre of the false teaching,[45] and end up believing their error rather than convincing them of the truth.[46]

The fact that the false teachers are elders, many of them presumably older than Timothy, is the worry Paul tackles in the second paragraph.

> Do not let anyone look down on you because you are young, but be an example for the believers . . . Until I come, give your time and effort to the public reading of the Scriptures and to preaching and teaching. Do not neglect the spiritual gift that is in you . . . Practise these things and devote yourself to them, in order that your progress may be seen by all. Watch yourself and watch your teaching. Keep on doing these things . . .[47]

Paul repeats to Timothy (and anyone else tempted to feel intimidated) that the way to make even those who are older respect him is simply to do his job properly: 'be an example for the believers' (task 3b). And then get on with task 3a – reading the Scriptures, preaching and teaching – the fundamental ministry of all church leaders.[48] As Timothy continues to falter, Paul reminds him that this is his spiritual gift, attested by God. And then he peppers him with commands to get on and do it. Give your time and effort . . . don't neglect . . . practise and devote yourself . . . watch yourself and watch your teaching . . . keep on doing these things . . . Surely even Timothy would be goaded into action by now! But no; Paul isn't done yet.

1 Timothy 5:19–25

On their own, verses 19 and 20 seem a straightforward explanation of task 1b (replacing unrepentant false teachers). 'Do not listen to an accusation against an elder unless it is brought by two or more witnesses. Rebuke publicly all those who commit sins . . .' But Paul comes straight in with verse 21, which completely changes the tone.

> In the presence of God and of Christ Jesus and of the holy angels I solemnly call upon you to obey these instructions without showing any prejudice or favour to anyone in anything you do.

Even if he said only 'Obey without showing prejudice or favour', we'd learn that he feared that Timothy was likely to sentence some too hastily, while yielding to pressure to let others off. But the strength of language Paul uses to bind Timothy over shows he thinks it's already happening; Paul knew that Timothy could never stand up to the elders on his own. 'In the presence of God . . . I solemnly call upon you . . .' Paul has used the oath 'before God' only once in his surviving letters before 1 Timothy. That was in Galatians.[49] We know, and Timothy above all knew, how sternly and strenuously Paul was having to speak there. But here it's not just 'before God'; he adds Christ Jesus and, for good measure, the holy angels too! It almost strains our belief that Paul could write in this vein to his beloved Timothy. Only the most desperate emergency would drive him to it.

But there's more: '*I solemnly call upon you* to obey.' It's another word of the strongest possible pleading. Literally, Paul says, 'I solemnly protest or witness before God . . .' It's the word he used to describe the heart of his mission: 'witnessing solemnly' to the Good News of God's grace.[50] It has something of the force of the children's affirmation, 'Cross my heart and hope to die.' Words simply don't exist to put it any more strongly. *That* is the word, virile and close to the heart of his own identity, that he picks up and holds like a gun to Timothy's head. 'By all you know that is dear to me, do it: stop the false teachers.'

Then Paul moves on to Timothy's task 2, appointing new elders.[51]

Be in no hurry to lay hands on anyone in dedication to the Lord's service. Take no part in the sins of others; keep yourself pure. Do not drink water only, but take a little wine to help your digestion, since you are ill so often. The sins of some people are plain to see . . . but . . . others are seen only later. In the same way good deeds are plainly seen . . .

Here again Paul's instruction isn't just a simple set of steps to take when the time comes. Three of the commands are negative; in Greek this often means, not 'Don't ever consider doing this thing', but 'Stop doing it now'.[52] The force of the first of the two sentences is less GNB's 'Be in no hurry . . . Take no part . . .' than '*Stop* being in such a hurry to appoint people elders, and so *stop* appearing to approve of their sins'. Whether because he can't say no to them or because he's a poor judge of character, Timothy is evidently choosing other false teachers (perhaps the 'next in line' in each house-church) to replace the ones he's just sacked. 'Not so fast!' says Paul. 'Give it time, and the qualifications of the right candidates to be the new elders will become obvious – even to you!'

Into this paragraph Paul slips one of his most famous sidelights on Timothy's character and story. 'Take no part in the sins of others by making them elders,' he says; 'keep yourself pure; stay clear of their contamination.' And that reminds him of another way Timothy has given in to their influence. 'Do not drink water only' – or, more precisely, 'Stop drinking only water.'[53] Timothy has obviously 'swallowed' their super-spiritual line on food and drink.[54] They thought it more 'holy' to be teetotal, and he's followed their lead. However holy the practice, unfortunately it was less healthy; the bad water was not helping Timothy's old tummy trouble. Come on, says Paul, you don't have to be *that* pure! Take a little wine (not too much!) to help your digestion; that'll make you feel better. You don't have to compete with the cranks and drive yourself into an early grave. Pay attention to the proper demands of your body. Look after yourself sensibly, kindly, medically.[55]

1 Timothy 6:11–14

But you, man of God, avoid all these things. Strive for righteousness, godliness, faith, love, endurance, and gentleness. Run your best in the race of faith, and win eternal life for yourself; for it was to this life that God called you when you firmly professed your faith before many witnesses. Before God . . . and before Christ Jesus . . . I command you to obey your orders and keep them faithfully until the day when our Lord Jesus Christ will appear.

In his anxiety Paul repeats himself again and again. 'Strive for righteousness, godliness', *etc.*; these are the same qualities he told Timothy to develop a mere two chapters ago.[56] 'Run your best . . .'; literally, struggle the good struggle of the faith. These words are almost identical to his plea in chapter 1, 'Fight the good fight.'[57] But this time the echo goes back still further than Timothy's commissioning; it repeats his conversion and baptism call to 'win eternal life for yourself'.[58] That's how far Timothy has slipped back under pressure. And once again Paul makes his appeal with an oath 'before God . . . and before Christ Jesus.'[59]

He pulls out every stop he can think of as he sums up the whole letter by repeating his blunt words of half a chapter earlier: 'I command you to obey your orders and keep them faithfully . . .'[60] How long for?'. . . until the Day when our Lord Jesus Christ will appear.' No father needs to speak to his son, apprentice and friend like this unless the younger man is veering dangerously off course.[61]

1 Timothy 6:20–21

Timothy, keep safe what has been entrusted to your care. Avoid the profane talk and foolish arguments of what some people wrongly call 'Knowledge'. For some have claimed to possess it, and as a result they have lost the way of faith.

God's grace be with you all.

The last words come as a shock: 'grace be with you *all*'. But they shed a sudden new light on the whole letter. Paul is speaking not just to Timothy but to all the church members in Ephesus. This makes more sense of his opening words too: 'From Paul, *an apostle of Christ Jesus by order of God.*'[62] Paul stresses his apostolic authority only when it is in dispute.[63] He's speaking through Timothy to the erring elders and their followers. In other words, the letter isn't a purely private note to Timothy. It's his official document of authorization to show, perhaps read aloud, to all the churches. It puts in writing what Paul expects him to do. It's to strengthen his position and stiffen his resolve.[64]

This is the setting for the last two verses of the letter. No string of the usual friendly greetings; just dark, dark foreboding. 'Timothy . . . Avoid the profane talk and foolish arguments . . . ' This is Paul speaking to his closest friend and helper of the last sixteen years. Why should he need to tell him to avoid the false teaching? Partly, as we have seen with alarming repetition, because he fears that Timothy isn't strong enough to resist it unaided; but partly too to label the false teachers for all to see.

Imagine the scene. Timothy visits one of the house-churches where the 'super-spiritual' teaching holds away. He reads out his letter of authority from Paul. What more devastating ending could there be than 'Avoid . . . what some people wrongly call "Knowledge". For some have claimed to possess it, and as a result they have lost the way of faith.' Those who've been teaching the new 'Knowledge' stand exposed. They're no longer fit to be church leaders. *That* should help Timothy rally the loyal troops. Without such a weapon in his hands, Paul fears, he'll never do it.

So this is what 1 Timothy is: notice of dismissal for the false teachers; a licence to appoint new leaders; and a reissue of Timothy's own job description. Was it enough to bring Timothy back into line? We've no chapter 29 of Acts to tell us, and no letter from Timothy to Paul to report the results. But we have got Paul's next preserved letter to Timothy, written about two years later. It gives us a clear idea of how Timothy got on in the meantime.

2 Timothy[65]

Paul is in prison again, probably arrested at Troas on his way back from Macedonia to Ephesus.[66] And this time the regime is harsher than the earlier house arrest: 'I suffer and am even chained like a criminal.'[67]

While in prison he received repeated visits from Onesiphorus of Ephesus: 'he cheered me up many times'.[68] But he evidently brought bad news of the churches in Ephesus and the surrounding province. 'You know that everyone in . . . Asia . . . has deserted me.'[69] Paul may be exaggerating in his despair; but it sounds as if there has been a general turning away from him on the news of his arrest. Things were bad in 1 Timothy, but now they're worse. Even those who *were* loyal to him have abandoned him.

Except for . . . Onesiphorus. We hope in vain for Paul to say that, of course, *Timothy* has stood firm. But plainly Onesiphorus was unable to report this. Instead, Paul holds the loyal Onesiphorus out as an example and a contrast to Timothy.[70] Of Onesiphorus Paul says wistfully, '*He* was not ashamed that I am in prison'; to Timothy he says, '*Do* not . . . be ashamed of me, a prisoner for Christ's sake.'[71]

This 'level 3' inference is borne out if we cut the letter back to its bare bones. It doesn't thank God or congratulate Timothy for his loyalty (which so many of the past letters took for granted); it's a prolonged four-chapter appeal to *be* loyal. It's a string of thirty-three verbs in command mode;[72] a series of staccato orders, urgings and pleas to Timothy. Pared down to these commands, Paul's mood and message become all too clear. We can deduce what he has heard about Timothy.

> Do not be ashamed, then, of witnessing for our Lord; nor be ashamed of me, a prisoner for Christ's sake. Instead, take your part in suffering for the Good News . . .
>
> Hold firmly to the true words that I taught you . . . and remain in the faith and love that are ours . . . keep the good things that have been entrusted to you . . .
>
> Be strong through the grace that is ours in union with Christ . . . Take the teachings that you heard me proclaim . . . and entrust them to reliable people . . . Take your part in suffering, as a loyal soldier of Christ . . .
>
> Think about what I am saying . . . Remember Jesus Christ . . .
>
> Remind your people of this, and give them a solemn warning . . . not to fight over words . . . Do your best to win full approval in God's sight . . . Keep away from profane and foolish discussions . . .
>
> Avoid the passions of youth, and strive for righteousness, faith, love, and peace . . . But keep away from foolish and ignorant arguments . . .

> Remember that there will be difficult times in the last days. People will be selfish . . . Keep away from such people . . .
>
> Continue in the truths that you were taught . . .
>
> I solemnly urge you to preach the message, to insist upon proclaiming it . . . to convince, reproach, and encourage . . .
>
> But you must keep control of yourself in all circumstances; endure suffering, do the work of a preacher of the Good News, and perform your whole duty as a servant of God.[73]

As in 1 Timothy, Paul has to command and warn and threaten and repeat, in his effort to persuade Timothy to stay true to his task and to the faith. Commentaries have traditionally taken a rather sentimental view of the Paul–Timothy relationship in 2 Timothy. One of them speaks of the letter as 'one of the most moving portions of Scripture . . . There is a paternal touch about the whole epistle . . . a beautiful and intimate companionship between this Father and Son'.[74] Our final estimate may come very close to these words; but if so, we shall mean them all the more deeply, after a great deal of pain. We shall notice what that commentary hardly notices at all: Paul's tone of frenzied concern and criticism about Timothy in almost every verse.

The heart of the letter

The section which deals most clearly with Timothy's performance since the end of 1 Timothy is 2:14 – 3:9.[75] It shows the false teachers still at work in Ephesus. Timothy has been unable to carry out task no. 1, which was to stop them. 'They have left the way of truth and are upsetting the faith of some believers by saying that our resurrection has already taken place.'[76] As in 1 Timothy there's a strikingly modern ring to their heresy. 'The "resurrection" isn't a literal return to life after we die. There probably is no afterlife. It's picture language for the new quality of life we experience here and now as Christians.'

Paul calls such ideas gangrene, a wasting disease like cancer, because they eat away at our faith and finally destroy it.[77] They lead to a collapse of Christian living. 'People will be selfish, greedy, boastful, and conceited; they will be insulting, disobedient to their parents, ungrateful, and irreligious; they will be unkind, merciless, slanderers, violent, and fierce; they will hate the good; they will be treacherous, reckless, and swollen with pride; they will love pleasure rather than God.'[78] At first sight these words sound to me like the pagan world all round us. But as I read on, the chilling fact dawns that Paul is talking about *church members*! 'They will hold to the outward form of our religion, but reject its real power.'[79]

To be exact, he still has in his sights the erring house-church leaders and their followers – people he and Timothy had appointed a mere ten years earlier. Once they had seemed orthodox Christians, but now they're quite the reverse. 'Some of them go into people's houses and gain control over weak women . . . these people are opposed to the truth – people whose minds do not function and who are failures in the faith.'[80] Timothy may have succeeded in removing them from leadership (task 1b), but his Christian living and teaching haven't won them back to the truth (task 3).

When we come to Paul's direct commands to Timothy in these paragraphs, they too confirm Paul's fears in 1 Timothy.

2 Timothy 3:1

'Remember that there will be difficult times in the last days.' Like most of the commands in this part of the letter, the form of the Greek word means something Timothy is to do continually.[81] 'Keep telling yourself these are the last days, when people will behave like this. Don't be taken off guard; don't let it sweep you off your feet.' Paul remains unsure that Timothy will keep his head in the crisis.

2 Timothy 2:16, 23; 3:5

Three times in twenty-two verses Paul reminds Timothy how to treat the false teaching.[82]

> Keep away from profane and foolish discussions, which only drive people further away from God . . . keep away from foolish and ignorant arguments; you know that they end up in quarrels . . . Keep away from such people.

Again the commands are all continuous: 'Keep on keeping away;

don't drop your guard and get lured in.' There's no need for Paul to repeat like this unless he's been given reason to fear that Timothy *isn't* keeping away.

2 Timothy 2:22

What Paul has heard makes his fear go deeper still. It's not just that Timothy gets distracted into wasteful, damaging quarrels; but that when he does, he's quarrel*some*. 'Avoid the passions of youth, and strive for righteousness, faith, love, and peace . . .'[83] As in 1 Timothy, this negative command isn't mere wise advice that may come in handy some day; it's direct censure of how Timothy is behaving now. 'Turn your back on your natural tendency to dispute and argue; make an all-out effort to stay true to Jesus' teaching and show love and peace towards your opponents.'

Paul continues: '. . . together with those who with a pure heart call out to the Lord for help'. He has heard that Timothy is abandoning his duty to pastor the flock, in his haste to snap and snarl at the wolves. 'Don't leave your real allies; work with the Christians who are staying true to Jesus, and draw on their support.'

2 Timothy 2:15

When it comes to how Timothy is actually teaching, we find a negative origin to a beloved text, usually quoted with no regard to its setting. 'Do your best to win full approval in God's sight, as a worker who is not ashamed of his work, one who correctly teaches the message of God's truth.' Many a Bible teacher has taken it as a motto, and a good one it makes. But Paul didn't write it for a bookmark or tapestry square when Timothy first joined the team; rather as a final desperate tug on the leash when he seemed about to abandon all it stood for. The point is, Timothy had reason to *be* ashamed of his work: he was *not* teaching correctly. So Paul used the reminder of God as his ultimate paymaster to pull him back on course.[84]

When we look at the verses between the commands, they seem at first glance not to mention Timothy at all. But they're really all about him.[85] And the same picture stares us in the face. He's falling down badly on the job.

2 Timothy 2:24–25

Straight after the commands, 'Avoid the passions . . . strive for righteousness' *etc.*, 'keep away from foolish and ignorant arguments', Paul continues:

> The Lord's servant must not quarrel. He must be kind towards all, a good and patient teacher, who is gentle as he correct his opponents, for it may be that God will give them the opportunity to repent and come to know the truth.[86]

In Paul's mind this wasn't, as in so many sermons today, a generalized cameo of the ideal Christian minister. It was a sustained rebuke to Timothy, made slightly less painful and easier to take by using 'he' instead of 'you'. But what Paul meant was, 'Timothy, *you* must stop all this quarrelling. You're teaching in the wrong way. You aren't living out a Christian example. You aren't being kind, patient, gentle. You're treating the elders as enemies and so driving them away, rather than winning them back to the truth.'

2 Timothy 2:19–21

These verses paint an even bleaker picture. They follow Paul's report of the latest false teaching at Ephesus (the resurrection has already taken place);[87] this is what dominates his mind and colours his illustration of the kitchen in a rich man's house (verses 20–21).

> In a large house there are dishes and bowls of all kinds: some are made of silver and gold, others of wood and clay; some are for special occasions, others for ordinary use. If anyone makes himself or herself clean from all those evil things, they will be used for special purposes, because they are dedicated and useful to their Master, ready to be used for every good deed.

The two types of dishes and bowls are literally 'for honour' (GNB translates 'for special occasions') and 'for dishonour'. These 'dishonourable dishes' were probably not 'for ordinary use' as

GNB puts it, but rather rubbish bins or bedpans for the slops. They were good only for throwing out. And they're a picture of – yes, of course – the false teachers. 'If anyone makes himself or herself clean from all those evil things [*i.e.* the false teachings], they will be used for special purposes.' A dishonourable false teacher can become an honourable teacher of the truth again.

But then comes the shock. The very next words are the command to Timothy. 'Avoid the passions of youth, and strive for righteousness . . .' *He* is the 'anyone' who must make himself clean from false teachings and dedicate himself afresh to the Master. Timothy is the dirty dish who must become useful again. He has been contaminated by the false teaching.

But if Timothy is the real subject of verses 20 and 21, isn't he also the main subject of verse 19?

> But the solid foundation that God has laid cannot be shaken; and on it are written these words: 'The Lord knows those who are his' and 'All who say that they belong to the Lord must turn away from wrong-doing.'[88]

Timothy must turn from the wrongdoing of involvement with the false teaching; and Paul reassures him that *his* solid foundation will in the last resort stand. It seems that Timothy was every bit as badly affected by the false teaching as Paul had dreaded in 1 Timothy. He didn't merely fight it with un-Christian aggression.[89] His own faith was beginning to waver; was he mesmerized by the idea of a 'spiritual' resurrection?[90] Perhaps his loud shouting grew from insecure fears that he couldn't see through the false teachings and hold his ground against them. In Onesiphorus' view at least, it was only a matter of time before Timothy became a false teacher himself. No wonder Paul howls to him from his Roman dungeon, 'Don't give in; don't give up. The Lord knows you and can hold on to you.'

So the central section of the letter turns out to be a dim, worrying report on Timothy's progress. He has failed to stop the false teaching (task 1 in 1 Timothy);[91] and he's failed to counter it with true teaching (task 3a). When he has seen through it, he's tried to attack it blow for blow in an un-Christian spirit (so failing in task

3b, which was to be a model disciple). But worst of all, he's nearly gone under to the false teaching himself.

The rest of the letter

If this is the right reading of 2:14 – 3:9, we shall expect the rest of the letter to support it. And indeed it does. Time and again Paul says to Timothy, 'Keep on doing what I told you. Don't give up.' When this message comes not once but six times in as many paragraphs, we can be pretty sure we're close to the letter's heartbeat. The horrible prospect jumps out at us at every turn: Timothy is on the point of giving up in despair, giving up his *job* certainly, but perhaps giving up his *faith* as well.

2 Timothy 1:5–7

> I remember the sincere faith you have . . . I am sure that you have it . . . For this reason I remind you to keep alive the gift that God gave you . . . the Spirit that God has given us does not make us timid; instead, his Spirit fills us with power, love, and self-control.

Paul simply wouldn't need to say that 'the Spirit . . . does not make us timid' unless Timothy was short of guts and staying power. Nor would he say (to his closest Christian friend), 'I am sure that you have [sincere Christian faith]', unless someone was casting doubt on it. Onesiphorus? Or even Timothy himself? He's clearly become a very demoralized, downcast disciple. So Paul takes him back to square one. 'You remember how you became a Christian; how the Holy Spirit came into your life; how he gave you living faith, power, love and self-control? Well, that's what you're missing now. You must have forgotten that the fire of the Spirit needs constant fuelling. Keep going, don't give up. Be strong, not timid.'

2 Timothy 1:8, 13–14

> Do not be ashamed, then, of witnessing for our Lord; nor be ashamed of me, a prisoner for Christ's sake . . . Hold firmly to the true words that I taught you, as the example for you to follow, and remain in the faith and love that are ours in union with Christ Jesus . . . keep the good things that have been entrusted to you.

Timothy looks in danger of turning away from Paul in prison; and even from witnessing to Jesus. So Paul says, twice over, 'Don't give up; keep holding on to (a) your faith and discipleship; and (b) your job of guarding and teaching the Good News.'

2 Timothy 1:15 – 2:1

You know that everyone in the province of Asia . . . has deserted me . . . Onesiphorus . . . was not ashamed that I am in prison, but as soon as he arrived in Rome, he started looking for me until he found me . . . And you know very well how much he did for me in Ephesus. As for you, my son, be strong through the grace that is ours in union with Christ Jesus.

Everyone else was timid; when Paul was arrested, they deserted. Onesiphorus was strong and not ashamed. 'Now you, Timothy, stop being timid like the others; let Jesus make you strong like Onesiphorus.'[92]

2 Timothy 2:3–6

Take your part in suffering, as a loyal soldier of Christ Jesus. A soldier on active service wants to please his commanding officer and so does not get mixed up in the affairs of civilian life. An athlete who runs in a race cannot win the prize unless he obeys the rules. The farmer who has done the hard work should have the first share of the harvest.

Soldier, athlete, farmer. Why does Paul use these three illustrations? Certainly not to give us in future generations some neat three-point sermons to preach! He knew he had to hammer the lesson home again and again, because Timothy was in no state to take it in first time round. 'It's tough being a Christian minister. But don't give up; be tough and ruthless with yourself – like a soldier,[93] loyal and single-minded; like an athlete, upright and uncheating; like a hard-working farmer, up before dawn.'

2 Timothy 3:14–15

But as for you, continue in the truths that you were taught and firmly believe . . . you remember that ever

since you were a child, you have known the Holy
Scriptures, which are able to give you the wisdom that
leads to salvation through faith in Christ Jesus.

Back again to square one. It is startling enough that twice in the
one letter Paul reminds Timothy of how he began as a Christian;
startling too that he says, yet again, 'Don't give up the true faith,
but continue in it.' Most startling of all, he appears to tell Timothy
to begin all over again: 'The Holy Scriptures . . . are able to give
you the wisdom that leads to salvation.' That's how far Timothy
has sunk in the two years since Paul last saw him.

2 Timothy 4:1, 5

In the presence of God and of Christ Jesus, who will
judge the living and the dead, and because he is coming
to rule as King, I solemnly urge you . . . you must keep
control of yourself in all circumstances . . . do the work
of a preacher of the Good News, and perform your
whole duty as a servant of God.

As the letter comes to an end, Paul loads up with the two weapons
he used in 1 Timothy, the two strongest, most devastating words
he knew. The oath 'before God' (and, he adds, before Jesus who is
coming as Judge and King), and the semi-oath 'I solemnly witness
against you'. He resorts to this language only because he knows
no other way to make Timothy yield to the plea he repeats again
and again and again: 'Control yourself: don't give up. Keep doing
the job I gave you.'

That's the thrust of 2 Timothy. Paul holds on to Timothy with
every ounce of his strength, because he's in imminent danger of
losing him. To hear some commentators talk, you'd think the letter
was a chummy fireside chat between a father and his favourite
son. In reality it's a distress flare, to stop the young man
committing spiritual suicide.

O Timothy!

What are we to make of the extraordinary decline in Timothy's
performance revealed in 1 and 2 Timothy? We saw hints of trouble
in Thessalonica and Corinth, where he persevered in difficult

conditions; but nothing to prepare us for this, where he falls down and is about to give up. On the earlier occasions Timothy could fairly argue that he was young and inexperienced, but now he should be in his prime. The letters positively groan with Paul's disappointment that Timothy should let him down after such promising beginnings and apprenticeship. What's happened? It's time to take a closer look at Timothy's character.

Timid?

The commonest word for Timothy's character in books about Paul or the New Testament is 'timid'.[94] A typical example is, 'Timothy always comes across as young, timid and unsure of himself.'[95] This has been repeated so often that people take it for granted and exaggerate it in their portraits of Timothy. In *Epistles to the Apostle*, Colin Morris has suggested what some of the letters written *to* Paul were like. This is the report he puts into the mouth of Timothy, and which in his view Paul was answering in 2 Timothy:

> Dearest Father in God,
>
> I was frankly terrified when you put me in charge of the Christian community here in Ephesus. I started badly and things have got steadily worse. I'll never make a preacher; never! No matter how carefully I prepare my sermons, the moment I see all those faces staring up at me, my legs turn to water and I stammer and stutter, losing my place in the manuscript and repeating myself over and over again. I'm afraid I'm not much credit to you . . . there are times when I am silent in the face of evil. It's not that I am afraid. I just can't think of anything to say until it is too late, so I'm scorned as either a fool or a coward. There is the usual bickering and quarrelling in the congregation that we experienced so often when I was travelling with you. But whereas you have the authority to rebuke and reprove, I just flounder, and I'm sure the followers of the Goddess, Diana, who are everywhere in this city, must think the Ambassador of King Jesus is a wooden donkey!
>
> Yours abysmally,
> Timothy[96]

We've seen evidence for some of this, but overall it's badly overdone. If Timothy was *that* wet, what had Paul seen in him? He was obviously not a complete jellyfish; he didn't turn tail for home as Mark had.[97] So, in reaction to this kind of caricature, some have gone to the other extreme and suggested there are no grounds at all for thinking Timothy was a nervous type. Who's right? Let's look at the components which make up the 'timid Timothy' picture in people's minds.

First, his *tears*. 'I remember your tears,' Paul tells him, 'and I want to see you very much.'[98] But tears were no sign of wimpishness in first-century Jewish or Greek men. Paul himself shed 'many tears' throughout *his* three years in Ephesus[99] – and few would call him timid! Tears are positively healthy and therapeutic. It's high time British society grew out of its dreadful tradition that 'big boys don't cry'. This was drummed so deep into me in my schooling that I still find it impossible to shed tears at any but the worst crises, even when I wish I could. Emotionally, Timothy was better adjusted than I am.

Then there are his *health problems*. We've seen Paul's disclosure that Timothy was 'ill so often', suggesting he had a weakish constitution, vulnerable to untreated water and to stress.[100] No surprise then to find him ill at Ephesus; plenty of stress there! But although a weak stomach slows you down, it doesn't mean a weak character. We all show stress symptoms at some point; we simply vary in the amount we can tolerate without discomfort, and in the form our symptoms take.

We're on surer ground in saying that Timothy had a *less strong personality than Paul*. That's obvious from the New Testament writings; Paul booms out of almost every verse from Acts 9 to the end of Philemon, while you have to listen hard to hear Timothy at all. Throughout the New Testament, of course, he was Paul's young sidekick, but clearly however long he lived he'd never be such a 'big noise' as Paul. But that doesn't make him a wimp. The point is not that Timothy was abnormally weak; rather that Paul was abnormally strong. Paul dwarfed him and made him look secondary and inferior. But then Paul would have done the same to us. Most of us are much more like Timothy than Paul. Paul was 'superhuman', Timothy 'human'.

Timothy does appear to have had a weakness in letting his *relative youth* inhibit him. Paul's instruction, 'Do not let anyone look down on you because you are young',[101] suggests that is just what they *were* doing. His advice on how to treat older men and women and his command to 'avoid the passions of youth'[102] show that Timothy felt young and acted young. This has surprised many readers, because by now he was no longer all that young; he was, on my calculation, around thirty-five. He must have come over as younger than he really was. And in those days (without today's cult of youth and fear of ageing), that was a handicap.

Some have read Timothy's over-awareness of his youth as *insecurity*. And insecurity would be readily understandable in someone who lost his father, his natural pattern of an adult male, early in life. Insecurity might well show itself as timidity, but again that doesn't mean the whole person is weak and wimpish all through. Timothy makes an interesting comparison with the twentieth-century world traveller, Sir Ranulph Fiennes. In his autobiography *Living Dangerously*, Sir Ranulph reveals a family home startlingly similar to Timothy's. His father died before he was born; he was brought up by his mother and grandmother. He describes how unprotected he felt, emerging from this background into the adult world.

> I had lived a sheltered life in an all-female family and I was totally unprepared for the way in which the world fell apart about me. My skin was paper-thin, my imagination fertile and my ability to fight back nil. Perhaps if some male relative had warned me of the impending problems adolescence would involve, I might somehow have forearmed myself. But I had no brothers, no uncles and no father.[103]

This opening chapter he titles, most significantly, 'A Timid Disposition'. Whether his later tough lifestyle and daring exploits are a way of compensating for his insecurity or simply the achievements of a late developer, they demonstrate forcefully that 'insecure' isn't the same as 'feeble'. Timothy also survived an extremely rigorous life in his twenties.

So there's nothing to look down on in these five mark of Timothy's character – tears, ill-health, a quiet personality, a certain immaturity and, underlying it, a feeling of insecurity. Indeed, quite the reverse. Full marks to Timothy for having a go at all, and for sticking at the tasks Paul set him, despite these counterweights. 'Timid' and 'brave' aren't opposites. A nervous person may well be more courageous than an impulsive go-getter, because he knows how difficult it all is for him. Insecurity and self-doubt aren' a sign of weakness in someone who perseveres despite them; they're a measure of his strength.[104]

Humble?

It may be the distorted view of male strength in the West today that casts Timothy in the rather feckless role so many give him. 'Real men don't cry, or report sick, or let anyone else tell them what to do, or look indecisive.' So by the twentieth century's arrogant standards, Timothy isn't a 'real man'. These modern values have a lot in common with the Roman empire in which Timothy lived; but they're at odds with the kingdom of Jesus which Timothy was learning to make his home. In that kingdom Timothy and Paul were the trail-blazers for a new understanding of maleness, which had room for a degree of proper weakness and didn't have to be a tireless parade of macho strength.

We can see this in the New Testament history of the word *tapeinos*, usually translated 'humble'.[105] The Greek world gave it a bad sense. The Corinthian rebels used it as an insult against Paul for being 'meek and mild', or in some other translations 'timid'![106] It *was* an insulting word to use of a man; if it had any positive value it was only for women, such as Mary who called herself God's 'lowly' servant.[107] Yet the early Christians took this humble, even humiliating, word and turned it into a badge of honour; it enshrined for them the right attitude of all Christians, men as well as women, towards other people. Jesus led the way by giving the word his magic touch. He called himself 'humble in spirit', like an ox in its plough-shafts.[108] He repeatedly tipped the world's values upside down: 'Whoever makes himself great will be *humbled*, and whoever *humbles* himself will be made great.'[109] This was the lead Paul and Timothy followed as they 'humbled' themselves at Corinth and worked 'with all humility' at Ephesus.[110] And they taught it as a cardinal virtue in the Christian way to live: 'Be always humble' and 'You must clothe yourselves with humility.'[111]

Jesus pointed to that most un-macho symbol, an undeveloped child, as the model of humility: 'The greatest in the Kingdom of heaven is the one who *humbles* himself and becomes like this child.'[112] So perhaps we should learn from Timothy as a truly humbled male, instead of adopting the pitying, patronizing tone that writes him off as 'poor, timid Timothy'. There's nothing necessarily demeaning about a Christian man weeping, or feeling ill, intimidated or unsure of himself. It's less manly to cover these things up and hide them from others. Shaking hands are more Christian than a stiff upper lip.

Cowardly?

Yet we're still left with things going very wrong for Timothy at Ephesus. If we've given his 'timid' character a clean bill of health, we must look elsewhere for the root of the trouble. So far we've defended Timothy against modern critics. We've seen that 'timidity' was natural in someone of his birth and background. But what did Paul think about it? He too calls Timothy timid. That is inescapable from the flow of his words:

> The Spirit that God has given us does not make us timid; instead, his Spirit fills us with power, love, and self-control.
> Do not be ashamed, then, of witnessing for our Lord; nor be ashamed of me . . .[113]

For Paul to say this at all shows he thinks Timothy is being timid and ashamed. But to Paul these aren't lifelong twists of Timothy's character. They're a spiritual decline from how Timothy used to be. 'God gave you his Spirit . . . You used to be full of power, love and self-control, when you became a Christian and then worked with me on the team. Don't fall back now into timidity and shame.'

The words Paul uses aren't the same as the English 'timidity'. His Greek 'timidity' means 'cowardice'; it always has a bad sense in the New Testament. It's being afraid in a way that Christians shouldn't. Jesus rebukes his disciples for it when they fear that the boat might sink in the storm: 'Why are you so *frightened*?'[114] He expects his followers to be able to replace cowardly fear with peace;[115] but Timothy was obviously far from at peace in Ephesus. Most ominous of all, 'cowards' are at the head of the list of people Jesus says are unfit for heaven.[116] The word implies running away from the hardships of *being a Christian*.

It's an apt partner for 'shame', the other word Paul uses. 'If a person is ashamed of me and of my teaching in this godless and wicked day,' says Jesus in the only other New Testament use of 'ashamed', 'then the Son of Man will be ashamed of him when he comes in the glory of his Father with the holy angels.'[117] No wonder Paul urged, 'Do not be ashamed.' He meant, 'Don't give up being a Christian.' And he pleaded his own case as the example to follow: 'I am still full of confidence [literally, I am not ashamed] because I know whom I have trusted, and I am sure that he is able to keep safe until that Day what he has entrusted to me.'[118] As far as Paul can see, Timothy is on the point of giving up everything (the mission entrusted to him, *and* Paul and Jesus who entrusted him with it) for lack of faith.

In the wrong job?

This seems to have been as perplexing to Paul as it is to us. How could Timothy flinch from persecution now, when he's been through beatings, prison and mob violence before? How could Timothy fall prey to the false teaching after years and years of not only listening to the truth, but teaching it effectively himself? I sense a touch of exasperation in Paul's repeated commands to Timothy to grow up: 'Avoid the passions of youth' and 'Do not let anyone look down on you because you are young'. He must have had to say exactly the same after Timothy's earlier solo missions. So why does Timothy still find he can't stand on his own two feet?

Two possible explanations occur to me. One is that Timothy has run into a 'mid-life crisis'. This sounds absurd only because of the modern name for it; but the experience itself has happened to people in all ages. Timothy was now in his mid-thirties at least. In the shorter life expectancy of ancient times, this was well into middle age, despite Paul's talk of Timothy's youth. It's natural to take stock of our lives at 'half-time' and ask what they amount to. What progress have I made towards what I hoped to be? Am I pursuing the right ambitions or wasting my time? Are there important things I've missed out on? Many people make major changes at this stage of life as a result of facing these questions. Some change career, others retire early. Some get married, others walk out of a marriage that has lost meaning. Some chase youthful fantasies before it's too late; others settle into a comfortable routine as they look ahead to the confines of old age and death; their risky, daring days are done.

Christians do this mid-life check-up as naturally as anyone else. And they're just as prone to make wild or lazy decisions. Some have left their wife or husband and run off with a younger partner; others have given up their faith. Many more have simply lost their Christian cutting edge. The faith no longer has its all-or-nothing lustre for them. They settle for creature comforts instead. Even 'full-time Christian missionaries' can become discouraged, tired and faint-hearted. They run out of steam after years of unremitting energy. Their powers wane and they begin to ask, 'Is Christian ministry worth it? What have I got to show for it? Is the Christian faith really true after all?' Maybe this is what happened to Timothy.

But there's another possibility. The New Testament contains only Paul's version of the Ephesus crisis. In his view, Timothy's faith is slipping and Timothy is to blame. Indeed, the whole 'timid Timothy' picture is drawn from what *Paul* says about him. But is this view the whole story, simply because it's in the New Testament? Timothy would surely have something to say in his own defence.[119] People often disagree and argue over the reasons they behave as they do. And the very fact that Paul keeps repeating his fears in 1 Timothy and his commands in 2 Timothy may be because Timothy was resisting him with another point of view. We seem to have unearthed an argument between Paul and Timothy, even a clash of wills.

Timothy must have found at least the second letter deeply hurtful. It's an implied rebuke to him for letting things slide from bad to worse. But surely this was Paul's responsibility. As he admits, it was *he* who forced Timothy to stay in Ephesus against his will. Perhaps there was no-one else to leave with Timothy or in his place. But should Paul have left so soon himself? Did he really need to? The result was the disaster we have traced in 2 Timothy. And Timothy himself always knew it would be.

For surely this is the most satisfying explanation of Timothy's 'wimpish' characteristics. He was in tears because Paul was leaving him alone to do an impossible job; he was pleading in vain for a change of mind. His tummy weakness flared because of stress too strong to bear on his own. He almost gave up because he wasn't the right personality to turn the Ephesian churches round alone; he knew he seemed a push-over to the false teachers. He felt too 'young' to exert authority, because he had no authority of his own. He felt insecure and incompetent for the simplest of reasons:

Paul wasn't there. He needed Paul as his leader, because he was a follower, not a leader, himself. Take the prop away and he collapsed.

Timothy understood himself; but Paul, it seems, didn't. He developed a regular habit of pushing Timothy into tasks that were beyond him. With Timothy he kept breaking his own 'rules': 'Be in no hurry to lay hands on anyone in dedication to the Lord's service . . . They should be tested first, and then, if they pass the test, they are to serve.'[120] Not just once, but at least three times Paul promoted Timothy beyond what his track record proved he could safely do. The first time or two, Paul could perhaps claim that Timothy was the unfortunate guinea-pig whose experiments led to the wise principles they later formulated. But by the time of Ephesus he should have known that Timothy would find the task beyond him. And of course, he *did* know really; his forebodings in 1 Timothy showed us he was well aware of the dangers.

He could see Timothy's weaknesses, but it seems he wouldn't accept them. The evidence of the earlier solo missions was quite clear: when he forced Timothy to be a lone leader, things didn't go well. But instead of concluding that Timothy must therefore stay with him or always work in a team, he forced him back into lone leadership at Ephesus. A bit unfair, then, to keep scolding Timothy for all the resulting problems.

Was Paul making the mistake of many fathers? He should have conceded that his 'son' was a different person from him. But instead, he kept pushing him to do jobs that he himself would have found straightforward. He expected Timothy to be a duplicate of himself. As a result he forced him into a mould and a job that didn't fit him. Many parents put this same pressure on their children (and team leaders on their juniors) – even without realizing it.

It's desperately dangerous. The unhappy, floundering figure of Timothy in Paul's second letter may be as much the product of Paul's own unreasonable demands and disapproval as of the conflict in Ephesus. Paul has almost lost his son. What can he do to win him back?

Key Bible passages: 1 Timothy 1:1–3, 18–19; 3:2–7, 15; 4:6–16; 5:19–25; 6:11–14, 20–21; Titus 1:5–6, 10–11, 13; 2:1–3, 6–8, 15; 3:9–10; 2 Timothy 1:5–8, 13–18; 2:1–8; 2: 14 – 3:9, 14–15; 4:1–2, 5.

Reflect

1. Do you know other people like Timothy, advanced in some ways, immature or insecure in others? What has helped them to grow as people?

2. Do you think Timothy would have handled his difficulties better if he (like Paul) had had someone to assist him? What advice can we give people who feel trapped in the wrong role?

3. One Study Bible suggests, 'When you face a challenge that seems beyond your abilities, read 1 and 2 Timothy.' Paul must have hoped his letters would have this uplifting effect. Try reading them in this light. Do you think they had the desired effect on Timothy? Would they on you?

Share

1. How accurate or fair do you think this (American) characterization is?

> Would you put this man in charge?
> He's young, rural, insecure, and has gastronomical problems. Why would Paul pin his hopes for an Ephesus project manager on such a dubious rookie? He has many other strikes against him. 'Am I too young for this job? Can I lead? How do these city folk think anyway? (Surely not like down home.) Will I fail Paul in this assignment?' Conflict troubles Timothy. He personalizes it too much.[121]

Was Timothy a wimp?

2. A UK Christian magazine once ran a feature on '25 key young Christian leaders – faces to watch for the future'. In the light of Timothy's story, what do you think of the idea? What report would you write on Timothy aged eighteen? How would you modify it by the time he was thirty-five?

3. Can you think of other cases (in any walk of life) of long-term colleagues falling out, or outgrowing each other? Is it avoidable, and if so, how?

Heir?

That's it, then. I quit. I'll go home. I've had enough.

What's the point of carrying on here if I can't do *anything* right? 'Stop quarrelling . . . stop ruining people . . . stop driving them away from God.' I'm not doing it on purpose, you know. Do you think I *want* to put people off Christianity? I'm only trying to do what you told me to.

'Keep away . . . keep away . . . keep away . . . avoid your passions.' If you think I ought to be so ashamed of what I'm doing, I'll run off and hide, somewhere where I can just be alone. It wasn't *my* idea to stay on in Ephesus. *You* told me to. I didn't want to. I *told* you it wouldn't work. But you wouldn't listen. You wouldn't understand now if I tried to write and explain.

'These people are opposed to the truth – but they will not get very far, because everyone will see how stupid they are.' Everyone except me, I suppose. I *know* I don't see things as clearly as you. But I can't help it. It's not my fault if I can't confront them. There are too many of them. They're too sure of themselves. They laugh at me. They don't want me here. *I* don't want to be here. I can't do it without you.

Oh, Paul, why did you have to go away?[1]

What can Paul do to save his son? He outlines his next move in 2 Timothy. After the crisis call to Timothy not to give up his faith and his mission, Paul has one more word to say: 'Come.'[2] The closing words of the letter echo it three times: 'Do your best to *come* to me soon . . . When you *come*, bring my coat . . .'; and then, probably in Paul's personally written PS: 'Do your best to *come* before winter.'[3]

One reason for this urgent summons at the end of the letter is that Paul's own circumstances have taken a new twist, perhaps even since he started writing. Suddenly he announces that he is about to die; he has finished his life; he is going to his coronation in heaven.[4] He's had a first court hearing, and emerged without a death sentence.[5] But it's only a temporary stay of execution; there will be no reprieve this time: 'The Lord will . . . take me safely into his heavenly Kingdom.'[6] Death sounds only a few days away at most: 'The hour has come for me to be sacrificed; the time is here for me to leave this life.'[7] But the short breathing space, or his previous experience of delays in the system, gives him hope that there's time for Timothy to come to his side, provided he gets a move on! 'Come to me *soon* [literally, *without delay*] . . . come *before winter*', when the sea would be too rough and no ships could sail. Next spring will be too late.

Exactly why does Paul want him in Rome? Is it mainly, as most commentators have assumed, the old man longing to see his favourite son before he dies? On Timothy's side, is it the release from unsuitable work that he must have pined for? Or is there more of a hint about his future? When we look for answers, we find that Paul's hope of seeing Timothy isn't only at the end of the letter.[8] It underlies everything else he says. This helps us to read his mind and trace a more detailed set of travelling instructions. The simple word 'come' includes a sequence of steps for Timothy to take.

Step 1

Pass your Ephesus teaching duties on to others.

> Take the teachings that you heard me proclaim in the presence of many witnesses, and entrust them to reliable people, who will be able to teach others also.[9]

Like so much else in Paul's letters to Timothy, this verse is usually lifted out of its original setting and treated as a pattern for Christian instruction in every generation. As we shall see, that ripple effect is certainly intended.[10] But it can't have been the first thought in Timothy's mind as he read, or Paul's as he wrote. The command 'Take and entrust' is in the form that means a single, definite action to take at once.[11] If Timothy is to leave Ephesus, he must see that his work carries on. The churches still need teaching. So he must prepare 'reliable people' – the elders who've stayed true to the Good News of Jesus, and the new ones he's appointed – to take over.

Still unsure of Timothy's own reliability, Paul reminds him what to pass on: 'the teachings that you heard me proclaim' over all those years we worked together. 'Entrust them,' he says, reminding Timothy that the teachings are a sacred trust from God.[12] But what if that's not enough to brace Timothy? Supposing he soft-pedals the teachings in the prevailing air of retreat? Paul calls on everyone who has heard them and worked with them in the past: 'the teachings that you heard me proclaim *in the presence of many witnesses*'; may they rise up and challenge you if you leave anything out!

Remembering, explaining, checking that the new teachers have got hold of it, will all take time. And there isn't much time left before winter. So do it now.

Step 2

Restore your relationship with me.[13]

1 Timothy was full of tension and implied rebuke. So is 2 Timothy. The rapport between Paul and Timothy, once so intimate, is in urgent need of repair. It's always better to sort out these misunderstandings face to face than by letter. So Paul calls Timothy to his side.

But this is more than just clinical patching up. Paul's deepest longing is to be reunited with the 'son' he still loves so warmly. It's the opening note of the letter. 'To Timothy, my dear son . . . I give thanks to God . . . as I remember you always in my prayers night and day.'[14] 1 Timothy began with no thanks at all; but here he prays for his beloved Timothy with gratitude and tender sympathy. 'I remember your tears, and I want to see you very much, so that I may be filled with joy.'[15] As he is about to die, the person Paul wants to see above all is Timothy. His greatest joy will be to soothe that memory of tears and distress.

The end of the letter tells the same story. The closing verses ache with Paul's loneliness. He feels betrayed and deserted. He writes of his grievance against Alexander the metalworker who, it seems, contrived his arrest.[16] And then, just when Paul would hope for the love and support of his team, Demas deserted him.[17] He dropped out of Christian mission work (and out of love with Jesus) to save his own skin. Watching it happen to one of his team can only have intensified Paul's fear that it was about to happen to another; the one he dreaded losing most of all.[18]

But this wasn't the end of Paul's fears and heartaches; Demas wasn't the only deserter. 'No one stood by me the first time I defended myself; all deserted me.'[19] Under Roman law Paul was allowed a lawyer to plead his case and witnesses to support it. But none could be found, even among the Roman church who'd welcomed him in the past.[20] It was now too dangerous to hold his hand in open court. '*The Lord* stayed with me and gave me strength, so that I was able to proclaim the full message for all the Gentiles to hear . . .'[21] But Paul always craved human company as well as the Lord's.

He had, alas, run very short of human company at this stage. His team was as small as it had been for many years. Others had left, for more legitimate reasons than Demas'. 'Crescens went to Galatia, and Titus to Dalmatia . . . I sent Tychicus to Ephesus [the usual formula to identity 2 Timothy's courier] . . . Erastus stayed in Corinth, and I left Trophimus in Miletus, because he was ill.'[22] It sounds as if all Paul's comforts had been stripped away one by one. He's even without his coat and books.[23] No wonder he cries out for Timothy to make good his loneliness.[24]

Yet Timothy isn't just a last resort when all else fails. Despite the sad list of losses, Paul isn't totally alone. Luke is still with him.[25] Mark should soon be on his way to replace Tychicus as another practical helper.[26] And some of the Roman church leaders and members must at least have been willing to visit him in prison, for 'Eubulus, Pudens, Linus, and Claudia send their greetings, and so do all the other Christians.'[27] But the cry of Paul's heart is for Timothy. The repeated call, 'Come . . . come . . . come', sounds the depth of his longing. Ephesus must wait: Timothy's place is with Paul. His 'dear son' is dearer to him at this moment even than the 'dear doctor' Luke, already at his side.[28] And so Paul signs off, in the last note we possess, with the most directly personal of all his letter-endings. To Timothy's colleagues at Ephesus, he says as he usually does, 'God's *grace* be with you all'; but for Timothy he prays, '*The Lord* be with your spirit.'[29] Timothy is special, his longest-serving and favourite companion, his son.

'Timothy's place is with Paul.' The letter eloquently voices Paul's emotional need. But Timothy needed this reunion too. Our future peace of mind depends greatly on seeing our loved ones before they die, and on being at peace with them; and on *making* peace with them when necessary, as it may have been for Timothy.

The letter, with its alarm call, its hints of Paul's loneliness, its mention of so many old friends, must have stirred a mix of strong feelings in him on top of the resentment we've already sensed:[30] fondness for the past, regret at so much trouble in the present, fear of bridging the gap that had grown between him and Paul? Probably they would both have to admit mistakes. The Ephesus adventure looks as if it was a false trail from the start. Timothy was perhaps really meant to be Paul's companion for life.[31]

There was a lot for them to set to rights. The letter isn't the slushy farewell card that many have painted it; it's a tough, bitter-sweet olive branch. Making up with each other would be hard and tearful – Timothy would find it extremely painful to look Paul in the eye after such stinging words in the letters – but they must do it. 'I want to see you very much . . . Come.'

Step 3

Take your part in suffering.

Paul doesn't merely want to see Timothy and hold him in his arms once more. There's something in Rome for him to do. The whole first section or 'movement' of the letter[32] focuses on this next step. Modern readers, nearly 2,000 years later, find it hard to hear exactly what Paul is saying. But a little digging can help us see beneath the text itself.

'Take your part in suffering, as a loyal soldier of Christ Jesus.'[33] This immediately follows step 1, 'Take the teachings . . . and entrust them'; after travelling to Rome and finding Paul, it will be the next thing to do. It's another command in the form that suggests a definite action for Timothy to agree to, and then take. And it's a repetition. Paul has already said, 'Take your part in suffering for the Good News, as God gives you the strength.'[34] It must be important for Paul to repeat it like this.[35] It dominates this first section of the letter as the recurring command.[36]

It means more than just 'Take your part in whatever suffering happens to come your way'; Paul has added three letters to the usual Greek word, to make it mean 'Come and suffer *with me*'.[37] To join Paul in Rome won't just be an emotional reunion; it will expose Timothy to the same danger and difficulties Paul is facing.

This throws light on the companion command dominating the opening chapter:

> Do not be ashamed, then, of witnessing for our Lord;
> nor be ashamed of me, a prisoner for Christ's sake.[38]

This isn't, as preachers usually take it, a general encouragement to Timothy to be a bolder Christian, or a plaintive hope that he'll think kindly of Paul from afar. It is, once again, a definite step to take. He is to follow the steps of Onesiphorus who 'was *not* ashamed that I am in prison, but as soon as he arrived in Rome, he started looking for me until he found me'.[39] The traditional picture of son reunited with father on his deathbed easily forgets that it's a condemned cell. It's risky. It may land Timothy in prison too, so that he literally suffers with Paul. It could lead to his death, as it clearly would for Paul, and presumably had for Onesiphorus.[40]

Perhaps Paul urges Timothy to these risks simply to 'cheer him up' by being there, as Onesiphorus had done.[41] But the plea for Timothy to witness without turning his back on Paul in prison would make fuller sense if it means appearing in court at the next hearing. 'Be my defence witness; don't disown me in embarrassment and fear, as everyone did last time I came to court.'[42]

Time was when Timothy would have risen to this challenge quite naturally, but, on recent form, Paul feels the need to urge him to think hard and let the Lord persuade him.[43] And the rest of this first movement of 2 Timothy turns out to be several more carrots and sticks to persuade Timothy not to flinch, but face the danger.[44]

As you're a Christian, God has equipped you with the resources you need to face danger. 'His Spirit fills us with power, love, and self-control. Do not be ashamed, then . . .'[45] God has given you the strength you need; simply draw on it.

You're not alone; we're in this together. 'For the Spirit that God has given *us* does not make *us* timid; instead, his Spirit fills *us* with power . . .' The 'us' doesn't mean all Christians in general, even though the statement would be perfectly true of us all. Paul means 'you, Timothy, *and me*; I'm not asking you to go beyond me'. 'Remain in the faith and love that are *ours* in union with Christ Jesus. Through the power of the Holy Spirit, who lives in *us* . . .'[46]

You needn't fear death, for Jesus has defeated it. 'He has ended the power of death and through the gospel has revealed immortal life . . .'[47] This isn't a digression, as some commentators suggest. Paul doesn't add these doctrinal truths simply to fill space. He's repeatedly reassuring Timothy, who feels real fear about a real danger. 'Remember Jesus Christ, who was raised from death . . . "If we have died with him, we shall also live with him . . ." '[48]

Our loyalty to Jesus and the Good News should outweigh our fear. 'A soldier on active service wants to please his commanding officer . . . Because I preach the Good News, I suffer and I am even chained like a criminal . . . I endure everything for the sake of God's chosen people, in order that they too may . . . obtain . . . salvation . . . '[49]

Think of the rewards of persevering – but also the result of disobeying. 'An athlete . . . cannot win the prize unless he obeys the rules. The farmer who has done the hard work should have the first share of the harvest . . . "If we continue to endure, we shall also rule with him." ' [50] What stronger encouragement could there be to face the danger bravely? But there's also the other side of the coin: 'If we deny him, he also will deny us.'[51]

Paul simply wouldn't wave all these sticks and carrots about if he didn't think Timothy needed them. The young Timothy had accepted suffering as an all-in part of the deal when he became first a Christian and then a missionary. But now the middle-aged church leader hesitates. It can happen to any of us. We become more comfortable, less courageous. But the cost and pain of following Jesus get no less. We may need regular doses of these truths to lure us back into the firing-line.

Step 4

If you live on after I've died, carry on with the task of defending and teaching the Good News.

Paul has prepared Timothy to face the 'worst' scenario of being put to death in Rome. But he hopes it won't come to that. He wants Timothy to take a fourth step after he himself has died. He repeats it again and again through the letter; it obviously fills his horizon beyond all else. It is in fact the same message we used for our backward look in the last chapter to deduce how Timothy was failing. 'Keep on doing the job I gave you – don't ever give up.' At that first viewing we took it as a frantic yell at Timothy to stay at his post *now this minute* in Ephesus. But Paul is also looking further into the future than just the next few weeks before Timothy sails for Rome: 'The time will come when people will not listen to sound doctrine . . .'[52] Many of the commands are in the 'continuous' mode, which carry the sense: 'Keep going indefinitely without stopping.'

Teacher

This further horizon was already in view in the first and second movements of the letter.[53] But it's in the third movement that step 4 appears most clearly.[54] Here it's the main subject. Paul sets the scene of the 'last days', the stretch of time between Jesus' ascension to heaven and his second coming to earth. They're bad times when faith*ful* Christians will suffer and faith*less* Christians will turn away from the truth. Against this depressing backdrop Paul's commands stand out in two clusters.

2 Timothy 3:14–17

Timothy is to go on believing and doing what he's learnt from his earliest days.

> But as for you, continue in the truths that you were taught and firmly believe ... ever since you were a child, you have known the Holy Scriptures ... All Scripture is inspired by God and is useful for teaching the truth, rebuking error, correcting faults, and giving instruction for right living, so that the person who serves God may be fully qualified and equipped to do every kind of good deed.

Here's another favourite nugget of the letter with a rather different point in Paul's mind from the usual interpretation these days. When we teach people to learn the last sentence ('All Scripture . . .'), we tend to explain it as, 'The purpose of the Bible is for *God* to teach *you*, rebuking, correcting and instructing; in the process he will equip you to do good and live Christianly as you serve him.'[55]

It's probably all quite true. But Timothy wasn't talking about the Bible as every Christian's bedside reading; he was pointing to it as the church teacher's textbook. He was saying to Timothy, 'God has given you all the Scriptures[56] to use in teaching *other people* the truth, rebuking *their* error and correcting *their* faults, and instructing *them* in how to live as Christians. The Scriptures are the full qualification and equipment for *you* to do every part of your work as a minister.[57] So don't drift away from the Bible or wander off into new ideas, but carry on teaching it in the future as you did for so many years with me, and should have been in Ephesus.' This understanding is confirmed by the resounding trumpet call which follows naturally on and perfectly sums up step 4.

2 Timothy 4:2, 5

> Preach the message . . . insist upon proclaiming it (whether the time is right or not) . . . convince, reproach, and encourage, as you teach with all patience.[58]

These commands are in the 'immediate action' mode. Paul is calling Timothy to commit himself afresh to the task he'd almost given up. 'Make up your mind now that, whatever the difficulties, nothing will ever stop you preaching and teaching God's message.'

A moment later he repeats this call for immediate action; here and now Timothy must sign back on for his lifetime commission. Paul shouts three quick-fire orders, the final left–right–left of step 4.[59]

> [1] Endure suffering, [2] do the work of a preacher of the Good News, and [3] perform your whole duty as a servant of God.

Order 3 is only three words in Paul's Greek: 'fulfil your ministry'. Timothy is to keep on with the job Paul gave him and see it through to the end. And what is that job? Orders 1 and 2 spell it out in simplest form: suffer and preach. 'After I've gone, Timothy, you're to carry on preaching; don't let suffering make you give up.'

There are surely many today who need to join Timothy in taking step 4. In the past they've wanted to teach the Bible, or they've actually done it – perhaps as church leaders or mission leaders, or working with children and young people, or through writing or drama. But other things have blown them off course. For one reason or another their time and energy have gone on activities which have left the Bible closed on the shelf. They've been part of the modern 'forget the Bible' movement, which leaves even

Christians more ignorant of it than any previous generation. Reserving top place for Bible teaching (in our own lives or in a church) is one of the hardest things in the world – perhaps because it's the most important thing in the world, and the devil resists it with all his might. There's now an acute need for mature adults to get to grips with the words of the Bible and hand them on – living, breathing, burning – to others. Paul would say to them (and perhaps you?), 'Teach God's book. It's never too late to turn to this all-important way of serving God. But it's also never too soon.'

Successor?

Step 4's look ahead to the future leads many commentators to describe it as Paul passing on the torch or the baton to his 'successor'; even to call the letter his 'last will and testament'. The address of 2 Timothy to 'my son'[60] certainly gives it something of this feel.[61] It's natural at such a moment for Paul to want to bequeath his responsibilities (his sacred 'trust' from God)[62] to an heir. And Timothy's name resounds through the letter as a uniquely special son in the faith, despite all their difficulties. But it's important to be clear what Timothy is heir to; exactly *what* he's to take over from Paul.

We've gathered that there were times when Paul had looked to Timothy to carry on his pastoral oversight of the churches they had founded.[63] But if he still wanted it at the time of his death, it seems he was disappointed. There's no scrap of evidence in the New Testament or the rest of church history that that is what Timothy did.[64]

But then there's no hint in 2 Timothy that Paul still wants Timothy to succeed him as pastor to all the churches. What he keeps telling him to be is a gospel-preacher and Bible-teacher. He says, 'Fulfil *your* ministry'; not 'Fulfil *mine*'. Or, inasmuch as he does appear to speak of Timothy as his heir, it's 'Fulfil that part of my ministry which is legitimately yours as well'. The part of his own work Paul talks about in 2 Timothy is preaching, teaching and suffering.[65] *That's* what Timothy can and will inherit. Paul doesn't say 'Look after the churches', but 'Look after the Good News'. Timothy is to be a preacher and teacher, not a founder-apostle.

This is partly because of Timothy's gifts, as more of a teacher than a leader. But more deeply it's because of Timothy's special place in church history. This brings us to the fifth step in Paul's marching orders.

Step 5

Build the bridge between the apostles and all future generations of Christians.

Here we come to the long-life content of Paul's instruction which formed step 1.

> Take the teachings that you heard me proclaim in the presence of many witnesses, and entrust them to reliable people, who will be able to teach others also.[66]

The immediate plan was to equip the Ephesus elders to carry on teaching the Good News while Timothy left for Rome. But it contained the seed of further growth; an ongoing line of Bible teachers to keep the Ephesus church alive for as long as Ephesus itself should last. The reliable elders would do the teaching in the house-churches at first; but in the process they could train a further generation of Bible teachers, who in their turn could . . . The emergency tactic was to become the permanent strategy. Every teacher of the Bible automatically inspires and begins to mould others, who will carry on and multiply the good work.[67] That's the normal growth pattern for all generations after the unique first one. They were the founder-apostles, who developed Christian teaching from the sayings of Jesus and the guidance of the Holy Spirit. We are their followers, holding in our hands the inspired guidebook they helped to write. And Timothy is the clearest example of the middlemen who connect them with us. He was the vital link who took Paul's teachings and handed them on to the first generation of elders.

This moment of history where Timothy stands is critically important. The apostles knew how vulnerable the story and teaching of Jesus would be when their eyewitness testimony died out. Peter wrote to a wide circle of Christians who had learnt the faith from him: 'I think it only right for me to stir up your memory of these matters as long as I am still alive. I know that I shall soon put off this mortal body . . . I will do my best, then, to provide a way for you to remember these matters at all times after my death.'[68] When Paul knew that *he* was about to die, he addressed his famous last words to Timothy. But for Timothy, we wouldn't possess this priceless letter where Paul lets slip what he thinks the church and its leaders are here for.

It's not a carefully considered statement. It's dashed off in the last-minute hope that Timothy can beat the axe-man to Rome. But white heat lights up the burning concern of Paul's mind. There's not a word about so many of the preoccupations of the modern church. Paul doesn't tell Timothy to be a social worker or political reformer; he doesn't urge him to dispense the bread and wine or lead inspiring 'worship'; he doesn't mention a single sign, wonder or healing. They're all fine things; but they won't sustain the church into the future. What fills Paul's horizon as the task for Timothy, and all the Timothys who follow, is plain to see.

> Hold firmly to the true words . . . keep the good things that have been entrusted to you . . . Take the teachings . . . and entrust them to reliable people, who will be able to teach others also . . . Do your best . . . as a worker . . . who correctly teaches the message of God's truth . . . a good and patient teacher . . . continue in the truths that you were taught . . . Scripture is . . . useful for teaching the truth . . . preach the message . . . insist upon proclaiming it . . . convince, reproach, and encourage, as you teach . . . do the work of a preacher . . .[69]

That's Paul's bequest to his son: his Bible and the command to teach it. It's the letter's bright legacy for the future; its abiding message for today.[70] Paul wants Christians after his death to learn and teach the truth. With such clear directions at the end of the New Testament, it's hard to see how churches who slight or ignore them can claim to be Christian. They're certainly not Pauline or Timothean.

Thankfully, though, there are many people and missions across the world that teach the Bible or train others to do so. They range from lay preachers to international agencies such as the Bible Society. All power to their elbows, hands, feet, minds and voices! In these days of corporate mission statements, I wonder if any have thought of taking Timothy and his final instructions, 'Take the teachings . . . and entrust them' or 'Preach the message . . . as you teach with all patience', as their logo.[71] Or, as there's always room for more of these initiatives, how about an informal 'Timothy tendency' within our churches? The Dominican Friars launched their 'Order of Preachers' in the Middle Ages. A century later in England John Wyclif despatched his 'Poor Preachers' or 'Lollards' (wandering chanters) to tell the Good News and popularize the Bible, newly translated into the people's own language. Perhaps in our generation we need some 'Timothy troupes' dedicated 'to the public reading of the Scriptures and to preaching and teaching'.[72]

This book has tried to show Timothy as the New Testament 'patron saint' of many groups of people – children with lone parents, or parents of mixed race and faith; Christians converted and discipled as teenagers; apprentices, assistants, team members and friends; people who are underestimated; men with a gentle masculinity, who are not strong natural leaders. Now we've added another: Bible readers, preachers and teachers.

But there's still one more to come. In my view it's the most important of all Timothy's claims to fame – most important because it affects all Christians, not just some. We shall uncover it by looking at the two titles the New Testament gives Timothy, 'apostle' and 'deacon'.[73] We've not yet given either its full weight.

Apostle

There are two groups of apostles in the New Testament. The first, more senior group was the apostles of Jesus. They were the original twelve Jesus chose. When Judas fell, the other eleven set out the qualifications for his replacement: he must be a witness of Jesus' life and resurrection.[74] Paul makes much of the fact that by Jesus' special intervention he became a member of that group.[75] These apostles were the original and unrepeatable foundation of the church, passing on what Jesus had taught or directly revealed to them.[76] There was room for only twelve candidates, because they were the 'ancestors' of the New Testament in the same way the twelve sons of Jacob were of the Old.[77] Timothy couldn't be Paul's successor in that job, because those apostles had no successors.

Yet Paul seems to have encouraged his mission teams to think of themselves as a sort of apostles. Timothy and Silas (his partners on his second missionary journey) twice appear with the title. Writing together to the Thessalonians, they say, 'We did not try to get praise from anyone, either from you or from others, even though *as apostles of Christ* we could have made demands on you.'[78] To the Corinthians, Paul identifies the three of them as the 'real apostles' supplanted in the church's affections by the lately arrived 'false apostles'.[79]

But Timothy was a minor and 'junior' apostle compared with Paul; an apostle with a small 'a'. The word 'apostle' is simply the Greek equivalent of the Latin 'missionary'. That's the more general sense in which Timothy was an apostle – the second group in the New Testament. He wasn't an eyewitness of Jesus. And neither he nor Paul claims that he had the authority of a 'big A' Apostle, to be recognized by all Gentile churches. He was more an 'apostle of Paul' than an 'Apostle of Jesus'.[80] He shared in Paul's apostolic task of planting and tending new churches; preaching the Good News to them and teaching them the Christian way of life; appointing and guiding elders to lead them; and spearheading their witness to Jesus in the surrounding area. But his authority in them was precisely because he was Paul's assistant and delegate. It lasted only while Paul was alive. After Paul's death he didn't, it seems, become a second-generation apostle, supervising all Paul's churches. He remained what Paul told him to be: a preacher and teacher, and a 'deacon'.

Deacon

This is another ambiguous word. By the end of the first century, a generation after Paul's letters to Timothy, 'deacon' was the title for a recognized job in church life: the deacon was the administrative right-hand person to the local bishop.[81] Deacons have occupied an official post in many sections of the church ever since. And there are signs of them emerging in the New Testament. Paul and Timothy address their Philippian letter 'To all God's people in Philippi . . . including [literally] the *bishops and deacons*'.[82] Similarly 1 Timothy gives instructions for appointing at Ephesus what Paul actually calls 'bishops' and 'deacons'[83]. In both places GNB translates 'deacons' as 'helpers' and this shows why the word is ambiguous. The Greek *diakonos* was the ordinary, common word for a servant. You're never quite sure whether the New Testament writers mean it in this general sense, or as some new special order of 'deacons'.[84] Most English translations make a guess, sometimes plumping for the general 'servant', sometimes the specialized 'deacon', sometimes the neutral 'minister' which comes somewhere in the middle.

It's interesting to look through Paul and Timothy's use of the word with eyes open to the possible alternative meanings. Paul uses it only six times in letters and speeches spread over ten years; hardly one of his most frequent words.[85] But it makes a rush of appearances in the sections of 2 Corinthians which, on my theory, look as if Timothy may have written them.[86]

> You yourselves are the letter we have . . . It is clear that Christ himself wrote this letter [served/ministered/deaconed] by us . . . The capacity we have comes from God: it is he who made us capable of [serving/ministering/deaconing] the new covenant . . .
>
> God in his mercy has given us this [service/ministry/deaconing] to do, and so we are not discouraged . . .
>
> All this is done by God, who through Christ changed us from enemies into his friends and gave us the [service/ministry/deaconing] of making others his friends also . . .
>
> We do not want anyone to find fault with our [service/ministry/deaconing], so we try not to put obstacles in anyone's way. Instead, in everything we do we show that we are God's [servants/ministers/deacons] by patiently enduring troubles, hardships, and difficulties . . .
>
> Of their own free will, they [the Macedonian churches] begged us and pleaded for the privilege of having a part in [serving/ministering to/deaconing] God's people in Judea.[87]

If this was indeed Timothy's choice of word, was it such a favourite because it expressed exactly how he understood himself? Another possible translation is 'assistant', which is of course the role he filled for so long. During his earlier years on the team, Timothy features in Acts as one of *Paul's* 'servants/assistants/ministers/deacons'.[88] In 1 Timothy, Paul says, at the heart of one of his personal appeals, 'If you give these instructions to the believers, you will be a good servant [assistant/minister/deacon] *of Christ Jesus* . . .'[89] And the last word of Paul's 'step 4' command in 2 Timothy is, 'Perform your whole duty as a servant [assistant/minister/deacon] *of God.*'[90] Paul's deacon, Jesus' deacon, God's deacon – it certainly sounds like a key 'T' word.[91]

No-one highlighted Timothy's position as an apostle; and it evidently faded further as time went on. On the other hand, the role of servant or deacon fitted him exactly. The name became more and more his badge. 'Complete your deaconing' is virtually Paul's last word to him in 2 Timothy;[92] it's the lasting impression of Timothy he leaves us with. Timothy was the apostle who became a deacon. He embodies the change from first-generation leaders in the church to those who succeed them in every later century.[93] After the apostles come deacons, ministers or servants. Timothy is the patron saint of them all. He was the most prominent deacon in the New Testament.[94]

The deaconhood of all believers. Timothy is a role model not only for those who call themselves 'deacons' (or 'deaconesses'). The title 'deacon' is unfortunate if it sounds like a special status, or obscures the fact that we are all called to be servants.[95] It's equally wrong to talk of only some Christians as having a ministry, or being in *the* ministry. We are *all* ministers, or servants; they're the same word. This is the essence of Christianity. Jesus was himself 'the Servant King'; he said: 'I am among you as one who serves.'[96] At his last meal on earth, he demonstrated this quite literally by washing the disciples' feet. He then drew the moral that his followers too are to be servants.[97]

Timothy took this calling seriously; for many years as Paul's assistant, he lived the life of 'a good deacon-servant of Jesus Christ'. He wasn't just a model missionary or team member. He was a model *Christian*. And that makes him an example for us all. Not that he did everything right; we've seen that. But he's by far the most fully recorded person in the Bible at exactly the same stage of God's plans as we are. We're meant to follow Jesus, of course, but we can only be struck by our distance from him as God's perfect Son. We're meant to follow the Apostles too; but they had a unique role in founding the church, never to be repeated. Timothy is the supreme New Testament example of an 'ordinary' Christian.[98] In one sense we can follow Timothy more fully than any other New Testament figure-head. Like us he lived after Jesus: like us he wasn't one of the Apostles. He's *the* model New Testament Christian. We're meant to be like him in learning to be deacon-servants.

Deacon-leaders. Jesus calls all Christians to serve; that's no great surprise. But he spoke his words at the Last Supper to his Apostles, the future leaders of the church. His insistence that Christian *leaders* are to be servants *was* a shock. He calmly stood every human idea of power, status and hierarchy on its head. 'You know that those who are considered rulers of the heathen have power over them, and the leaders have complete authority. This, however, is not the way it is among you. If one of you wants to be great, he must be the servant of the rest; and if one of you wants to be first, he must be the slave of all.'[99]

The impact of these words is quite revolutionary. For four years I helped to lead a group of children aged seven to eleven in our church. One Good Friday, one of our number challenged us, the adult leaders, to get down on our knees and wash the children's feet. And so we did. There were no giggles, no ribald comments as I'd feared and expected; just an awed silence at such a reversal of the natural order of things.[100] Obeying Jesus' command is a great deal more than one symbolic gesture, of course; but it was a start. I *hope* we learned to carry this attitude of the servant into all our dealings with the children from then on.

If we managed it, we were following the lead not only of Jesus, but also of Timothy the deacon-leader. 'For it is not ourselves that we preach,' he wrote (on our theory) on behalf of Paul and himself to the Corinthian church they had founded together; 'we preach Jesus Christ as Lord, *and ourselves as your servants* for Jesus' sake.'[101] Timothy turned out to be a reluctant and ineffective leader in the strong, apostolic mould of Paul; but all along his servant's heart was in the right place. In his basic attitude, if not always in his actions, he was a model Christian leader.

But again he's important less for his achievements than for this unique niche he fills in church history. He personifies the movement from apostle-leadership to deacon-leadership. There's precious little support in the New Testament as a whole for the modern movement that tries to revive 'apostles', with absolute powers over the faith and private life of church members. It savours of the domineering heathen leadership Jesus spoke against. But there's strong support for the emerging glory of deaconhood. This is the pattern of leadership for all post-apostolic generations of Christians: leaders who serve; live a model Christian life; see their job as reading, preaching and teaching the Scriptures; train others to do the same; and suffer for their pains.[102] Leaders, in short, just like Timothy.

Timothy was the heir of Paul as preacher and teacher. But he was a deacon-teacher, not an apostle-teacher; the first one clearly defined in the New Testament. Christian leaders today are the heirs of Timothy.

Key Bible passages: 2 Timothy 1:2–4, 7–8, 10, 13–14; 2:2–6, 8–12, 15, 24; 3:10 – 4:22; Acts 19:22; 1 Thessalonians 2:6–7; 2 Corinthians 3:2–3, 5–6; 4:1, 5; 5:18; 6:3–4; 8:3–4; 11:4–5, 13; 1 Timothy 4:6.

Reflect

1. Is there anyone you need to make peace with? Especially an older Christian who might die with a dispute or misunderstanding unresolved?

2. Are you happy with the part the Bible plays in your life at present? If not, how could you adjust? How could you recommend it to others?

3. If you're a leader of a group or activity, who will you hand the job over to? How do you know they're suitable?

Share

1. Plan a celebration of the Bible or the Christian Good News with the group you're discussing these questions with. Would you prefer to keep it to yourselves as a chance to encourage each other, or throw it open to guests?

2. The apostle Paul gave way to the deacon Timothy. So is there any place in churches or Christian organizations today for one-person leadership?

3. List the qualities you would look for in a church minister or missionary today. One major denomination requires 'spirituality, relationship ability and leadership skills'. Would you agree? Or add or replace anything?

Saint and martyr?

Timothy received Paul's letter in late summer. 'Do your best to come to me soon.' He dreaded a painful reunion with Paul, but he couldn't run away from it. All the ties of their long partnership pulled him towards Rome. He must go; and move fast. It would soon be October when the rough seas closed down all shipping till spring. 'Come before winter.' It would be a race against time.

'Get Mark and bring him with you': Timothy sent word to Mark to drop everything and meet him at Troas *en route* for Rome.

Then he turned to Paul's other immediate instruction, 'Take the teachings and entrust them to reliable people.' The urgency of a short-term task and timetable concentrated his mind. He gathered his thoughts and his notes. What were the most important themes in Paul's teaching? How could he sum them up in a simple, memorable outline? He formed a teaching team with Priscilla and Aquila, two of the senior elders and old friends of Paul's;[1] also with Tychicus who had brought Paul's letter, and was planning to stay in Ephesus while Timothy was away. With their help, he went back over all he knew.

He called together the few elders who had remained true to the Good News, and some other faithful souls he knew he should have had the courage to appoint. Every night for two weeks he guided them through the parts of the Old Testament where Paul saw Jesus so clearly forecast – the stories of Adam and Abraham, the words of Moses and David. Then he remembered the letters he and Paul had written, to the Thessalonians, the Corinthians and the Colossians, and he repeated some of the main things they'd said.

All the while he was not only showing them what to teach others; he was reviving himself. The mists of fear and doubt began to lift; he rediscovered his faith and his nerve. By the time he'd handed over all he knew, he was ready and eager to go. He longed to be in time to put everything right with Paul.

He found a small boat on its way up the coast from Ephesus to Troas, and was there in three days. Good old Mark was already at the quayside. They called on Carpus and collected Paul's coat and books.

From the harbour it was easy to pick up a boat for the two-day crossing to Neapolis. They walked the few miles along the Egnatian Way to Philippi. They hugged all the old friends there and stayed the night with them.

One of them took them in his mule cart the week's ride across Macedonia. They relived all their memories of Paul. This made them ache and weep. But knowing they'd *both* disappointed him in the past comforted them. And they felt fresh love for him and his exacting demands on them. They prayed they'd find him still alive.

When they reached Dyrrhachium on the Adriatic coast, October had begun. But they caught the last ship making the hop over to Italy, and arrived safe in Brundisium. From there it was straight up the Appian Way, walking fast and hiring lifts when they could, to Rome.

They followed Onesiphorus' footsteps, asking the Roman Christians the way to Paul's prison. There they found him, with Luke in attendance.

It was a deeply tender and emotional reunion. All the hurts and strains were forgotten in the embrace of father and son. They cried and cried and held on tight to each other. Mark and Luke joined them in a huddle of praise and prayer.

It was two days before Paul's second trial. This time he didn't stand alone. Timothy, Luke and Mark came with him as advocates and witnesses. They presented his citizen's papers. But they could hardly deny the charge against him – so-called 'treason against the divine emperor'. He did indeed worship another King, Jesus. Paul pleaded guilty, and once again set off on a passionate explanation of who Jesus was, until the Senate cut him short and voted for him to die.

The three friends stayed with him through the days till his execution. Paul's mind was busy with what they should do once he was gone. His documents he gave to Mark and Luke. It was vital they should put together reliable records of Jesus' life and teaching. Mark had also been in touch with Peter and his fund of memories; he would be best placed with the church in Rome. Luke from his base in Philippi was the natural choice to help the Greek churches forward. Timothy must return to Ephesus, as the largest and most influential church centre in Asia Minor. With his renewed vision and vigour he wouldn't fail Paul this time.

Paul gave him his coat, the large, warm poncho of black hair from the goats near Tarsus. It wasn't just a treasured heirloom from father to son. It was an echo of Elijah's mantle passing to Elisha. Every time Timothy looked at it, felt its rough fabric and put it on, it said to him, 'Now it's your turn, Timothy. You're God's spokesman, in line of descent from Elijah, John the Baptist and Paul. Follow their faithfulness and courage. Teach God's Word and preach the Good News, as my last owner did. Go where he went and go where he still wanted to go when he died.'[2]

Timothy walked with Luke and Mark beside Paul as he went to his death. The soldiers and executioner marched him out of the city. Roman citizens had the dignity of a private ceremony in the countryside. The road took them past miles of tombs to the spot where Paul's own would be. Dismal surroundings, but the four Christians weren't depressed; they were strangely excited, elated even. Paul was walking through the tunnel to the winner's rostrum.

'There is waiting for me the victory prize for a righteous life,' he kept telling them, 'the prize which the Lord, the righteous Judge, will give me.'

They sang the hymn Paul had quoted in his letter to Timothy:

> If we have died with him,
>   we shall also live with him.
> If we continue to endure,
>   we shall also rule with him.

They reached the spot. Paul wrapped his arms round each friend in turn and blessed him. Timothy he held last and longest.

'My dear, dear son, the Lord be with your spirit.'

Timothy could find no words for an answer; just tears and a tighter embrace.

At last Paul repeated his letter again. 'The Lord will rescue me from all evil and take me safely into his heavenly kingdom.'

He slipped gently out of Timothy's arms, knelt beneath the swordsman's blade, and was gone. Timothy stared at the empty shell, which only a moment ago had been so full of Jesus.

More of Paul's words came back to him: 'But the Lord stayed

with me and gave me strength, so that I was able to proclaim the full message for all the Gentiles to hear.' Taking Luke and Mark by the arm, he said the words out loud.

'That means me now,' he said.

'And us as well,' answered Luke.

Or perhaps that wasn't at all how it was.

Timothy hesitated. He couldn't bring himself to face Paul. The commands and reproaches in the letter froze him into inaction. It took Tychicus, Priscilla and Aquila several days to lift him into anything like life. They sent for Mark, and together they sought out the reliable elders in Ephesus, and explained what they had to do.

After much dithering, Timothy at last agreed to go with Mark, and with heavy feet they made their way to Troas. They enquired at the harbour, but they were too late. No more sailing till April.

What should they do? Trudge back to Ephesus, or ask to stay with the Christians in Troas? The thought of going back brought Timothy close to despair. He remembered the house where Carpus lived, and the two of them knocked on his door.

He looked appalled to see them, made as if to shut the door in their faces, then bundled them inside.

'You surely haven't come down Harbour Street in daylight,' he hissed.

'Well, yes', they said, mystified.

'But didn't Paul warn you about Alexander the metalworker?' he asked.

They instantly remembered the letter. 'Be on your guard against him yourself, because he was violently opposed to our message.'

'His shop's on the seafront', said Carpus. 'He's bound to have seen you.'

They retreated deeper into the shadow of the room. Where could they go? But too late. A loud hammering on the door. It was Alexander, with soldiers. He looked slowly round the room. His eyes stopped at Timothy.

'That's the one,' he said with quiet relish. 'Right-hand man to the one they call Paul. Been speaking against emperor-worship right across the Empire.'

Strong arms clapped Timothy in irons and flung him into the jail next to the barracks. For days he sat in deepest depression. Mark was allowed to visit and came repeatedly. But he couldn't get a word out of Timothy.

Still, he persevered. He and the church in the town prayed. And those who visited took simply to reading aloud from the Old Testament Scriptures and their collection of the teachings of Jesus. Gradually the darkness lifted. After total numbness Timothy found he was able to think again. It wasn't the end. He'd been in prison before. He'd been sentenced to death before. And he'd survived. Perhaps he would again. Perhaps Jesus would . . . perhaps Jesus could and would forgive him. He began to pray and to mend.

Timothy wasn't a Roman citizen,[3] so his trial needn't take place in Rome. He appeared before a local court and several of the leading Christians in Troas spoke in his defence. Everything worked to his advantage. The local judges were concerned only with what he'd done in Troas.

'Yes,' said the church leaders, trusted and respected men, 'he did preach in Troas nearly ten years ago. But no, he said nothing against the emperor.'

Alexander snarled and kept repeating what Timothy had said in Ephesus, but that was no concern of the judges. They released him on grounds of insufficient evidence.

Timothy was overjoyed. God was at work again; Jesus still loved him and wanted to use him. He itched to be on the move.

There were still two months till he could sail, so he stayed in Troas and made himself useful to the church. After appearing in court, he could do no overt teaching or evangelizing that Alexander would hear about. He had to bite his tongue twenty times a day. But he served the others with all his heart. He visited the sick, he helped the poor and weak, he comforted the bereaved. It was like the early days of his Christian discipleship at Lystra again. And quietly, persistently, in the spare moments he wrote a record of Paul's teachings. It was what he should have done at Ephesus. He would present it secretly to the church when he left.

At last the seas opened and he sailed for Italy. He sped along the road to Rome, and asked for Paul. He found the house of Linus, the oldest elder in the city.

'Brother Timothy,' he said gently, 'we thought you would never come. Whenever Paul heard footsteps approach his cell, he

IN THE STEPS OF TIMOTHY

thought it was you. His face fell each time. If only you could have come . . . before winter.'

'Then he . . .?'

'Beheaded in December. His last prayer was for you.'

Timothy leant his head against the wall. He thought his despair would overwhelm him again. After all he'd been through . . . he'd come all this way for nothing . . . it was a sick, cruel joke . . . would nothing ever go right again?

But after a few moments the wave of self–pity drained away. Amazing peace and calm took hold of him. So Paul was with Christ – which is a far better thing. It was the second time he'd lost a father. But this time, no fear, no pain, no bitterness. He would see him again. Before long! And by then Paul would have cause to be proud of him again. He turned back to Linus.

'I must go back to Ephesus. There is work to do.'[4]

We come to the last chapter in Timothy's story. And we slip off the edge of the Bible into later history which we can't trace for sure. We don't know which of those two opening scenes is nearer the truth. We can't be certain whether Timothy became the 'saint and martyr' later generations called him.[5] But some things are clear. We can be sure of what is in the Bible; we need to be more cautious with later traditions.

Timothy's last years

Date	Age	Event
before 70	under 40	**Imprisoned and released: still travelling (Heb. 13:23).**
95?	65	'Bishop' in Ephesus.
96?	66	Receives Revelation (2:1–7).
96/97	66/67	? Martyred in Ephesus in reign of Domitian/Nerva.

Bible

Losing Paul

We don't know whether Timothy saw Paul die. But undoubtedly he had to face life without Paul, the 'father' he'd known for twenty years, all his adult life; the father he'd worked with, travelled with, suffered with, shared everything with. He'd loved and learnt from him; he'd inherited his faith and purpose in life. He'd looked like losing him several times before, until – each time – Jesus snatched him back from the teeth of death.

But not this time. Now he really was gone. The shock and the pain would take time to become real. But once they took hold, they would be savage. We have the priceless comfort of knowing that Christians who die go to heaven. But we still miss them terribly. We're not spared the human pangs of bereavement.

There's an old Ethiopian manuscript called *Conflicts of the Apostles*. It quotes a letter claiming to be written to Timothy by Dionysius, one of Paul's few converts in Athens.[6] In this nineteenth-century translation, it echoes the grief Paul's followers must have felt at his loss.

> O brother Timothy, now art thou, am I, orphan and alone. Behold, thy course has been suddenly cut short; he will no longer write to thee, saying: O my beloved son! He will no longer send for thee to come to him, thy teacher, from city to city. O brother Timothy, there came to him the day of trouble and of joy; but unto thee one of mist and darkness.[7]

Our eyes are mistier, the world is darker – at least for a time – for loss of those we have been close to.

The recent strains in Timothy's friendship with Paul will only have added to the pain. On top of loss came doubt and guilt. 'Did I really put things right? Or did he die still thinking I'd let him down? Was he proud of me or ashamed? Did I spoil his last moments on earth by making him worried and sad?'

If Timothy did not reach Rome in time, it must have been a lingering regret for the rest of his life. I've already mentioned the rather 'Paul-like' Christian leader I worked with in my late twenties.[8] We had a number of disagreements, the warmth between us cooled, my work changed and I moved out of his orbit. A few years later he became bedridden and sent a message that he wanted to see me. I was rather flattered he'd thought of me, and looked forward to visiting him. But I was busy and put it off. At last I got round to ringing up to fix a date. 'Oh dear,' said the voice of his nurse. 'He died last week.' He was never afraid to voice his disapproval. So I fear I'm in for another rocket when I get to heaven! But more sadly, I have to live now with a relationship I never patched up. He held out the olive branch, but I was too slow to take it.

And so Timothy found himself for the first time in the world without Paul. I've summed up his adult life so far as, 'With Paul, success; without Paul, failure.' If that's right, he now faced the supreme test. How would he get on, without Paul as the main source of his strength and health?

Going to jail

The Bible tells us definitely about only one more incident in Timothy's life – he had another spell in prison, but was then released.

> I want you to know that our brother Timothy has been let out of prison. If he comes soon enough, I will have him with me when I see you.[9]

This verse from the letter to the Hebrews teases us by what it doesn't tell us. We don't know the 'I' who wrote it. The 'our brother' suggests it was someone who knew Timothy from working with Paul; but that's as far as we can go.[10] Nor do we know the 'you', the people he was writing to. Long tradition suggests a group of 'Hebrew' or Jewish Christians at Rome, perhaps one house-church in the city. Timothy could certainly have known such a group, from his stay during Paul's first imprisonment.

We don't know where or when Timothy was in prison. There's no obvious slot in our reconstructed date-chart for it before Paul's death; and the fact that Hebrews doesn't mention Paul makes it likely it was written after he died.[11] So perhaps Timothy was jailed on his way to see Paul in Rome (as in one of the opening scenes to this chapter), or on his next journey soon after. We don't know *why* he was jailed; but it's hard to think of any reason other than persecution of known Christian leaders at that time under the emperor Nero. Lastly, we don't know whether Timothy made the proposed journey with the writer to the readers, or what happened after that.

And yet we do know some things! Timothy was imprisoned (level 1). Very soon after he got 2 Timothy, he found himself following its command to share the same kind of suffering as Paul.[12] The writer's words, 'I want you to know that Timothy has been let out of prison', show (level 2) that he'd been in prison long enough for the readers to know about it before this; it wasn't just a night or two in the cooler. The 'I want you to know' implies (level 3) they've been concerned and praying about Timothy in prison. He'd been in prison before,[13] but with Paul now gone he was all the more vulnerable. How would he cope with this setback at such a turning-point in his life?

Timothy isn't, of course, the only New Testament character imprisoned for his faith. But he's one of the patron saints of the long roll-call of Christians since then who've lost their freedom for staying loyal to Jesus. It still happens in parts of the world today. It could happen to us. We'd be foolish to assume that the freedom of religion enjoyed in most western countries is guaranteed for ever. If we have to follow Paul and Timothy to prison, let's pray we can learn the attitude they taught from Paul's first Roman jail: 'Don't be afraid of your enemies; always be courageous, and this will prove to them that they will lose and you will win, because it is God who gives you the victory. For you have been given the privilege of serving Christ, not only by believing in him, but also by suffering for him.'[14] With God on our side and at our side, we can't lose; we're bound to win. Whether in prison or out, Jesus is still in charge. If he wants us released, he'll find the way; if not, and he leaves us there till we die, that'll be an even better freedom as we join him in heaven.

Timothy *was* released. This is the second 'level 1' fact we know for sure. Unlike Paul's, his imprisonment wasn't fatal or final. This meant that Jesus had more for him to do on earth. Paul had understood in his first Roman jail that 'by continuing to live I can do more worthwhile work'.[15] Every Christian God brings out of prison has a fresh chance to serve him in freedom. That was the good news for Timothy, the challenge to put the past behind him and make the future better.

On the timescale we've followed in this book, he was touching forty – young enough to be active and energetic still, with many years of mature and experienced service to give, and yet past half-way through the life expectancy of those days. His ministry at Ephesus had shown some of the cracks and wobbles of mid-life. Here was his chance to seize its positive side. He could get back on the field after half-time and make the second half count for more than the first. The touch Jesus gives to the ageing process is nothing short of golden. As Paul and Timothy said in 2 Corinthians, in a passage Timothy may well have written himself: 'Even though our physical being is gradually decaying, yet our spiritual being is renewed day after day.'[16] As he steps out of prison at the end of the New Testament, and faces the unknown future, this is the question. Can he recapture that ringing faith and vigour of 2 Corinthians, to lift him over the hurdles of middle and old age?

Our final sight of him suggests (level 3) that at least the first step was in the right direction. 'If he comes soon enough, I will have him with me when I see you,' says the writer of Hebrews. Timothy seems headed towards an old friend and colleague, and a supportive church group who care about him. In that company he will receive not only comfort and healing for past wounds, but every encouragement to pick up his Bible to start reading, teaching and preaching again. Timothy shows us that failure need never be final for ordinary Christians. The rest of the family are there to welcome us back into fellowship and discipleship.

And that's where God's inspired record leaves Timothy and us. Whatever our age and circumstances, God gives us the same equipment and much the same task. It's not easy to remain a faithful Christian for the rest of our lives. But our church should be the family of fellow-Christians to keep us spiritually healthy. From among them or the wider Christian body, there will be one or two to work with us on the special job Jesus wants us to do for him. And part of that job is bound to be sharing the Good News with people who need to hear it or see it in action.

Paul said to Timothy, 'Watch yourself and watch your teaching.'[17] Timothy's life story says the same thing, in a slightly more general sense, to us. 'Keep an eye on your own progress as a Christian, and see to it that you help others to make the journey with you.'

Tradition

Returning to Ephesus?

We haven't quite reached the end of the book. There's a repeated tradition that Timothy went back to Ephesus, and continued his work there. The next datable events in his story are set there about thirty years later; but the tradition implies he was there a long time before then, perhaps ever since Paul's death. It's only tradition; it isn't in the Bible, and therefore doesn't carry the demand that Christians believe it and learn from it. But a book about Timothy should certainly investigate it.

There's nothing unlikely about it. If Timothy was in time to see Paul before he died, he may well have received a fresh commission to serve the churches in one of the strongest Christian outposts – Asia Minor, with its commercial centre Ephesus. But if Timothy missed Paul, how true to his best instincts to go back to the last place where Paul had assigned him. Things hadn't gone well there so far, but now was his chance to make a better fist of them.

During the early centuries of the Christian era, the churches developed great respect, even reverence, for their founders and leaders (especially any who were killed for their faith). It became the habit to commemorate martyrs and early bishops in the communion service on the anniversary of their death – the origin of what many Christians still celebrate as 'saints' days'. From these 'calendars of early saints', which started as a simple list of names, there developed books telling the stories of each hero. It became quite common for a later bishop to write the stories of his predecessors.

At Ephesus, there was just such a book claiming to be by Polycrates, who was bishop about AD 190–200. This is very early, and some have said it must be a forgery by someone later, just pretending to be Polycrates.[18] But the stories he tells are not only accurate in the historical details we can check; they're entirely free of the 'miraculous' exaggerations that began to distort these books from the third and fourth centuries onwards.[19] Polycrates includes the story of Timothy and of his death in AD 96 or 97. If it's genuine, it's unusually strong evidence for anything in ancient history. Written about 100 years later, it's only one generation after those who were alive at the time and could vouch for the events as eyewitnesses.[20] When I started writing this book I doubted these traditional stories outside the Bible. But the purity and sheer age of Polycrates' account has won me over.

Both Polycrates and the much later Metaphrastes[21] insist that Timothy worked at Ephesus as a church leader for many years after Paul's death. Let's take their accounts at face value and try to piece together what he is likely to have done there, if they're right.[22]

John's assistant? One difficulty in imagining Timothy at Ephesus is that there's an even stronger tradition that the apostle John went and worked there. If it's true (and Polycrates and Metaphrastes, as well as many others, are equally insistent that it is), we don't know when he went there. The last sight of John in the Acts of the Apostles is very early, probably before Paul's conversion.[23] But Paul mentions him as still in Jerusalem at the time of his own second visit there in AD 45 or 46.[24] After that, we know nothing of where John was till the tradition of his long stay in Ephesus. He could hardly have started there before Paul's death, as there's no mention of him at Ephesus in Acts; he had in any case been party to the agreement that Paul would have freedom of manoeuvre as apostle to the Gentiles. But, once Paul had died, John may have moved there very soon to help consolidate such an important group of churches.

So it's quite possible that if Timothy went back to Ephesus, he found John already in residence; or that John arrived soon after Timothy's return. The situation looks almost doomed for a power struggle. John is the senior man in every sense, an original apostle of Jesus; but Timothy represents Paul, the founder of the church. The one comes from the Jewish strand of Christianity, the other from the Gentile. Who would the churches support? How would Timothy handle the potential clash? Would he fight his corner, or run away and hide? The answer seems to be neither. The only evidence we have is that there was no trouble at all. This speaks volumes for the graciousness of John and the humility of Timothy.

For, reading between the lines, Timothy took the junior position. Metaphrastes tries to sort out their relationship.

> Timothy did not succeed John, for he [Timothy] was the first bishop of Ephesus [Metaphrastes is referring in later, 'bishop' language to Timothy's earlier role at Ephesus as Paul's go-between]; however, for as long as

John, apostle of Christ and evangelist, was present, although he [John] was not tied to a single see, yet he exercised principal authority.

John evidently took apostolic oversight of the whole of Asia Minor. Timothy was his subordinate, perhaps concentrating on Ephesus alone; but not, according to Metaphrastes, a jealous or protective subordinate.

> For the divine Timothy was not only swift in under-standing, but also very ready to speak out, and most adept at using eloquence skilfully, and happy to expound divine things, and especially suited to build-ing up and taking charge of the church . . . not only did the Spirit charm him through Paul's wonderful lyre, but he also conversed with John, the specially beloved disciple, and was put by him in charge of the see of Ephesus, when he had heard and learnt from him what he, John, had in turn received from the Holy Spirit.

In this account, Timothy recognized an apostle's authority in John, and readily fitted in with it. More than that, he lapped up all he could learn from John's store of knowledge as 'the disciple whom Jesus loved'.[25]

This would show us Timothy once again at his most comfortable in the role of junior, learner and assistant. Well into his middle age, he appears as the 'permanent deacon'. It's the perfect position for his temperament. Far from putting his nose out of joint, it made his job easier and more effective. He worked better as a teacher and church leader under someone else's wing than out on his own. There are many others like this, happier as number two in an outfit than as number one. I've known some of them demote themselves from leading an organization, or return to a previous job, when they recognized a more suitable chief to take over. I don't want to belittle the great humility they showed in stepping down and making the new relationship work so well; but *they* were more conscious of God releasing them into a position where they could give more time to their real gifts, with less of the stress of leadership.

Timothy's main work over the next twenty-five to thirty years was, according to Metaphrastes, 'to expound divine things to build up the church'. Helping Christians understand and obey God's teaching in the Bible must be one of the two most important jobs in the world (alongside bringing the Good News to people who aren't yet Christians). But it has a negative side too; the constant battle against false teaching. It seems that a false teacher called Cerinthus came to live in Ephesus, and much of John's work was to argue against his wrong ideas. John took the corrupting effect of false teaching so seriously that – according to tradition – when he heard that Cerinthus was in the same bath-house as him, he leapt straight out of the water and ran! Timothy was well schooled to help in this fight for truth. He and Paul endlessly had to try to root out the weeds of false teaching among the new churches they planted. That was the job Paul had left him to do at Ephesus in the first place.[26] And in their letters to the Corinthians and the Colossians, they'd countered teaching very similar to that of Cerinthus; the idea that really spiritual people advance beyond the simple Good News of ordinary Christians to a superior, private knowledge of God.

Tradition hints at something else that Timothy may have done during these years as John's partner at Ephesus. One of the service books for St Timothy's day describes him as 'a co-author and herald of the holy Gospel'. A seventeenth-century editor of these earlier snippets suggests that the phrase perhaps means that 'while he was intimate with John at Ephesus, he might have collected together the commentaries on Christ's deeds written by the three evangelists and other holy men, which John is then said to have edited and excerpted'.[27] He isn't saying John compiled Matthew, Mark and Luke as well! Rather, he helped people in Ephesus to learn what the other gospel-writers were teaching. In the process he was inspired to write a fourth gospel to fill in the gaps.

And an ancient memory says Timothy was his 'co-author'. It seems highly possible. Not in the sense that he could add any first-hand accounts of Jesus; but if he was John's junior colleague, isn't it likely he'd lend a hand in such an important project? He was an experienced co-author with Paul. He'd worked with Luke and Mark, and may even have been present with them at Paul's death, when they would have seen the critical need for reliable written records of Jesus' life and teaching. If he did indeed help John with this process of passing on the contents of the first three gospels and composing the fourth, it casts Timothy's shadow over another vast chunk of the New Testament.[28]

John's replacement? In AD 95, the Emperor Domitian allowed free rein to his notorious bad temper. He carried out vicious purges of Jews and Christians. One prize scalp was the apostle John, dispatched into exile on the island of Patmos. But with Timothy in Ephesus, the obvious stand-in was ready to hand.

> When the venerable John had been ignominiously exiled to that place, Timothy took up the bishopric of Ephesus in his stead . . . [writes Metaphrastes].

This would put Timothy in the isolated 'top slot' once again. But surely, now aged about sixty-five, he would be far more secure and stable than when Paul had pitched him into the same position thirty years before.

From the wording of these early 'biographers', it's confusing to know when exactly they thought Timothy was 'the bishop' and when he wasn't.[29] Part of the problem is that they're using language differently from the way Timothy himself would have done. There's no evidence that anyone thought of only one 'bishop' per town or area before Ignatius, about fifteen years after John's exile. In the New Testament the word 'bishop' or 'overseer' is a straight alternative to 'elder'; they're interchangeable titles for the same thing.[30] And as we've seen, the practice of Paul and other church-planters was to appoint a team of elders in each church.[31] The New Testament pattern is several bishops per church, not several churches per bishop.

This helps us with a question sometimes asked about Timothy. Was he the first diocesan bishop, or (if 'bishops' then looked after only one church) the first vicar? A quick glance at 1 and 2 Timothy, and then at these later 'Lives of the saint', might suggest he was something of the kind. Paul speaks to him as if he were the overall leader of the Ephesus churches; and Polycrates and Metaphrastes keep referring to him as 'the bishop'.

In fact, though, his position was different. His authority to take charge over several churches in Ephesus was only as a stand-in for an apostle; Paul's go-between, and later John's substitute. It's true that the New Testament churches remained answerable to the apostolic mission team who'd founded them and appointed their elders. So it's arguable (though far from certain) that something equivalent to modern area superintendents or diocesan bishops perform a valid apostolic function. But Timothy isn't a precedent; he never held the job in his own right.[32]

The local level of leadership in New Testament churches was the group of elders. You may feel that lone ministers are a legitimate development of this; or (like me) you may not. But it's quite clear that you shouldn't claim Timothy as a New Testament prototype for such ministry. He was acting as a sub-apostle, not as a super-elder.[33]

John's 'angel'? During his year on Patmos, John wrote down the visions and messages Jesus gave him. The result was the last book of our Bible, the Revelation to John.[34] Chapters 2 and 3 consist of seven 'letters' or messages from Jesus to the churches in Asia Minor, where John had been apostle-in-charge. Or rather, each is addressed to the 'angel' of the church in question. The word 'angel' needn't mean a heavenly being. It simply means 'messenger', and could here refer to the 'church secretary', the person who would receive the letter and read it to the rest of the church members.

Who more likely to be this person in Ephesus (perhaps in all seven churches)[35] than Timothy, if he was John's stand-in and representative? Early scholars assumed that at least the Ephesus letter was addressed to Timothy.[36] Many commentators since then have followed this view, and it seems entirely reasonable. Modern scholars tend to prefer a vaguer sense for 'angel', something like the 'spirit' of the church. I know of no evidence that the word could mean something as vague as this in the first century. Their reasoning is that the message from Jesus via John was meant for the church as a whole. This is probably true; but it's in no way contradicted by understanding 'angel' as the messenger who would pass it on to the rest of the church.

My 'level 4' hunch sides with the older commentators' 'level 3' inference that John actually addressed the words of Revelation 2:1–7 *to* Timothy. But let's put that on one side. If Timothy was, as tradition insists, a central member of the Ephesus fellowship, he was at least *one* of the people Jesus was speaking to. And as the words are in the singular (speaking to just one person),[37] he must have had a sense of Jesus talking direct to him. They're extraordinarily relevant. So let's read them in that light.

'To the angel of the church in Ephesus write:

'This is the message from the one who holds the seven stars in his right hand and who walks among the seven gold lampstands.'[38]

Timothy hears Jesus remind him that *he*, Jesus, is the true guardian of the seven churches (pictured as stars or lampstands, ablaze with God's light in the dark night). He's close to them all, watching over them, caring for them. It's an encouraging, but sobering, truth for any church leaders tempted to think they carry the burden and the power alone.

'I know what you have done; I know how hard you have worked and how patient you have been . . . You are patient, you have suffered for my sake, and you have not given up.'[39]

It's a cheering progress report on both Timothy and the church fellowship. Thirty years earlier Paul saw them on the verge of crumbling in the face of difficulty. They've rallied and kept going; they've developed dogged endurance.

'I know that you cannot tolerate evil people and that you have tested those who say they are apostles but are not, and have found out that they are liars . . . you hate what the Nicolaitans do . . .'[40]

This is a still more remarkable change from 1 and 2 Timothy. *Then* the churches were riddled with false teaching, and Paul feared Timothy would go the same way. *Now*, a generation later, things have turned right round and false apostles are shown the door. The Nicolaitans – a sect who seem to have been encouraging Christians to lower their standards by eating food from idol sacrifices and by committing sexual sin – couldn't force their way in.[41] Fifteen years later, Ignatius in *his* letter to the Ephesians verifies this new rigour in understanding the Christian faith and living by it: 'I have heard of some who have passed by you, having perverse doctrines; whom you did not suffer to sow among you, but stopped your ears, that you might not receive those things that were sown by them . . .'[42] Obviously John must take much of the credit for this turn-around. But if he was there, Timothy was also a major influence on the churches' growth.

So far Jesus has spoken with praise and appreciation.[43] But at the heart of his message there is a rebuke.

> 'But this is what I have against you: you do not love me now as you did at first.'[44]

It's fatally easy, in the passion for truth and for defending the Good News against all assaults, to lose the love, and to become harsh and cold. If these words apply to Timothy, the drift from his first love for Jesus and his people[45] probably began in the wear and tear of his earlier years at Ephesus. He returned determined to do a better job; not to let Paul down again. He worked hard; he did his best; he succeeded. But he never quite dared let himself love with the original carefree abandon. He served Jesus at arm's length. It's a common faltering in those who see themselves as not as young and 'naïve' as they were.

So Jesus shows him (and the rest of the church) the road back.

> 'Think how far you have fallen! Turn from your sins and do what you did at first.'[46]

People lose their love for many different reasons – the heat of the battle, the passing of time, or the sheer busyness of life. But here are three short, simple steps for them all. Step 1: *think* – look back and remember, and see how far things have slipped. Step 2: *turn* – make a clean break with anything sinful, and come back to Jesus for forgiveness. Step 3: *do* – get back to how you were at first. It's never too late to find again the open-hearted love of God, neighbours and fellow-Christians which marked the start of our Christian walk.

Timothy certainly needed to take these steps thirty years earlier when Paul wrote to him. We can't be certain how far he still needed to take them now, or to take them again. Perhaps he'd already taken them, and the message for him now was to lead the rest of the church through them. For Jesus' next words in the verse just quoted are a warning primarily about the church (the 'lampstand'); 'If you don't turn from your sins, I will come to you and take your lampstand from its place.'

210

Strikingly, Ignatius' letter to the Ephesians fifteen years later, already partly quoted, shows they've taken this warning to heart. After commenting on their valour for truth, he goes on: 'You are . . . full of God: his spiritual temples, full of Christ, full of holiness . . . *you love nothing but God only.*'[47] Helping the Ephesians to love nothing but God only – was this the task Timothy took on when he received Revelation? If so, it was the last task he undertook.

Dying violently?

Polycrates, Metaphrastes and all the other early biographers agree that Timothy died by martyrdom in 96 or 97. They describe it in detail; this is the 'business end' of their 'Lives' – the death was the main reason for writing them.[48] Polycrates' is the earliest and presumably most original account.

> The remnants of their early idolatry had remained among the inhabitants of the city, that is to say certain wickedness which they called the feast of Katagogia . . . They put costumes on, and veiled their faces so that they could not be recognized by their features, and bearing clubs and images of idols, and bawling out foolish songs, they leapt indiscriminately upon eminent free-born women, and even perpetrated murders and many other unlawful and wicked acts, and shed much blood in particular parts of the city. And they did not cease from doing these things . . . very frequently St Timothy, then the archbishop [*sic*!], tried to prevail upon them.
>
> Not managing to prohibit their madness by teaching, the saint, on the very day of this their abominable festival, went to meet them in the middle of the city gate, and exhorted them saying, 'Men of Ephesus, do not rage in idolatry, but clearly recognize him who is God.' The workers of the devil, indignant at his teaching, murdered the just man with the . . . clubs and stones which . . . they were carrying. But the servants of God laid him down, still breathing, on a mountainside near that splendid city, in the region adjacent to the gate, and there he gave up his holy soul to God in peace.

It's an early and widespread tradition; there's no reason to doubt it. God at last took at face value words which Timothy had probably written himself almost forty years earlier at a time of great stress and strain: 'And now we sigh, so great is our desire that our home which comes from heaven should be put on over us.'[49] He must have felt the similarities to one of his first sights of Paul – stoned in the gate at Lystra. Perhaps snatches of Paul's words came back to him: 'you have observed . . . my persecutions, and my sufferings. You know all that happened to me in . . . Lystra, the terrible persecutions I endured! . . . Everyone who wants to live a godly life in union with Christ Jesus will be persecuted . . .'[50]

Paul had got up again and lived; Timothy didn't. He was one of many in that first generation of Christians who reached a day when following Jesus cost them their lives. They were the forerunners of literally hundreds of thousands (probably millions) of Christians who've had to make this final sacrifice during the centuries since. Timothy's last message to us is to be ready to die for our loyalty to Jesus; to stand up for him right to the end. He was by my reckoning sixty-six or sixty-seven – much the same age as Paul when he died.

Polycrates and Metaphrastes say that Timothy died before John got back to Ephesus. It must have happened very soon after he sent Revelation. We can see now what a perfect preparation for martyrdom Timothy would have found in Jesus' closing words to the Ephesus angel.

> 'He who has an ear, let him hear what the Spirit says to the churches. To him who overcomes, I will give the right to eat from the tree of life, which is in the paradise of God.'[51]

'He who overcomes' emerges again and again in Revelation as the Christian who stays faithful all the way to a martyr's death. Timothy overcame; he now enjoys the fruit in God's garden.

But the Spirit also says this to the churches; to all Christians; to each and every one of us. We too may have to go through pain to paradise – even the pain of execution. But it will be worth it, to join Jesus round his tree.

In AD 356 the Emperor Constantius built a temple in Constantinople. He embellished it in the most pious way he knew – by transferring to it the remains of any apostles or their companions he could persuade the present custodians to part with. He secured Andrew, Luke – and Timothy.

Polycrates, Constantius, Metaphrastes – these earlier generations of Christians have found value in tracing the life of Timothy. This book has tried to do the same. He was no super-hero; not a strong personality. He's the patron saint of the ordinary Christian. He had his weaknesses and he made mistakes. The assessment of him as 'like a common clay pot' he probably wrote himself.[52] I think he was very like me. Perhaps, too, a bit like you. And yet – like you and me too, I pray – God loved him, persevered with him, and put him to good use far beyond anything he can have expected.

Key Bible passages: Hebrews 13:23; Revelation 2:1–7; 1 Timothy 4:16; 2 Corinthians 4:7.

Reflect

1. What similarities and differences do you see between Timothy's (a) qualities and (b) experiences, and your own?

2. Who is the person (now dead) you owe most to? How do you honour that person's memory and what he or she gave you? Should you do more – or less?

3. What are your hopes and prayers for middle age . . . old age . . . death? How could you help yourself be ready for imprisonment or martyrdom if God brought you to them?

Share

1. The 'official' day for commemorating Timothy (and Titus) is 26 January. What items would you include in a 'St Timothy's Day' service? How could you feature some of the causes which can claim him as 'patron saint' (see p. 187)?

2. Before 1969, some churches celebrated St Timothy's Day on 22 January (the traditional date of his death), and others on 24 January. With the current celebration on the 26th, this makes almost a week of 'Timothy-tide'. How else could we fittingly honour his memory and example during that season?

3. In about AD 435, Salvian of Marseilles wrote a letter *Ad Ecclesiam* ('To the Church'), using Timothy as his pseudonym. He criticized Christians for their greed and failure to give to those in need, urging any who died childless to leave their possessions to the poor. Try writing the letter you think Timothy would write today, either to the whole church, or to your own fellowship.

Notes

Introduction

[1]I know of only two attempts to write a full, self-contained 'life story' of Timothy before the book you are now reading. One was in the second century, the other in the tenth (see chapter 9, page 203–204, and note 20, for detail). It seems that Timothy gets a book to himself only about every thousand years.

[2]I have come across only one picture of Timothy, a miniature illustration from the Bible of St Cecilia in the Vatican Library, dated 1097. But, typical of so much in Timothy's reputation, it is inaccurate. It shows Paul handing him the letter to the Romans for delivery. But Phoebe was the courier who delivered Romans (Rom. 16:1–2); Timothy sent his greetings in the letter, not in person (16:21).

[3]W. K. Lowther Clarke (ed.), in *Liturgy and Worship* (SPCK, 1932), p. 220, mentions one church dedicated to St Timothy in the sixteenth century. St Timothy's, Crookes, Sheffield, was dedicated in 1908.

[4]For example, in Acts 17:15 we simply hear that Silas and Timothy are *not* in Athens; in 19:22 only that Paul sends Timothy and Erastus off to Macedonia. This doesn't mean that Luke thinks Timothy is unimportant. After all, Luke says next to nothing about himself, although it's clear he took part in three phases of the Acts (16:10–17; 20:5 – 21:18; 27:1 – 28:16). This is simply because he wasn't aiming to write his or Timothy's life story. His aim was 'to write an orderly account' (Lk. 1:3) of Jesus' ministry and teaching (Acts 1:1) from their beginning (Lk. 1:3) through to the events which followed Jesus' ascent into heaven (Acts 1:2). His main focus in Acts is Jesus' continuing activity through the two apostles Peter and Paul. Other characters appear only when they are necessary to the stories of Peter and Paul. Luke probably devotes so much attention to Paul (even to the exclusion of his companions) because he intends this book as an all-important defence document for Paul's trial in Rome (Acts 25:10–12).

[5]We shall look at this fully in chapter 7.

[6]When my uncle heard I was writing a *book* about Timothy, he said he would be hard pressed to write two paragraphs – or even the back of a postcard!

[7]H. V. Morton, *In the Steps of St Paul* (Methuen, 1937), p. 217.

[8]See chapters 2, 5 and 7.

[9]There is a remarkable parallel to Timothy's relationship with Paul

in the case of Robert Louis Stevenson and his step-son Lloyd Osbourne. In the introduction to Stevenson's *New Arabian Nights* (Heinemann, Tusitala edn., 1923, p. xiii), Osbourne tells of his first meeting with the writer. 'How incredible it would have seemed to me then had some prophetic voice told me that this stranger's life and mine were to run together for nineteen years to come; that I was destined to become his step-son, his comrade, the sharer of all his wanderings; that we were to write books together; that we were to sail far-off seas; that we were to hew a home out of the tropic wilderness; and that at the end, while the whole world mourned, I was to lay his body at rest on a mountain peak in Oceana.'

[10]For more on the Paul–Timothy relationship, see chapter 4 as a whole, but especially pp. 90–97.

[11]For more on Timothy as the patron saint of 'ordinary' Christians, see chapter 8.

[12]Acts 16:1.

[13]2 Tim. 1:5.

[14]Acts 16:3, my translation following I. Howard Marshall, *Acts*, Tyndale New Testament Commentary (IVP, 1980), p. 259.

[15]You may be alarmed at the thought of speculation and hunch playing a part in reconstructing a life story. And it should go without saying that these 'level 4' hunches carry no demand that Christians should accept them in the way that the 'level 1' facts do. But as I hope these examples in the introduction show, my hunches are not unreasonable; they are based on all the evidence available. There may seem too much hunch in the book as a whole for some tastes. But this is necessary only because Timothy has been neglected for so long.

[16]Luke called them Lycaonians (Acts 14:6, 11) after the name of the Roman region.

[17]*The Bearing of Recent Discovery on the Trustworthiness of the New Testament* (Hodder and Stoughton, 1915). He also writes, 'the fact that the father was accepted as the husband of a Jewess may be safely assumed to prove that he was a person of some standing in Lystra' (*The Cities of St Paul*, Hodder and Stoughton, 1917 p. 418).

[18]Acts 16:3.

[19]1 Tim. 4:12.

[20]*Against Heresies* ii.22.5, about AD 180.

[21]Throughout this book I follow the time-scheme calculated in *The Illustrated Bible Dictionary* (IVP, 1980), Part 1, pp. 279–283. The evidence for the date of 1 Timothy is that Acts (which closes in AD 64) doesn't have time for Paul to visit Ephesus and leave Timothy there (1 Tim. 1:3). The ancient tradition that this happened after Paul was released from his first imprisonment in Rome is virtually certain to be right.

[22]Acts 16:3.

[23]Perhaps the very year Jesus launched his public ministry in the temple at Jerusalem (Jn. 2:13; Lk. 3:23).

[24]Chapter 9 of this book looks at what we know – if anything – about Timothy after his late thirties.

Chapter 1: Child

[1]In Acts it is Stephen who prays these words (7:59). But Paul witnessed them (8:1); what more likely than that he would echo them when he faced the same death himself?

[2]The four 'levels' of supporting evidence for Timothy's life story are explained in the Introduction.

[3]Acts 16:1, 3; 2 Tim. 3:14–15; 1:5.

[4]Acts 16:1.

[5]Acts 16:3.

[6]Dt. 7:3–4; Ezr. 9 – 10; Mal. 2:10–12. A custom had arisen of holding a mock funeral for Jews who 'threw themselves away' on a Gentile partner. Eunice may have been cut dead in this way.

[7]Why *circumcision* rather than, say, a ring in the nose or a tattoo on the left arm? Isn't it that God marks and claims his menfolk in the deepest recess of their personality – their sexual identity and activity? They are not free to sow wild oats like their pagan neighbours. They are cut out (literally) for faithful monogamy, reflecting their exclusive commitment to God. Love for one partner mirrors love for one God.

[8]2 Tim. 3:14–15.

[9]As with so many Jews, this early training will have inclined Timothy to be both clever and moral.

[10]Strictly speaking, it is misleading to call the Old Testament the 'Jewish Bible', and circumcision the 'Jewish birthmark'. The word 'Jew(ish)' became current only after the Old Testament was written. Many aspects of Jewish faith and custom are later developments of what is in the Old Testament, even distortions of it. But I continue to use the word in the main part of the book, even if rather loosely, because Timothy, Eunice and Lois were called Jews by their contemporaries.

[11]Once Paul had given Timothy the operation, the Jews' objections to him lapsed (Acts 16:3–4).

[12]Circumcision (among other Jewish practices) was a constant subject for scorn and ribaldry among first-century pagan writers.

[13]2 Tim. 1:5. Lois is as distinctive a Bible character as Eunice. This verse is the only mention of the word 'grandmother' in Scripture.

[14]There may be another reason here why Timothy was uncircumcised. Infant circumcision was a naming ceremony in which the father

took an active part (see Lk. 1:59–62). Perhaps Timothy simply inherited his name from his father.

[15]Acts 16:3, AD 48. See Introduction, page 11.

[16]2 Tim. 3:15.

[17]Acts 14:6.

[18]Acts 13:50–51. They followed Jesus' 'order of the boot' (Mk. 6:11).

[19]Acts 14:19.

[20]Acts 14:6–20.

[21]Acts 14:7.

[22]Acts 14:20, 23. Paul's stoning came right at the end of their stay.

[23]Acts 14:15–17 is not a gospel sermon, but an agonized plea to the pagans in the crowd to worship God rather than his human messengers. Seeing Paul speak and then command a lame man to be healed, they had assumed that he and Barnabas must be two of the Greek gods, Hermes and Zeus, come to earth; so they tried to offer them a sacrifice (verses 8–12).

[24]Acts 13:16–41.

[25]The Roman province of Galatia was large – too large for Paul's letter to be addressed to the whole of it at once. For a long time scholars assumed he was writing to some churches in North Galatia; these churches are not mentioned in Acts, and there is no definite evidence that they ever existed. During this century another view has gained ground and is now held by most British commentators. This is that Paul was writing to the churches of South Galatia; namely, Antioch in Pisidia, Iconium, Lystra and Derbe. If it is right, this theory means an early date, making Galatians the oldest letter of Paul that has survived, perhaps the first he wrote. I follow this theory throughout the book.

[26]Gal. 3:1.

[27]Cf. Gal. 3:3, 2.

[28]2 Tim. 1:5.

[29]John Pollock suggests that Eunice, Lois and Timothy became Christians in Antioch, and then escorted Paul and Barnabas through Iconium to Lystra (The Apostle, Lion, 1969, pp. 66–68). He bases this on Paul's reminder to Timothy, 'You know all that happened to me in Antioch, Iconium, and Lystra, the terrible persecutions I endured!' (2 Tim. 3:11). It's an ingenious and possible reconstruction. But it isn't demanded by the words. Timothy almost certainly saw Paul's persecutions in Lystra with his own eyes. But he could still 'know all that happened' at Antioch and Iconium even if he had only heard Paul and Barnabas' description of it.

[30]Acts 13:46–47; 14:1, 15.

[31]Acts 13:17–25.

[32]E.g. Acts 13:26–41.

[33]Gal. 2:15 – 3:14, where Paul recalls the Galatians becoming Christians, and what they had heard and understood at that time.

[34]E.g. Acts 18:4. Some writers even wonder if Paul and Barnabas were staying in Timothy's house. It is quite possible: when Paul arrived in a new town, he lodged with Jewish inhabitants (e.g. Acts 18:2–3).

[35]2 Tim. 1:2; 1 Tim. 1:2; 1 Cor. 4:17, compare verse 15.

[36]Paul's letters to Timothy around twenty years later refer at least once to his baptism (1 Tim. 6:12; 2 Tim. 1:6; see below). This is remarkable in itself. Elsewhere Paul made a habit of forgetting people's baptisms (1 Cor. 1:16)! Yet he clearly took a close and detailed interest in this one.

[37]E.g. Acts 2:37–41; 8:12–13, 36, 38.

[38]1 Tim. 6:12.

[39]1 Cor. 12:3; Acts 16:31.

[40]E.g. the Ethiopian official in Acts 8:38.

[41]2 Tim. 1:6.

[42]The occasions they suggest are either when he joined Paul's team, or at the outset of his assignment in Ephesus where he was when Paul wrote the letter. They may be right, as the language is so similar to 1 Tim. 4:14, which certainly seems to talk of some such commissioning. But note that there the elders, rather than Paul, lay hands on Timothy. I am not alone in thinking 2 Tim. 1:6 refers to Timothy's baptism. Two authorities I can cite are Michael Green, Called to Serve (Hodder and Stoughton, 1964), p. 25, and David Pawson, The Normal Christian Birth (Hodder and Stoughton, 1989), p. 226.

[43]The link between verses 6 and 7 is very close: 'keep alive the gift that God gave you . . . for the Spirit that God has given us does not make us timid'. The GNB takes Paul to mean the Holy Spirit, and it may well be right. But Paul's words are, literally, 'God did not give us a spirit of cowardice, but of power and of love and of self-control.' It is not certain whether he means the Holy Spirit or simply a human attitude or disposition. In the end, of course, it comes to much the same thing, as power, love and self-control are the fruit of the Holy Spirit in our lives. If it sounds odd for Paul to tell Timothy to 'keep the Holy Spirit alive', the oddness is more in GNB's translation than in Paul's Greek. His word means 'fan the flame of' or 'keep burning'. It is a perfectly possible idea to connect with the Spirit; it is the positive alternative to 1 Thes. 5:19, which tells us, literally, not to 'quench' the Spirit. As chapter 7 will show, by the time of 2 Timothy Paul needs to take Timothy back to the very first steps of Christian discipleship.

[44]Acts 8:15–17; 19:5–6; Heb. 6:2.

[45]At least, it wasn't Paul's practice in Corinth four years later (1 Cor. 1:14–15).

[46]I don't want to pre-empt your thought or discussion. So please don't look up my suggested answer till you have done your own work. If and when you are ready, you will find it in chapter 8, especially note 98.

Chapter 2: Youth

[1]Gal. 1:6–9.

[2]Gal. 3:1, 3–4.

[3]Acts 16:2.

[4]Acts 14:21–22.

[5]Acts 14:22.

[6]I've done some unscientific and unofficial research into the staying power of members of Christian youth fellowships in England. The results are very disturbing. They suggest that fewer than 25% are still active Christian adults twenty years later.

[7]Acts 14:23.

[8]1 Tim. 3:2. Reducing the New Testament requirements for elders to their bare essentials, we are left with just these two: elders must be (1) exemplary disciples, and (2) able teachers.

[9]And so it was later in Ephesus (1 Tim. 5:17).

[10]A well-balanced team of youth leaders often includes an elder or two. While it is invaluable to have the help of students or young adults just a step or two further along the Christian road than the teenagers themselves, it is equally good to have a 'parent figure' or even a 'grandparent figure' to offer wisdom, stability and comfort. It is not true that all older people lose sympathy for the young. Many retain a soft spot and a natural feel for the growing pains of adolescence throughout their lives. Treasure such people and ask them to pray and care for your church's youngsters.

Paul and Barnabas commended the elders to the Lord with prayer and fasting (Acts 14:23). This too is a good idea with youth leaders. To call them out by name in a meeting of the whole church shows the importance we give to their ministry and invites every church member to support them in prayer. Paul and Barnabas probably laid their hands on the heads of the new elders as they prayed. (This was how they themselves had been commissioned; Acts 13:1–3.) This is another custom worth following as it expresses both our prayer that God will give them his power to do the job (stretching out his hand to strengthen them), and our own tangible support for it (wanting to back them up). On top of this, to fast during that day brings home to all of us that we think thorough work among young people and God's blessing on it are even more important than daily food!

[11]1 Tim. 4:6.

[12] 2 Tim. 3:14–15.

[13] 2 Tim. 3:16.

[14] This is only the background to 2 Tim. 3:16. Paul's real reason for writing it and what he meant by it become clear in chapter 8.

[15] Acts 14:22.

[16] The other idea in the sentence – that we fully enter God's kingdom only in the future – is equally out of fashion. We want everything *now*. Our surroundings mould us into expecting instant pleasures, instant satisfaction, instant solutions. Why wait for anything? But churches can begin to re-educate us for heaven. Build a dimension of life in the youth fellowship that looks ahead to tomorrow and the day after. Offer Christian holidays for which teenagers have to save up, week by week. Give practice in adult responsibilities which they'll soon be taking on. Hold talent-spotting contests and then train the raw potential you discover; keep leading on to the next stage of ministry, the bigger and better opportunity, which lies a little further on in the future.

[17] And it seems this was not his only suffering in Lystra. When Paul wrote to the Corinthians some nine years later, he catalogued his apostolic afflictions: 'Once I was stoned'; and in the same breath: 'three times I was whipped by the Romans' (2 Cor. 11:25). These Roman whippings were inflicted by 'lictors', men who accompanied the magistrates and carried wooden canes for the purpose. But the lictors existed only in Rome itself and in cities which had been promoted to the status of a Roman colony. The only three colonies Paul had visited by the time of writing were Philippi (where Luke records the beating, Acts 16:22); Antioch in Pisidia (where he does not, though it is presumably included in the 'persecution' of Acts 13:50); and – Lystra. A scourging for good measure was probably the Roman officials' titbit on top of expulsion from the city. That is how Pilate treated Jesus: he had him whipped for doing nothing wrong (Lk. 23:14–16). Paul may have endured his flogging – unbearable thought – the morning after the stoning. Or perhaps he met it now on his return visit, as a vicious visual aid to his teaching that we enter the Kingdom through tribulation.

As well as *seeing* Paul suffer, the Lystrans will also have heard him and Barnabas talk about previous persecutions. Other items in the grisly catalogue of 2 Cor. 11:23–27 had probably happened by this time.

[18] 2 Tim. 3:10–11. For the sufferings in Antioch and Iconium see chapter 1, note 29.

[19] 2 Tim. 3:12. In teaching this Paul was simply following Jesus (Jn. 15:20; 16:33; Mt. 5:11).

[20] But even in England I've seen bloody noses and broken teeth

handed out for no worse crime than refusing to retaliate, insult for insult, punch for punch.

[21]2 Cor. 6:4.

[22]Jn. 15:18; Ps. 23:4.

[23]2 Cor. 1:5.

[24]The 'South Galatian' theory means that Timothy was one of the people for whom Paul wrote Galatians. (See chapter 1, note 25.) The theory itself is a 'level 2' deduction from the evidence. This middle section of the chapter on Galatians is a 'level 3' inference that if the letter went to Lystra, Timothy will have heard it read. The chapter's opening scene showing Timothy the gifted reader (1 Tim. 4:13–14) reading the letter to the church is a 'level 4' hunch.

[25]Acts 15:5. Paul himself had also been a Pharisee, but he turned his back on his past status and achievements, even counting them so much dung or rubbish compared with knowing Jesus as Lord (Phil. 3:5–8). These Jerusalem Pharisees were much less revolutionary.

[26]Acts 15:5. Circumcision was the entry to the old covenant, and carried a commitment to obey the whole Old Testament Law. It became their battle-cry: 'You cannot be saved unless you are circumcised' (Acts 15:1). So much so that Luke and Paul call them 'the circumcision group or party' (the most direct translation of Acts 11:2 and Gal. 2:12).

[27]Paul crossed swords with them both when he visited Jerusalem (Gal. 2:4–5) and when they visited his 'home church' in Syrian Antioch (Acts 14:26 – 15:1; Gal. 2:12–14). One of the confusions about Paul's missionary journeys is that there were two Antiochs. Same name but different places, just as there are at least two towns in England called Newcastle.

[28]Gal. 3:1; 5:7, 10.

[29]Paul's words seem clear that he is still in time to stop them capitulating (Gal. 4:9; 5:3, 10).

[30]Gal. 1:6; 3:3.

[31]Gal. 5:12. Such self-mutilation was, in fact, practised by the worshippers of a local pagan goddess; and it would disqualify the Pharisees from remaining Jews (Dt. 23:1). But it's still hardly a gentle or tolerant thing to say!

[32]Acts 8:3; 9:1–2. Galatians is a clear example of what the Corinthians complained of: 'Paul's letters are severe and strong' (2 Cor. 10:10)! He is uncompromising in his fight for the gospel, but his mood towards the Galatian churches is more perplexity than anger (1:6; 3:1–5; 4:20).

[33]Gal. 4:19.

[34]See chapter 1, pp. 30–31.

[35]Gal. 4:4–7 GNB First Edition, which retains Paul's male language.

[36]One who does, Bishop J. B. Lightfoot, hazards this explanation: 'The appeal is driven home by the successive changes in the mode of address; first, "we, all Christians, far and wide, Jews and Gentiles alike" (5); next, "you, my Galatian converts" (6); lastly, "each individual who hears my words" (7)' (*St Paul's Epistle to the Galatians*, Macmillan, 1876, p. 170). I can't help wondering if my 'level 4' hunch isn't nearer the truth: as he dictates the letter, Paul's mind focuses on his concern for Timothy, so he starts talking directly to him.

[37]Gal. 6:6. This translation in the First Edition of the GNB is correct. The command for 'him' to share all good things with his teacher is a good example of helping to 'carry one another's burdens' (verse 2), but I have read no convincing explanation why it should be in the singular. Perhaps Paul is already thinking of the help one particular disciple could give him in carrying his own load (verse 5). The GNB Second Edition moves to inclusive language, so it abandons Paul's masculine singular and puts the verse into the plural.

[38]Jn. 8:44. His agents are busy corrupting and distorting the truth (2 Cor. 4:4; 1 Tim. 4:1).

[39]Gal. 5:19–21, 26.

[40]Gal. 6:2, 6, 10.

[41]Acts 15:36 – 16:3.

[42]Acts 15:1–19.

[43]Acts 15:22–29. It went on to ask the Gentile converts to meet Jewish concerns half-way by observing four Old Testament ceremonial laws – but significantly these did not include circumcision. 'Sexual immorality' may sound more than merely ceremonial, but it probably refers here to the various relations the Israelites were forbidden in Lv. 18 to marry.

[44]Acts 15:36, 41; 16:4.

[45]Acts 15:37–38.

[46]Acts 15:40. Silas had been one of the bearers of the Jerusalem letter (15:27); like Barnabas, he commanded the full respect of both the Jerusalem and the Antioch church (15:22, 32). He had one further advantage; like Paul, he was a Roman citizen (16:37–38).

[47]Acts 16:5.

[48]Acts 16:3.

[49]Acts 13:5. The Greek word *hyperētēs* had come to mean any assistant or attendant doing a supportive job. It differed slightly from the commoner 'deacon', in that the word carried a sense of being a potential partner, learning from the senior team member; the assistant's work was no humbler or less important than his superior's. It is perhaps revealing that Timothy seems to have chosen the humbler 'deacon' as his own trademark (see chapter 8).

[50]See Introduction.

[51] 1 Tim. 4:13.

[52] His only disadvantages were that he was not, like Mark, an eyewitness of Jesus' arrest in Gethsemane, or a representative of the Jerusalem church – but Silas filled this latter gap.

[53] The evidence for this is Paul's need to circumcise Timothy (Acts 16:3). See p. 49.

[54] Timothy was an ideal partner for Paul's tactics (described at a time when Timothy was working with him): 'While working with the Jews, I live like a Jew in order to win them . . . when working with Gentiles, I live like a Gentile . . . in order to win Gentiles' (1 Cor. 9:20–21; AD 56/ 57, see chapter 5, pp. 109–110).

[55] Acts 16:2.

[56] Luke's Greek actually says, 'All the *brothers* . . . spoke well of Timothy.' This may mean the same as all the believers, but more likely refers to the elders or other members of Paul's team (see chapter 4, p. 85). It does not affect the point here that Paul heard Timothy commended by people whose opinion mattered to him.

[57] He seems to have fulfilled many of the qualifications Paul framed many years later to guide Timothy himself in appointing suitable deacons: 'Church helpers must also have a good character and be sincere; they must not drink too much wine or be greedy for money; they should hold fast to the revealed truth of the faith with a clear conscience. They should be tested first, and then, if they pass the test, they are to serve . . . Those helpers who do their work well win for themselves a good standing and are able to speak boldly about their faith in Christ Jesus' (1 Tim. 3:8–10, 13). Many young Christians have admirable excitement and enthusiasm; but they need to be tested for stamina before too rapid promotion.

[58] The reasons usually suggested for Mark's defection are: resentment at Paul's growing ascendancy over Barnabas; homesickness; and disagreement with the new policy of preaching the Good News to Gentiles. There's an interesting exploration of Mark's story (much of it on what I would call in this book levels 3 and 4) in Hugh Osgood with Glenn Myers, *The Failure File* (Scripture Union, 1991).

[59] Timothy was part of the very first crop when God 'opened the way for the Gentiles to believe' on the first missionary journey (Acts 14:27). This prepared him perfectly to be associated with Paul's work as apostle to the Gentiles.

[60] Teenagers should even be on committees where part of their contribution could be to loosen up the bureaucratic, adult way of doing things!

[61] Acts 16:3.

[62] Joni Eareckson gives an amusing and poignant example. Soon after the accident which left her almost totally paralysed, she prayed

for someone to come and help her faith. 'Do you know who God sent? A tall, lanky, 16-year-old boy with a paper route. An unlikely candidate, wouldn't you say? By my standards, this guy really missed the mark. I mean, here was no super youth director or intellectual seminary student. He was just a teenager – only with a big, black Bible. But I was listening! And God used the long hours I spent with Steve Estes, a high school junior, to lift my spirits and help me understand God's word' (*A Step Further*, Pickering and Inglis, 1979, p. 47).

[63]If you want the addresses of these or similar agencies, ask your minister or a Christian bookshop. The UCCF's address is opposite the Contents page of this book.

[64]Acts 16:3.

[65]There must have been a further, subsidiary value in Timothy's circumcision. The immediate task was a visit to churches where the circumcision issue was still live. Paul was carrying a letter asking Gentile Christians to forgo some of their Christian liberty for the sake of their fellow-Christians who still had Old Testament scruples. Timothy was a living example. Once again he became a physical demonstration of what the mission was about: going as far as possible without compromising the truth to express Christian unity and reconciliation. He had been a born a Jew, so he could be circumcised without contradicting the Good News.

[66]We should adapt in this way not only to the outsiders we're evangelizing, but also to the local Christians who belong to the same background; they are the front-line missionaries to that society.

[67]A Jewish Christian I talked to thinks Timothy would have wanted to be circumcised, as Christianity would have made him more appreciative of his Jewish roots and heritage. We can't know, as the New Testament doesn't tell us.

[68]That is what Luke says; and, while the language could probably also cover a visit to a surgeon arranged and financed by Paul, many rabbis received the necessary surgical qualifications in their training. If Paul did perform the operation, their physical, emotional and spiritual collaboration can only have deepened the relationship between them.

[69]1 Tim. 4:14. Neither this passage nor 1:18–19 (see p. 51) says that the prophets spoke and the elders prayed at this stage of Timothy's story, nor that they are referring to the same occasion. Luke doesn't record a commissioning in Acts 16, but that doesn't mean there wasn't one. It is highly likely there was, because Paul himself was commissioned at the start of the second missionary journey (15:40); also at the start of the first (13:1–3), which probably set the pattern for all later departures, and has striking similarities to the passing references in 1 Timothy.

[70]The speakers may have been Silas and Paul; Silas was certainly a prophet (Acts 15:32), Paul possibly (Acts 13:1; 1 Cor. 14:19). But there may have been other prophets in the churches. And anyway, God could speak through anyone, not necessarily a recognized prophet. It is also worth saying that the words were not necessarily unpremeditated. When God speaks, he does not always take his mouthpiece by surprise. *Any* Christian speech is prophetic if it conveys what God wants to say.

[71]Paul's Greek wording is *dia prophēteias*. All other translators and commentators understand this as genitive singular, which means 'by means of a prophetic message'. But it is hard to understand how anyone would receive a 'spiritual gift' (such as teaching or evangelism) by or through a prophecy. It could be a shorthand way of saying that the prophet announced that Timothy was receiving a *ministry* and that he was already suitably gifted to exercise it, or would be from now on. But that would be better expressed by understanding *dia prophēteias* as accusative plural. In that case it would mean 'because of, or on the basis of, prophetic messages'. These plural 'prophecies' find confirmation in the echoing 'words of prophecy' of 1:18 (if it is indeed referring to the same event).

[72]1 Tim. 4:13. Michael Griffiths shows helpfully that 'reading and preaching' (*i.e.* expounding a Bible passage after reading it aloud) were a standard part of the Jewish synagogue service. They would naturally have carried over into the earliest Christian congregational meetings. This was an obvious arena for Timothy to use his gift (*Get Your Act Together, Cinderella* (IVP, 1989), pp. 113, 117–118). Paul also lists 'preaching and teaching' as gifts of the Holy Spirit in Rom. 12:6–7.

[73]1 Tim. 1:18–19.

[74]These were among the qualities we deduced in Acts 16:2 that everyone else saw in Timothy (see p. 47.)

[75]1 Tim. 6:12. The baptism sermon referred to the strenuous, athletic struggle of living as a Christian disciple; now at his commissioning Timothy is to take on the militant warfare of working as an evangelist and teacher for Jesus.

[76]Acts 14:22.

[77]And not for the last time; 1 Tim. 1:18 may refer to more than one occasion of prophetic encouragement.

Chapter 3: Missionary

[1]Chapters 4–6 cover the same period, but look at different parts of Timothy's job in greater depth.

[2]The fact that Luke says so little about Timothy doesn't mean he wasn't there, taking an active part in events. The reason for Luke's

'silence' is that Acts isn't a book about Timothy (see Introduction, note 3). But Luke has already shown from Acts 16:1–3 what an important new ingredient Timothy was from the second missionary journey onwards.

[3]Examples of Paul having to cope on his own against his will are his time in Athens (Acts 17:16–34; compare 1 Thes. 2:17 – 3:5, and see chapter 3 and chapter 4, p. 88); and some of his later trials and imprisonments (Acts 21:27 – 26:32; 2 Tim. 4:16–17, and see chapter 8, pp. 177–178).

[4]Acts 9 – 28 focuses on Paul's exploits. A quick reading of passages like Acts 19:1 – 20:1 and 28:16–31 can subconsciously reinforce the impression that Paul worked alone. But Luke's context makes clear that there was, in fact, a team in attendance (especially 19:9, 22, 29; 28:16).

[5]See 2 Thes. 3:7–10 and p. 86 for examples.

[6]Acts 16:4–5. My preceding statement is 'level 2' deduction bordering on 'level 1' fact. Paul has co-opted Timothy to his team. It is right and natural to assume Timothy is with Paul from now on, unless and until Luke tells us (or clearly implies) otherwise.

[7]Acts 16:6–8.

[8]Paul and Timothy both had problems with their health (Gal. 4:13; 1 Tim. 5:23). Some scholars have inferred from 2 Cor. 12:7–10 that Paul had chronic ill health, but this is not the only possible interpretation of the words.

[9]Again, why does Luke use the unusual name 'Spirit of Jesus' for the Holy Spirit's second intervention? He may simply be trying to keep the story interesting by varying his language; but, to judge from the careful way he writes, it is more likely that his change of wording holds a clue to his meaning. Is it that Paul saw and heard Jesus in person, as he had on the Damascus road (Acts 26:13–16, 19) and again in the Temple (Acts 22:17–18)? And if to Paul, did the vision appear to Silas and Timothy too?

[10]There is no hint that they could afford to own donkeys or a carriage. They may at times have been able to pick up a lift, but much of their overland travel was on foot. They would do well to average more than 15 miles a day. Their journey was about the length of England, from Land's End to Hadrian's Wall. A modern mission board would grow impatient at so long without any meetings or converts!

[11]Acts 16:9–10.

[12]Perhaps *Luke* was the Macedonian in the vision; he may have lived and trained as a doctor in Philippi. He seems to have stayed on at Philippi at the end of Acts 16: compare '*we* went inland to Philippi' (16:12) with 'Paul and Silas travelled on to Thessalonica' (17:1).

[13]*Cf.* Acts 16:11–18. This was a move of incalculable importance for the future history of Christianity. The faith is now usually regarded (quite wrongly) as a white, European religion. This error stems from this successful European mission of the Asians Paul and Timothy, and the Judean Silas.

[14]Acts 16:17.

[15]1 Tim. 4:13–14. See chapter 2, pp. 50–51. This is 'level 3' inference.

[16]My opening scene for this chapter is 'level 1' fact for Paul and Silas, but 'level 4' hunch for Timothy.

[17]Acts 16:19–34.

[18]Acts 16:35–40. It seems they were in Philippi for 'several days' (verse 12), then 'many days' (verse 18), then one more night and morning (verses 25–35), probably no more than a fortnight in all. This gave no time to establish the church and appoint elders; presumably this is why Luke needed to stay behind.

[19]They may have rested at the towns *en route*, Amphipolis and Apollonia (Acts 17:1). Some scholars question whether Timothy made this journey from Philippi to Thessalonica with Paul and Silas. But in my view they have insufficient grounds – see chapter 6, note 3.

[20]1 Thes. 2:2.

[21]Acts 17:2–7. Luke doesn't mention Timothy by name, but there are three strands of evidence that he was there. The first is the flimsiest; he *was* in Philippi and he *was* at the next port of call, Berea (verse 14); so it's reasonable to assume that he was also at Thessalonica in between. Strand 2 depends on how we read the Jews' accusation in verses 6–7: 'These men have caused trouble everywhere! Now they have come to our city, and Jason has kept them in his house. They are all breaking the laws of the Emperor, saying that there is another king, whose name is Jesus.' The interesting word for our purposes is 'all' in 'They are *all* breaking the laws'. It could mean Jason and the other Christians. But the flow of the Greek more naturally runs: 'These *men*, Paul and associate(s), have caused trouble elsewhere; now *they* have come here and Jason has harboured *them*; *they*, Paul and associate(s), are *all* breaking the law by preaching Jesus.' If Paul had only one associate, it would make no sense to call the two of them 'all'. A third associate would make sense of it all! And we would have instant confirmation that Timothy was one of the preachers announcing Jesus as Messiah.

Strand 3 leaves us in less doubt still. It is the fuller record of events in 1 Thessalonians. 'We brought the Good News to you, not with words only, but also with power and the Holy Spirit, and with complete conviction of its truth . . . When we brought you God's message, you heard it and accepted it, not as a message from human beings but as God's message, which indeed it is' (1:5; 2:13). Who are the 'we' who did all this? Presumably the people in whose name the letter is written: Paul, Silas *and Timothy* (1:1).

[22]For Paul there would be the well-known case of his arrest in Jerusalem which led to prisons in Caesarea and Rome (Acts 21:33–28:31). But we learn of Timothy in prison as well (2 Cor. 6:5, see p. 70; Heb. 13:23, see pp. 200–201).

[23]1 Thes. 2:8, 12. Both 1 and 2 Thessalonians talk throughout about the whole team, not Paul alone. They are written as 'we', not 'I'. This makes them 'level 1' source material for Timothy's life story. He is deeply woven into their fabric, as chapter 5 explores more fully.

[24]Both Thessalonian letters give us clear ideas of *what* Paul, Silas and Timothy taught the new converts: their lifestyle should aim to please God (1 Thes. 2:12), especially their sex life (1 Thes. 4:1, 6); they would suffer persecution (1 Thes. 3:4); they should earn their living as responsible, respectable citizens (1 Thes. 4:11, 2 Thes. 3:10); the Lord would come on his Day, but not before the 'Wicked One' appears (1 Thes. 5:2; 2 Thes. 2:3–5).

[25]1 Thes. 2:11.

[26]1 Thes. 2:9. Although they were staying with Jason they paid for their board and lodging. Their example formed the model which they taught and expected the new Christians to follow (2 Thes. 3:7–10).

[27]Perhaps Paul was teaching him a handicraft to make him self-sufficient at the same time as he was training him to teach and preach. Paul's trade is usually called tent-making, which is the literal meaning of the Greek word. But in the first century it covered a much wider range of leather-work (rather as, in English, a 'saddler' makes many more things than just saddles). Paul worked with 'cilicium', a material from goats' hair, which originated in his native province of Cilicia and was used for making coats and curtains as well as tents.

[28]It seems they were in Thessalonica for a great deal longer than the three weeks we might deduce from Luke's highly compressed account alone (Acts 17:2). There was time to receive repeated financial support from the infant church they had left in Philippi (Phil. 4:16). The Jewish riot against them (Acts 17:5–10) took place at the end of their stay.

[29]1 Thes. 3:4.

[30]The GNB does not get to the heart of Acts 17:9; the Greek word it translates 'required amount of money' means pledge or surety. The idea of an agreement to remove Paul from the scene of the trouble is the suggestion of Sir William Ramsay, *St Paul the Traveller and the Roman Citizen* (Hodder and Stoughton, 1895), p. 231. I follow it in my reconstruction of what happened.

[31]Acts 17:10.

[32]Acts 17:11–12.

[33] 1 Thes. 2:17–18.

[34] Acts 17:13.

[35] Acts 17:14.

[36] Acts 17:15 gives clear evidence of Paul's dislike of being alone. His summons would leave Silas and Timothy in Berea for only ten days or so. For what they did there, see chapter 6.

[37] Acts 18:1, 5.

[38] 1 Thes. 2:17–18.

[39] Acts 17:16. The Athens incident in Acts is really a diversion from the main story. It's what happened to Paul filling in his time *'while waiting for Silas and Timothy'*.

[40] 1 Thes. 2:14.

[41] 1 Thes. 3:1–2.

[42] Some think Timothy travelled alone from Philippi to Thessalonica (see note 19 above), and again from Thessalonica to Berea. But I'm not convinced by their reason; see chapter 6, note 3.

[43] It's from *this* trip to Macedonia that Timothy and Silas return safely in Acts 18:5. For more on Timothy's mission to Thessalonica, see chapter 6. The fact that Silas arrives in Corinth with Timothy suggests that he followed him from Athens to Thessalonica – or if, as seems likely, he was under the same ban there as Paul, to some other part of Macedonia (Berea or Philippi).

[44] We have seen this 'big city' strategy develop through Thessalonica and the hankering for Ephesus.

[45] Acts 18:3–4. Very likely Timothy and Silas joined Paul in staying with Aquila and Priscilla. Their home was probably the base for operations in Corinth as Lydia's had been in Philippi.

[46] Acts 18:5.

[47] 1 Thes. 3:6, 8–9.

[48] Margaret Mitchell points out that it was conventional to express 'joy' of this kind in first-century diplomatic correspondence (see chapter 6, note 2, for details of her article). But from all we have seen of the team's stake in Thessalonica, it must be clear that their joy was more than merely polite convention.

[49] 2 Cor. 11:8–9 (another of the New Testament's hidden references to Timothy); Phil. 4:15.

[50] 1 Cor. 9:12.

[51] 1 Thes. 3:2.

[52] 2 Cor. 1:19.

[53] 2 Cor. 4:5; 1 Cor. 1:23; 15:15.

[54] 2 Cor. 11:4. Timothy and Silas may have had one other job as they preached. Paul insists to the Corinthians that he did not baptize many of them: 'I thank God that I did not baptize any of you except Crispus and Gaius. No one can say, then, that you were baptized as my

disciples. (Oh yes, I also baptized Stephanas and his family; but I can't remember whether I baptized anyone else.) Christ did not send me to baptize. He sent me to tell the Good News . . .' (1 Cor. 1:14–17). It seems Paul baptized only the very earliest converts (presumably before Silas and Timothy arrived). As events have turned out, Paul is glad about this, because in their immaturity the Corinthians are splitting into sects and attaching more importance to their human disciplers than to the one and only true leader. The question remains: if Paul didn't baptize them, who did? The answer may well be that Crispus, Gaius and Stephanas did. They were leaders in the community and in the church (Acts 18:8; Rom. 16:23; 1 Cor. 16:15–16); and they may have exercised their eldership almost as soon as they were converted and established. Just possibly, though, baptisms remained for some time in the hands of the mission team; but Paul, in his single-minded devotion to Christ's priority ('not to baptize, but to tell'), perhaps left the baptizing to his colleagues.

[55]2 Thes. 3:2. Paul even needed a special vision of Jesus to comfort his fears and dissuade him from giving up (Acts 18:6, 9, 12).

[56]Acts 18:11.

[57]Acts 18:19–23.

[58]In the light of Paul's later remarks to him about widows, Timothy surely took good care of his mother and grandmother so long as they were alive: 'If a widow has children or grandchildren, they should learn first to carry out their religious duties towards their own family and in this way repay their parents and grandparents, because that is what pleases God' (1 Tim. 5:4).

[59]See notes 2 and 6 above.

[60]Acts 19:1.

[61]Acts 19:22.

[62]They probably stayed with Priscilla and Aquila whom they had left at Ephesus at the end of the second missionary journey (Acts 18:19).

[63]Acts 20:34. So I have no hesitation, as a 'level 2' deduction or 'level 3' inference, in including Timothy in Luke and Paul's accounts of what Paul did.

[64]There seem to have been at least three others in the team: Erastus, Gaius and Aristarchus (Acts 19:22, 29).

[65]Acts 20:19, 35.

[66]Acts 19:8–9; 20:18–19.

[67]The phrase doesn't appear in all the early copies of Acts. But there is nothing unlikely about it.

[68]The heat was ferocious. Even in May the temperature is in the 90s Fahrenheit by 11 a.m.

[69]Acts 20:20–21, 31.

[70] Acts 19:10. See also chapter 6, note 11.

[71] Acts 19:11–12. Some casual readers pick up the idea that in those early days, life was one long succession of miracles. Not so. In the six or seven years of Timothy's partnership with Paul so far, Luke has recorded only one other healing miracle: the deliverance of the Philippian slave-girl (Acts 16:18). Paul claimed 'many miracles and wonders that prove I am an apostle' at Corinth (2 Cor. 12:12); but Luke didn't think them important enough to mention. (It is possible that most of these miracles happened when Paul first arrived in Corinth, feeling especially vulnerable (1 Cor. 2:3–4), before Timothy and Silas arrived.) Luke's theme is the spread of the Christian Good News, not the acts of the apostle (despite the title others have given to his book!). So to his mind these miracles at Ephesus were important for the growth of Christianity; something quite abnormal, as he stresses with the word 'unusual'. The closest parallel in the New Testament was Jesus' healing of the woman who touched his cloak (Mk. 5:29). But that was only one person on one occasion; here there were evidently many. And Jesus was at least inside his cloak at the time; the woman was in effect touching *him*. Here Paul's leather-working overalls were carried round like relics.

[72] Diana is the goddess's Roman name, by which she is better known. The GNB and most other modern translations use (as Luke did) her Greek name Artemis.

[73] Such as the sons of Sceva who feature in the next incident Luke records (Acts 19:13–16).

[74] Acts 19:19. Other magic names were carved on to lucky charms called 'Ephesian letters'. Small wonder that Paul says in his, very different, 'Ephesian letter': 'I ask that your minds may be opened to see . . . how very great is his [God's] power at work in us who believe. This power working in us is the same as the mighty strength which he used when he raised Christ from death and seated him at his right side in the heavenly world. Christ rules there above all heavenly rulers, authorities, powers, and lords; he has a title superior to all titles of authority in this world and in the next' (Eph. 1:18–21).

[75] Acts 19:17.

[76] Acts 19:15.

[77] Writing to the church in Corinth near the end of his three years, Paul said, 'I will stay here in Ephesus until the day of Pentecost [the same time of year as the annual Diana-festival, which attracted huge crowds from all around the Aegean and Mediterranean seas]. There is a real opportunity here for great and worthwhile work, *even though there are many opponents*' (1 Cor. 16:8–9).

[78] 1 Cor. 4:9, 11–13.

[79] Even if Timothy didn't see Paul flogged at Lystra or Philippi (see

chapter 2, note 17, and p. 61), he must have visualized it in his mind.

[80]1 Cor. 15:30–32.

[81]Some think he's referring to the riot in the amphitheatre, sparked off by Demetrius the silversmith (Acts 19:23–41). But while it must have been a frightening moment, it fizzled out without any harm, least of all to Paul, who was successfully kept out of sight. In any case, Paul left straight after the riot (20:1), and therefore must have written 1 Corinthians before it.

[82]2 Cor. 1:8–9. 2 Corinthians is written in the name of Paul and Timothy together. Much of it speaks, as here, of 'we' and 'us'. So I take it as 'level 1' source material for Timothy's life. Some think the reference to a 'death sentence' here is metaphorical for serious illness. But the next quote from 2 Cor. 6 talks of being killed rather than merely dying. (For a fuller look at the letter, see chapter 5.)

[83]2 Cor. 6:5, 8–9.

[84]Acts 19:31.

[85]2 Cor. 1:10.

[86]For the likely date of Acts, see note 131 below.

[87]Mk. 8:34.

[88]See chapters 7 and 9.

[89]1 Corinthians shows they had split into factions (1:10–12); there was a case of incest (5:1); they were taking each other to court (6:1); and their meetings were turning into something near a riot (11:17–22; 14:23). 2 Corinthians shows new threats from unbelievers (6:14 – 7:1) and false teachers (10 – 13).

[90]1 Cor. 5:9; 2 Cor. 2:1; 13:1.

[91]1 Cor. 1:11; 7:1.

[92]1 Cor. 16:5.

[93]Acts 19:21–22. Luke mentions only Macedonia (Philippi, Thessalonica and Berea) on Timothy's itinerary. But Paul tells the Corinthians that Timothy is on his way to them as well (1 Cor. 4:17; 16:10–11). Timothy's visit to Corinth is covered in chapter 6.

[94]1 Cor. 4:17.

[95]2 Cor. 10 – 13.

[96]2 Cor. 1:23 – 2:4; 7:8, 14. Titus is an even more shadowy figure in the New Testament and church history than Timothy. Luke never mentions him at all!

[97]1 Cor. 16:8.

[98]2 Cor. 2:12–13.

[99]2 Cor. 2:13. An extraordinary admission – Paul was too worried about the Corinthians to preach! It must be the only place where Paul didn't preach, even though God had opened the door for it. Yet the people of Troas didn't miss their chance; the unmentioned Timothy was there to take Paul's place.

[100]2 Cor. 8:1 and 9:2 imply that at the time of writing they have recently spoken to all the churches in Macedonia.

[101]2 Cor. 7:5.

[102]2 Cor. 7:7.

[103]2 Cor. 8:16–18.

[104]2 Cor. 1:1.

[105]2 Cor. 1:3–4.

[106]Acts 20:2–3; Rom. 15:19. With great compression, Luke records Paul's next move as the long-delayed visit to Corinth: 'Then he came to Achaia, where he stayed three months' (note the typical non-mention of Timothy!). These were almost certainly the winter months of 58–59, a whole year after meeting Titus. It's hard to see when, other than this neglected year, to fit a visit to Illyricum into Paul's history; but in any case he makes it sound like the most recent staging post in his Gentile mission before writing Romans.

[107]2 Cor. 4:8–9.

[108]Rom. 16:21.

[109]Acts 11:25–30, probably AD 45. When James, Peter and John recognized him as an apostle to the Gentiles, they asked him to carry on helping the Jerusalem poor. Paul agreed eagerly; it was a good way to cement their approval for his mission to the Gentiles (Gal. 2:6–10, at the conference about Gentiles becoming Christians, AD 48, after the first missionary journey).

[110]2 Cor. 8:13–15 is how Paul taught this truth.

[111]1 Cor. 16:1–2.

[112]Acts 19:21. The GNB misses the thrust of Luke's Greek, which is that 'Paul purposed in spirit to go to Jerusalem by way of Macedonia [north Greece] and Achaia [south Greece]'. In other words, the relief fund has become the next item on his agenda, and the visits to the Greek churches are part of it.

[113]Acts 19:22.

[114]For more on Timothy's Macedonian mission, see chapter 6.

[115]2 Cor. 7:2.

[116]2 Cor. 9:1–2, 4–5.

[117]Acts 20:4. The GNB unwarrantably moves Timothy to the end of the list. Luke actually places him next to Gaius from Derbe. Timothy of course came from Derbe's neighbouring town Lystra, and he may to some extent have seen himself as a representative of Galatia.

[118]1 Cor. 16:3. Originally Paul had planned not to go with them himself; but now he had decided he should (Acts 19:21).

[119]Even though Luke once again doesn't mention him – so Timothy's involvement in Acts 20 and 21 looks like another 'level 2' deduction. But he is clearly one of the 'they' in Acts 20:5–6; so his inclusion in the 'we' from the amazing death and resuscitation of

Eutychus in Troas (verse 7–12) onwards is really 'level 1' fact.

[120]Rom. 15:30–31; Acts 20:3.

[121]Acts 20:18–35.

[122]Acts 20:23; 21:4, 10–11.

[123]Acts 20:36–38; 21:5–6.

[124]Acts 21:12–14.

[125]Acts 21:27 – 24:27.

[126]Luke records that Aristarchus sailed with them to Rome, and would surely have mentioned Timothy if he'd been there (Acts 27:2).

[127]Acts 28:30–31.

[128]Although there are other theories, I follow tradition in assuming this is their origin.

[129]Phm. 23; Col. 4:10.

[130]Phm. 10–13.

[131]Phil. 2:25–30; Phm. 24; Col. 4:7, 10, 14. There were also visitors: 'the brothers and sisters' (probably a technical term for church workers) and 'all God's people' in Rome (Phil. 4:21–22).

Luke's presence calls for one other comment. The fact that he ends Acts with Paul still under house arrest suggests he wrote it at this time. If so, Timothy at the very least heard about its contents. But with Luke being such a careful historian, he is almost bound to have consulted Timothy's memory of many of the events he records. The following passages cover periods when Timothy was present but Luke absent: Acts 17:1–14; 18:5–23; 19:1–22; 20:1–4.

[132]Compared with some of Paul's earlier imprisonments, it was a relaxed regime. Paul's talk of 'chains' is probably a figure of speech (Eph. 6:20; GNB translates as 'prison'). The Bible illustrations showing him writing his letters with one hand while the other is handcuffed to a soldier may be over-literal.

[133]For more on how Timothy helped Paul with the letters, see chapter 5.

[134]Paul probably never appointed an official 'number two', although, as we shall see in chapter 5, he hints at Timothy as his heir-apparent, at least in one sphere of his mission field. And the second-century apocryphal *Acts of Peter* confirms this view of Timothy as Paul's senior assistant in Rome. In the absence of Paul, Timothy and Barnabas (in that order), the Roman Christians lament that 'there was no man to comfort us' in difficulties. Titus was of course older than Timothy and had been part of Paul's team longer; he was able to handle situations that were beyond Timothy (see chapter 6). But he was with Paul far less often and so was less available to be Paul's 'number two'.

[135]Col. 4:3.

[136]Phil. 2:19, 23. For more on this proposed visit to Philippi, see

chapter 6. There are further sidelights on it in chapters 4 and 5.

[137]Phil. 2:24.

[138]2 Tim. 4:16.

[139]Phil. 2:19–22. We must shield some of the others from the apparent criticism. The 'everyone' concerned with their own affairs are only those who are alternative candidates for the journey to Philippi. By definition they must be still in Rome with Paul, available to travel, and free then to return to Rome, since the aim of Timothy's trip is to bring Paul news of the Philippians. Tychicus has already left to deliver Colossians (Col. 4:7–8) and Ephesians (Eph. 6:21–22). At the time of Colossians, Mark sounded on the point of leaving (4:10), so presumably he has gone too. Philippians includes no greeting from Luke who had the strongest links with Philippi, so he must also be out of the frame. He may already be back there, and be the 'faithful partner' Paul addresses in 4:3. If Epaphras and Aristarchus were still prisoners, they couldn't be considered. Paul could ill afford to spare Timothy, his closest associate. Very likely he asked Demas or some of the Roman brothers. But no, they were too busy with their own concerns. Only Timothy cared enough to go.

[140]Phil. 2:4–5.

Chapter 4: Son

[1]Chapter 3's picture of Timothy and Paul in constant motion leaves little room for reflective Bible study. But there are the two gaps in the story we know nothing about (AD 51–53 and 59–62). Obviously this Psalm 23 meditation is 'level 4' hunch, but based on 'level 3' inferences and 'level 2' deductions about their relationship, amplified in this chapter.

[2]Phil. 2:20, 22.

[3]First-century information in this section comes from William Barclay, *Educational Ideals in the Ancient World* (Collins, 1959).

[4]See chapter 3, p. 63.

[5]It's striking that the New Testament uses the same word 'strengthen' to describe first what Paul did *for* Timothy at Lystra (Acts 14:22), then what Paul did *with* Timothy in the rest of Galatia (16:5), and finally what Timothy did on his own at Thessalonica (1 Thes. 3:2).

[6]Plan for the overlap when you don't know in advance who your successor will be, *e.g.* in some elected posts.

[7]2 Tim. 3:10. See chapter 2, p. 39.

[8]William Barclay, *Daily Study Bible: The Letters to Timothy, Titus and Philemon* (Saint Andrew Press, rev. edn., 1975), p. 195.

[9]1 Tim. 4:6; 2 Tim. 1:13; 2:2; 3:14.

[10]1 Tim. 4:13.

[11]For Troas, see chapter 3, p. 71. Paul also visited Corinth from Ephesus (see p. 71) and may well have left Timothy in charge of the preaching and teaching while he was away. There were probably other occasions too.

[12]Acts 19:9; 20:20, 31. See chapter 3, p. 68.

[13]Scandalously, most 'sermons' or 'talks' are delivered in polite gatherings where the listeners are not expected to comment or reply. So there is no attempt to find out what they have learnt, if anything. In my observation, the positive results are pitifully small. Paul and Timothy in their discussion and personal tuition were not conducting monologues! They would be aware instantly of any failure to explain or convince; they would have to think again and do better; they would have to listen to their hearers' point of view and understand it.

[14]Acts 20:20, 27.

[15]Guy King, To My Son (Marshall, Morgan and Scott, 1944), p. 35. However tongue-in-cheek the comment, it is nonetheless a slur on Timothy, Paul and ministry to children!

[16]2 Thes. 2:15; 3:6. And even earlier in Philippi he was announcing how to be saved (Acts 16:17, see pp. 60–61).

[17]Paul was equally outstanding as teacher and evangelist; a rare blend of gifts. There is just the hint in his letters that Timothy, like most Christian speakers today, developed more strongly in one direction than the other. On the one hand, Paul identifies Timothy's gift as reading, preaching, and teaching (1 Tim. 4:13–14); on the other, he has to urge him to 'do the work of an evangelist' (2 Tim. 4:5, NIV). Evangelism remained part of his duty; but it may not have come so naturally to his temperament, less outward-bound and aggressive than Paul's. Time and circumstances seem to have channelled him into being a specialist teacher of Christians. On Paul's team he became, perhaps, 'Director of After-care' for new converts.

[18]Paul repeatedly urges his disciples to follow his way of life (e.g. 1 Cor. 4:16; 11:1; Phil. 3:17; 4:9). That's what discipleship means: T. W. Manson argues that behind the New Testament Greek word for 'disciple' lies the Aramaic word Jesus would have used, which means 'apprentice' (The Teaching of Jesus, Cambridge University Press, 1945, pp. 239–240). If he's right, all new Christians should think of themselves as spiritual apprentices.

[19]2 Tim. 3:10–11.

[20]1 Cor. 9:16; Rom. 1:14; Phil. 3:13–14.

[21]1 Tim. 1:2. Paul's Greek doesn't say 'son in the faith', which might imply 'my apprentice in teaching Christianity' but 'son in faith'.

[22]2 Cor. 6:6–7, 11. It is highly significant that we come to know Paul so well through 2 Corinthians, and that this chapter quotes the letter

again and again. About half the letter is steeped in the partnership between Timothy and Paul – so much so that I believe they collaborated on it (see chapter 5). It is as if his relationship with Timothy made Paul more self-revealing, perhaps even more accessible, to others.

[23]2 Tim. 2:2. For a closer study of this verse, see chapter 8, pp. 176–177 and 185.

[24]Joni Eareckson, the American Christian suffering from quadriplegia, tells how Steve Estes has helped develop her thinking and faith over many years. She calls it a 'Timothy and Paul relationship' (*A Step Further*, Pickering and Inglis, 1979, p. 9).

[25]Paul himself had a long 'hidden' learning period (Gal. 1:15 – 2:1); we know next to nothing about it.

[26]There are, of course, differences between a local church and Paul's travelling mission team. But he repeatedly said there were also ways in which the team set a pattern for churches and their leaders to follow (*e.g.* 2 Thes. 3:7; Phil. 3:17). I suspect that apprenticeship was one of them. It would surely be more strategic for church leaders to give a significant proportion of their time to apprenticing new ministers and disciples, than to feel they have to bless every church social or business meeting with their presence.

[27]Chapter 3 charted Timothy's growing influence and seniority within Paul's team.

[28]The responsibility for success rests on both sides. The managers need to be as good at training as the novices are at learning. Many junior pastors or secretaries leave sadly soon because they have bad leaders to work with.

[29]See note 58 below.

[30]Phil. 2:22.

[31]1 Thes. 3:2, 'fellow-worker of God'; 2 Cor. 6:1; Rom. 16:21.

[32]1 Thes. 3:2.

[33]The Greek word doesn't have the 'men only' implication of 'brother' in English. The GNB Second Edition rightly translates 'brothers *and sisters*' to convey what Paul meant.

[34]For all the evidence, see E. Earle Ellis' article 'Paul and his Coworkers' in *New Testament Studies* 17 (1970/71), pp. 435–452.

[35]Not 'our brother', as in GNB – 2 Corinthians, Colossians and Philemon.

[36]The letter-headings which introduce Timothy as 'brother' give Paul's parallel rank or status as apostle (2 Cor. 1:1; Col. 1:1) and 'prisoner of/for Jesus' (Phm. 1).

[37]For the first time in this chapter since the opening psalm-meditation, we move from 'level 1' direct statements to 'level 2' deduction and 'level 3' inference. That reflection on Psalm 23 showed

some of what Paul did for Timothy; now we look at what Timothy did for Paul.

[38] Acts 15:41. It could be that Paul was temporarily without Silas at this stage. But as Luke has only just (in the previous verse) told us of Paul co-opting Silas, it's unlikely. Either way, though, it shows Paul working *independently* rather than *interdependently*.

[39] Acts 16:9–10.

[40] Acts 16:13, 15.

[41] Acts 16:6–7.

[42] H. V. Morton, *In the Steps of St Paul* (Methuen, 1937), p. 248.

[43] 1 Thes. 2:7–8, 11–12.

[44] Gal. 4:19. As throughout, I continue to follow the view that Galatians is earlier than Thessalonians. See chapter 1, note 25.

[45] 1 Thes. 2:6–7.

[46] H. V. Morton, *In the Steps of St Paul*, p. 249.

[47] 2 Cor. 8:20–21.

[48] *E.g.* Acts 17:32–34.

[49] A literal translation of Acts 17:6. Many people apply these words to the early Christians in general. The charge was in fact levelled at Paul, Silas – and Timothy.

[50] Not *all* assistants should remain assistants; for some, this is part of their apprenticeship in becoming leaders. But others (including, I suspect, Timothy) have found their true vocation when they become lifelong assistants. There are many church or committee secretaries, for instance, who aren't cut out to be in the chair, and shouldn't progress automatically to that position.

[51] Phil. 1:1; 2 Cor. 6:4.

[52] 1 Cor. 16:10.

[53] 2 Cor. 4:1, 15–16; 5:5–8.

[54] 2 Tim. 3:10.

[55] The traditional translation of 'a painful physical ailment' in 2 Cor. 12:7.

[56] 2 Cor. 6:10.

[57] F. W. Farrar speaks eloquently, if sentimentally, of how Paul regarded Timothy. 'In all his wanderings, in all his sickness, in all his persecutions, in all his imprisonments, in all his many and bitter disappointments, the one spot invariably bright, the one permanent consolation, the one touch of earthly happiness, had been the gentle companionship, the faithful attendance, the clinging affection of this Lycaonian youth' (*The Life and Work of St Paul*, Cassell, 1913 ed., p. 667). There is no 'level 1' proof of any of this; but it resonates through the way Paul talks to and about Timothy.

[58] The Jewish Talmud (the detailed law-code applying the Old Testament to daily life) spells out the duties like this: 'A son is bound

to feed his father, to give him drink, to clothe him, to protect him, to lead him in, and to conduct him out, and to wash his face, his hands, and his feet' (quoted in Alfred Edersheim, *Sketches of Jewish Social Life in the Days of Christ*, 1876, Eerdmans, 1990, p. 99).

[59]Beatings: Acts 16:23; 2 Cor. 6:5; 11:24–25. For the evidence for Paul's chronic health problems, see chapter 3, note 8. Luke was the team doctor when he was with them (Col. 4:14). But in his long absences, Timothy would have to do the best he could. Paul also expresses concern for Timothy's health (1 Tim. 5:23; see chapter 6, p. 129, and chapter 7, p. 154); and on at least one occasion he was beaten too (2 Cor. 6:5). It may be that both nursed each other – another bond linking them as partners and friends.

[60]Phil. 2:20. The GNB may come close to Paul's underlying meaning, though it isn't a direct translation of what he wrote. The Greek words say nothing about 'sharing my feelings'. Translated literally, they read: 'I have no-one like-minded (or equal-souled), who will genuinely care for your affairs.' The surface meaning, which the Philippian readers would have understood, must be: 'I have no-one else who shares *Timothy's* feelings, his heart and mind, in genuine care for you.' Among Paul's current companions, Timothy was the only one who really cared about the Philippians. But that of course made him a colleague who matched Paul in what he called the daily 'pressure of my concern for all the churches' (2 Cor. 11:28). And the words Paul chooses in Phil. 2:20 suggest there was more in his mind than just that surface meaning. The word 'equal-souled' (*isopsychon*) deliberately echoes the word 'encouraged' or 'cheered in soul' (*eupsychō*) in the previous verse: 'I hope that I will be able to send Timothy to you soon, so that I may be *encouraged* by news about you.' Trying to put Paul's word-play into English, it goes something like: 'He will "psych me up" (make my soul well); his psyche is unique – it chimes with mine.' He wrote, 'I have no-one else like-minded with Timothy'; but must at the same time have thought, 'and no-one else so like-minded with *me* as Timothy is'.

[61]Ps. 55:13. With his Pharisee's training, Paul would have known the Old Testament verse by heart; he deliberately echoed it as he applied the word to Timothy.

[62]A. S. Way, *The Letters of St Paul* (Macmillan, 1901).

[63]They were from similar social backgrounds. Like Timothy, Paul was a Greek-speaking Jew (Acts 21:37–39). But unlike Timothy, both his parents were Jews. And probably unlike Timothy, he was a Roman citizen.

[64]Acts 9:15–16.

[65]Jn. 13:23; 19:26; 20:2; 21:7, 20.

[66]We don't know when Paul was born. Luke calls him 'young' (*i.e.*

under forty) at the time of Stephen's death in, say, AD 34/35 (Acts 7:58). It's perfectly reasonable to assume he was roughly contemporary with Jesus. That would make him thirty years older than the age I have attributed to Timothy.

[67]J. Oswald Sanders, *Bible Men of Faith* (H. E. Walter, 1965), p. 106.

[68]Hesiod, quoted in Stephen Gaukroger and Nick Mercer, *Frogs in Cream* (Scripture Union, 1990), p. 124.

[69]A recent and wholly fanciful example is Gore Vidal's *Live from Golgotha* (André Deutsch, 1992).

[70]2 Tim. 1:3–4.

[71]A literal translation of Paul's disclaimer in Rom. 3:4 and elsewhere.

[72]The theory has been espoused by John Spong, Bishop of Newark in New Jersey, USA. On BBC Radio 4's *Sunday* programme on 10 February 1991, he advanced the idea on the shaky grounds that (1) Paul never married (almost certainly untrue, see note 96 below); (2) he was negative towards women and the human body (highly disputable); (3) he said nakedness cannot separate us from Christ's love (Rom. 8:35 – a highly questionable interpretation; GNB translates 'poverty'); (4) he spoke of civil war raging in his soul (true, but this is universal Christian spirituality, not limited to *gay* Christians!).

[73]Acts 21:13. See chapter 3, p. 74.

[74]1 Cor. 7:8.

[75]1 Cor. 7:32, 35.

[76]Rom. 1:27.

[77]1 Thes. 4:3–4, 6, 8.

[78]1 Thes. 2:10; 2 Tim. 1:3.

[79]Nero, who was Emperor for most of the years Timothy and Paul worked together, publicly married both a boy-wife and (casting himself in the female role) a husband.

[80]The chief authority here is Elizabeth Moberly, in her books, *Psychogenesis: The Early Development of Gender Identity* (Routledge and Kegan Paul, 1983) and *Homosexuality: A New Christian Ethic* (James Clarke, 1983). Another authority, Leanne Payne, refers to several cases of boys brought up, just as Timothy was, by their mothers and grandmothers, stumbling into affairs with older men (*The Broken Image*, Kingsway, 1988, pp. 76–77).

[81]1 Tim. 5:1–2. Paul's instructions to Timothy incidentally include a beautiful vision, relevant to Christians in all ages, of the church as an extended family, where we care deeply and intimately for one another without sexual desire or pressure.

I have also heard 2 Tim. 2:22 ('Avoid the passions of youth...') twisted into a harangue at teenagers about sex. But as the immediately following words (verses 23–25) show, Paul isn't thinking of *those* youthful passions at all! He's talking about the argumentative spirit that loves to win heated quarrels by its own cleverness, the brash, dogmatic temper of an insecure young man; he's telling Timothy how to handle the false teachers in Ephesus – with love and peace, not anger and aggression. (See chapter 7, p. 160.)

[82]1 Tim. 4:12.

[83]1 Tim. 5:11–15.

[84]1 Tim. 5:1. Verses 1 and 2 are a single sentence in Paul's Greek.

[85]Phil. 2:22.

[86]I myself received help this way. If you want the story, and a fuller explanation of this understanding, see my booklet *No-gay Areas?* (Grove Pastoral Series No. 38, 2nd edn., 1992).

[87]Paul's appeal for chastity wasn't asking Timothy to take a vow to stay for ever single. Unlike the false teachers they were up against at the time, Paul saw marriage as one of God's good gifts which no-one should forbid (1 Tim. 4:1–3). But it's important to stress that the New Testament doesn't expect every mature adult to get married. Both Jesus (Mt. 19:11–12) and Paul (1 Cor. 7:25–38) teach that some should stay single. In neglecting this, the twentieth-century church has become unbalanced and failed its members.

[88]Paul calls Titus exactly the same in his letter to him (Tit. 1:4).

[89]2 Tim. 1:2; 1 Cor. 4:17. In Paul's surviving letters, Timothy is the only individual 'son' also called 'dear'.

[90]1 Cor. 4:14. The distinction Paul stresses here is that, unlike the Corinthians, Timothy is *faithful* as well as dear (verse 17).

[91]2 Tim. 4:9, 21.

[92]1 Cor. 16:10–11.

[93]Phil. 2:19–20, 22.

[94]Mk. 12:6.

[95]Phm. 12.

[96]Paul's own circumstances are a puzzle. Acts 26:10 clearly implies that he was once a member of the Sanhedrin, the Jews' ruling council: 'I received authority from the chief priests and put many of God's people in prison; and when they were sentenced to death, I also voted against them.' One qualification to be a member of the Sanhedrin was that you should be married. We don't know what became of Paul's wife after he became a Christian, except that he no longer lived with her. He advises 'the unmarried and ... the widows ... *to live alone as I do*' (1 Cor. 7:8). Presumably she had divorced him at her own request, or had died in the meantime. We hear nothing of any children by Paul's marriage. It's simplest to assume he had none. If he had, they too must have died or become estranged from him on account of his Christian conversion.

[97]Timothy has an unlikely modern counterpart in Sir Ranulph

Fiennes the explorer. Both have travelled the world in the face of superhuman obstacles. But, more to the point here, both lost their fathers in early life; Sir Ranulph's father died in the Second World War before he was even born. He closes his autobiography in his late thirties – around the age we have reached in Timothy's story. These are the final words. 'Forty years after my father's death we [he and his mother] flew to Naples together and drove to the military graveyard east of the city. We knelt together beside the headstone ... I thought of the man I had never known, of the father whose guidance I still miss' (Ranulph Fiennes, *Living Dangerously*, Macmillan, 1987, p. 250). Every Christian finds the guidance of a divine Father who will take care of us when our own parents abandon us (Ps. 27:10). But Timothy found in Paul a human father's guidance more complete than his Greek dad in Lystra could ever have given.

Chapter 5: Letter-writer

[1]The passages quoted in this reconstruction are Phm. 1–2, 5, 7–10, 12–14, 16–19, 21, 23–24. The background story of Onesimus and Paul is 'level 2' deduction. Timothy's feelings and hand in composing the letter are 'level 4' hunch. But they are educated hunch verging on 'level 3' inference because the letter comes from him as well as from Paul (verse 1). He is associated with all Paul's feelings, prayers and requests in it. Ignatius' *Epistle to the Ephesians* (about AD 115) names their bishop as Onesimus. It's not necessarily the same Onesimus, but it could be. In that case, Timothy helped to save one of his own successors as a church leader at Ephesus.

[2]Robert Funk has showed that Paul made his apostolic presence felt in 'his' churches in three ways: (1) his physical presence; (2) his presence via an envoy acting in his name; (3) his presence via a letter ('The Apostolic *Parousia*: Form and Significance' in W. R. Farmer, C. F. D. Moule and R. R. Niebuhr, eds., *Christian History and Interpretation: Studies Presented to John Knox*, Cambridge University Press, 1967, pp. 249–269). Chapter 3 has looked at how Timothy helped him with the first way. Chapter 6 will look at the second. This chapter looks at the third.

It's worth noting that the letters don't appear in the New Testament in chronological order. The Pauline letters are arranged in two groups: (1) those to churches (Romans to Thessalonians); and (2) those to individuals (Timothy to Philemon). In both groups they appear in order of descending length. The one apparent exception to this, 1 Thessalonians with five chapters, comes after Philippians and Colossians with four each, so as to remain next to its partner 2 Thessalonians which has only three.

[3]1 Thes. 3:6.

[4]1 Thes. 3:10.

[5]I continue to follow the *Illustrated Bible Dictionary* and the majority of British scholars in assuming that Galatians is earlier than Thessalonians. See chapter 1, note 25. Richard Longenecker argues that the absence of any mention of Timothy is the strongest indication that Galatians was written before Timothy became Paul's colleague (*Galatians*, Word Books, 1990, pp. lxx–lxxi).

[6]1 Thes. 1:2, 7 (Macedonia was northern Greece, where Thessalonica was the capital city; Achaia was southern Greece including Corinth, where Paul and the team were writing from); 2 Thes. 1:3–4. (True to its policy, GNB Second Edition adds 'and sisters' where the letter just says 'brothers'. If the letter is addressed to the whole church, the translators have done the right thing. But E. E. Ellis suggests this is the specialized use of 'brothers' to mean church leaders (see chapter 4, p. 85, with note 34). If he's right, 2 Thessalonians is addressed to the elders rather than the church as a whole. This doesn't affect anything I say about the letter here.)

[7]Gal. 1:6. See chapter 2, note 32.

[8]1 Thes. 4:1; 2–3, 8.

[9]Gal. 3:1, 3. 2 Thessalonians tackles another error in Christian living equally tactfully, and again more gently than Galatians (2 Thes. 3:6–15; compare Gal. 1:9).

[10]I detect his influence too in the 'new' way that the Thessalonian letters open, with thanks to God and praise for the recipients (1 Thes. 1:2–10; 2 Thes. 1:3–4). It was a first-century convention to begin letters in this way. But Galatians didn't; whereas all the Pauline letters to churches from now on do. Something caused a change of approach. The tone of thanksgiving and compliment isn't a mere opening formality; it runs on throughout the letters (see 1 Thes. 2:13; 4:9–10; 2 Thes. 3:4). If Paul already believed in building people up by encouraging them like this, the presence of Timothy as someone who had suffered the opposite approach in Galatia helped to draw it out of him. But if this affirming style came less naturally to him, perhaps Timothy helped him to learn it.

[11]1 Thes. 5:9–10. Compare 2 Thes. 2:16–17.

[12]1 Thes. 1:2.

[13]Two of them are his standard practice of adding a few words at the end of the letter in his own handwriting, rather than the secretary's (1 Thes. 5:27; 2 Thes. 3:17). The others are 1 Thes. 2:18, 3:5; 2 Thes. 2:5.

[14]1 Thes. 2:17–18; 3:1–2, 5.

[15]1 Thes. 1:1; 2 Thes. 1:1.

[16]Or Paul may have added the 'I' passages after the rest was

written, while he checked it all through, or had it read to him. This isn't my own brainchild. It's the conclusion reached by that foremost Bible scholar, the late Professor F. F. Bruce, after a lifetime's study. See his volume 45 of the Word Biblical Commentary: *1 and 2 Thessalonians* (Word Publishing, 1982), p. xxxiii. It is particularly clear in the case of the fifth 'I' (2 Thes. 2:5). In the notoriously difficult teaching about the final Rebellion and the Wicked One, who must appear before the Day of the Lord will take place, 2:4 reads, 'He will oppose every so-called god or object of worship and will put himself above them all. He will even go in and sit down in God's Temple and claim to be God.' Verse 6 continues, 'Yet there is something that keeps this from happening now, and you know what it is.' But they are interrupted by verse 5: 'Don't you remember? I told you all this while I was with you.' It sounds as if Paul has added a comment of his own in the margin. If we had the original manuscript and could see the handwriting, it might show us exactly this.

One writer who accepts Timothy's collaboration in the writing of 1 Thessalonians at face value is Hans-Ruedi Weber in *Experiments with Bible Study* (World Council of Churches, 1981), p. 238.

[17]The half-verse is 2:18; the four verses are 2:17-18 and 3:10–11; the eight verses are 3:1–3, 5–9.

[18]The evidence for this is researched and presented in Michael Prior, *Paul the Letter-Writer (Journal for the Study of the New Testament* Supplement Series 23, 1989), pp. 38–39.

[19]For Silas' standing, see Acts 15:22.

[20]Some commentators persist in saying that Paul indiscriminately switches from 'I' to 'we'. They need to explain why he does it so seldom here, and why never at all in Galatians. They may be afraid that the idea of Timothy's collaboration would dethrone the letters' apostolic authority; but it doesn't. Clearly Paul was the team leader and so his name comes first at the head of the letters. For the same reason he added a handwritten greeting at the end. He was authorizing the letters by putting his name to them. They say what he wanted said. But their content didn't spring from his mind alone (his 'I' sentences make most sense as extra notes added to the first draft). By first-century convention, the heading 'From Paul . . .' needn't mean that Paul thought up and dictated every word, any more than that he wrote them with his own hand.

[21]1 Thes. 1:2; compare 2 Thes. 1:3.

[22]1 Thes. 3:10–12; compare 5:23; 2 Thes. 1:11; 2:13, 16–17, 3:5, 16.

[23]1 Thes. 1:3.

[24]1 Thes. 1:5–6, 9–10; 2:1–2, 5–15; 3:4; 4:1, 6; 2 Thes. 1:10; 2:5, 13–14; 3:1, 6–10.

[25]1 Thes. 3:6. This is the closest we come in the New Testament to

hearing Timothy *speak*. But the thesis of this chapter is that we can read a fair amount of what he *wrote*.

[26] 1 Thes. 5:11; compare 4:1, 10; 5:1–2.

[27] There's the further testimony that 'you became an example to all believers in Macedonia and Achaia. For not only did the message about the Lord go out from you throughout Macedonia and Achaia, but the news about your faith in God has gone everywhere ... All those people speak about how you received us when we visited you, and how you turned away from idols to God' (1:7–9). How did they know this? Partly perhaps from travellers or letters coming to Corinth; but most likely these are Silas and Timothy's own words based on the trips to Macedonia through Achaia, from which they've just returned. With 2 Thessalonians, by contrast, written a few weeks or months later, they seem to be replying to news that someone else has brought: 'We say this because we hear that there are some people among you who ...' (3:11).

[28] 1 Thes. 2:18–19; 4:13. The letter also gives further teaching on other topics which must have been areas Timothy spotted as weaknesses, or questions the Thessalonians themselves asked him. See chapter 6, p. 129, with note 29.

[29] 1 Thes. 3:1–2, 6.

[30] See p. 105, and note 16 above. On top of this, A. Q. Morton's statistical study has found differences in vocabulary between Thessalonians and the Paul-only letters. See M. Levison, A. Q. Morton and W. C. Wake, 'On Certain Statistical Features of the Pauline Epistles' (*Philosophical Journal* 3, 1966), pp. 129–148; A. Q. Morton, 'The Authorship of Greek Prose' (*Journal of the Royal Statistical Society*, Series A 127, 1965), pp. 169–233; A. Q. Morton, 'The Authorship of the Pauline Corpus' in W. Barclay and H. Anderson (eds.), *The New Testament in Historical and Contemporary Perspective* (Blackwell, 1965), pp. 209–235; A. Q. Morton, *The Integrity of the Pauline Epistles* (Manchester Statistical Society, 1965).

[31] 1 Pet. 5:12; Acts 15:32; 16:38. Exhibitions of the paintings of Rembrandt and Allan Ramsay in London in the early 1990s drew special attention to the part played by their 'schools' of assistants and students. Sometimes parts of a picture (*e.g.* the background landscape or the costumes), sometimes a whole painting, were the work of a collaborator working under the tutelage of the old master who has ever since been credited as the creator.

[32] 1 Cor. 4:21; 11:22.

[33] The letter is Paul's attempt to put right some troubles he's heard of at Corinth; and he uses part of it to answer a number of questions the Corinthians have written to him about (1:11; 5:1; 7:1; 11:18).

[34] 1 Cor. 1:4.

[35] 1 Cor. 2:2; 13:1; 15:9–10.

[36] The apostle 'we's' are 3:4 – 4:1; 4:9–10; 9:9–10, 15:10–12. The team 'we's' are 1:23; 2:6–7, 13 (where GNB incorrectly translates the first two verses as 'I'); 4:11–13; 9:11–12; 11:16; 15:14–15, 30.

[37] 1 Cor. 9:11–12, which blends references to the second-journey team which founded the church, and to the third-journey team at the time of writing. All the team 'we's' may have this extended, present-and-past reference. But 4:11, 13 and 15:30 clearly focus primarily on the time of writing, and 15:15 on the original mission to Corinth.

[38] Acts 18:17, compare verse 8. Paul seems to have developed a habit of inviting one of the 'firstfruits', one of the earliest converts in a town, on to the mission team. (Timothy himself was part of the early harvest in Lystra.)

[39] This makes 1 Corinthians a departure from first-century convention in a way that the Thessalonian letters weren't. The earlier Galatians is also unconventional. It claims to be from Paul 'and all the brothers who are here' (1:2, GNB First Edition). These presumably include Barnabas as co-leader of the missionary journey that had planted the Galatian churches, and the other church leaders at Antioch, adding their weight to Paul's opposition to the false teachers. Although this is definitely an 'I' letter, it's unlikely in that culture that Paul would name them as collaborators if they were entirely passive partners. It would be surprising if he didn't draw on their advice in writing such an important letter. In his biography of Paul, John Pollock pictures Barnabas and the Antioch church leaders sitting round Paul throughout his dictation of the letter (*The Apostle*, Lion, 3rd edn., 1987, pp. 79–83).

This may well suggest that Sosthenes had an active consultative role in composing 1 Corinthians. In addition, he may have been the secretary. Paul as usual indicates that only the postscript is in his own writing (1 Cor. 16:21). The rest of this long and delicate manuscript was perhaps in the hands of his highly useful ally .

[40] See, in this case, 1 Cor. 16:19–20.

[41] 1 Cor. 4:17. The words 'I am sending Timothy' may, of course, mean no more than that he is coming as a personal envoy from Paul (see chapter 6, especially pp. 131–34). But with no other messenger mentioned, it's more than likely that Timothy is also bearing the letter. Gordon Fee, in his important commentary, *The First Epistle to the Corinthians* (New International Commentary on the New Testament, Eerdmans, 1987, p. 188), argues against this idea because Paul does *not* name him as co-author and because he sounds so uncertain about when and whether Timothy will arrive in Corinth. Either view may be right. We simply don't know.

[42]See chapter 3 for the circumstances in which 1 Corinthians was written.

[43]1 Cor. 16:10–11.

[44]2 Cor. 1:1.

[45]2 Cor. 1:4, 6.

[46]2 Cor. 2:14, 4:5, 7; 5:14. Casual readers would probably assume that the first and third of these are 'inclusive' we's, referring to readers as well as writers. But comparison with 2:15 – 3:1 and 5:13 makes it quite clear they aren't. They refer to the author(s).

[47]Indeed, they clearly distinguish between themselves, as the co-writers, and Titus and the others who are on this occasion the postmen (2 Cor. 8:16–18, 22). As before in dealing with the prickly Corinthians, there is a careful boosting of the couriers' reputation and dissociation of them from the writers in case too close a connection should prove a problem.

[48]2 Cor. 1:15 – 2:13; 7; 10 – 13.

[49]2 Cor. 8 – 9. This is where the letter turns from grateful joy at the reconciliation between the Corinthians and Paul (and Timothy!), to the more ticklish task of persuading them to rejoin the Jerusalem fund-raising. It reads as if Paul and Timothy fear that, although they introduced the Corinthians to Jesus, their wishes may not be strong enough inducement; so Paul adds the weight of his apostolic authority (although reluctant to lean too heavily!). So we find a 'we' paragraph reinforced by a set of 'I' statements: 'You are so rich in all you have: in faith, speech, and knowledge, in your eagerness to help and in your love for *us*. And so *we* want you to be generous also in this service of love. *I* am not laying down any rules. But by showing how eager others are to help, *I* am trying to find out how real your own love is ... *I* am not trying to relieve the others by putting a burden on you ...' (8:7–8, 13). The two flanking paragraphs in chapter 8 are 'we' sections, each with an 'I' insertion (verse 3 in 1–7 and verse 23 in 16–24)! Chapter 9 is virtually 'I' throughout.

[50]2 Cor. 1:3–14; 2:14 – 6:13.

[51]2 Cor. 5:11. Compare 1:13–14; 6:12–13.

[52]Some have suggested that chapters 6:14 – 7:1 and 10 – 13 were written at different times and have become attached to the letter inaccurately, as they don't seem to fit the tone of the rest. But there are no early copies of the letter without these passages, so it seems best to try to understand it with them included.

[53]Acts 20:2. Luke typically refers to Paul alone; but 2 Corinthians makes clear that Timothy was with him. See chapter 3, p. 72.

[54]2 Cor. 7:5; compare 11:28–29.

[55]Paul was of course the senior of the two writers. The letter says it's 'From Paul and Timothy' – not 'Timothy and Paul'!

[56]Of course they may *not* be inserted postscripts. Paul and Timothy may have worked together on the 'we' passages. But I can see nothing in the stage their relationship has reached to make this inherently more likely than my hunch.

[57]See note 47 above.

[58]I call it 'my' conclusion. The detail is indeed mine. But Michael Prior has done all the spadework, and points towards this conclusion. See chapter 3 of his *Paul the Letter-Writer* (see note 18 above).

[59]The 'we' passages – 2 Cor. 1:3–14; 2:14 – 6:13; 8:1–7, 16–24.

[60]We mustn't get carried away. But I feel I can almost hear the two voices in a sequence like 2 Cor. 1:23–24:

FORCEFUL PAUL: 'I call God as my witness – he knows my heart! It was in order to spare you that I decided not to go to Corinth.'

TACTFUL TIMOTHY: 'We are not trying to dictate to you what you must believe; we know that you stand firm in the faith. Instead, we are working with you for your own happiness.'

[61]2 Cor 1:9. People are understandably reluctant to lose the echoes of Paul himself in such well-loved passages. This theory doesn't ask them to do so. It doesn't exclude Paul from these sentiments and experiences. It merely includes Timothy in them and makes him the spokesman for the two of them. A rare case of modern writers accepting this passage at face value as a collaboration is that of Joni Eareckson *with Steve Estes* in *A Step Further* (Pickering and Inglis, 1979), p. 74. Perhaps it takes two co-authors to recognize others!

[62]2 Cor. 5:19–20. Here again I'm not attempting to drive a wedge between Paul and Timothy; merely to associate Timothy (as Paul's apprentice preacher) with a passage usually treated as exclusively Pauline.

[63]2 Cor. 5:16–18.

[64]Rom. 1:1, 8. Romans and Ephesians are the only two church letters in which he does this. Virtually all the 'we's' in Romans are inclusive (meaning 'I the writer and you the readers together'). But one exception is Rom. 10:8, which is a glimpse of Timothy as Paul's colleague – 'the message of faith that *we* preach'.

[65]Although Paul already knew at least eleven of the people he greets in 16:3–15, there were presumably other key leaders he hadn't met.

[66]Rom. 15:23–24. For the first time in this survey, he isn't responding to the church's agenda or trying to solve their problems.

[67]For once, we know who the letter's secretary is, for he greets the readers in person: 'I, Tertius, the writer of this letter, send you Christian greetings' (16:22). Clearly he's a Christian, but we know nothing else about him. He never appears in a list of Paul's fellow-workers. So perhaps he was a professional scribe in Corinth, specially hired; if so, this would be another sign of extra care taken over this letter.

[68]Rom. 1:16 – 11:36. This understanding of Romans is convincingly argued by N. T. Wright, *The Climax of the Covenant* (T. and T. Clark, 1991), p. 234.

[69]Rom. 16:21. For Paul and Timothy's circumstances at the time of writing, see chapter 3.

[70]Rom. 2:1, 17, 21.

[71]I sense Timothy's shadow alongside Paul in the second half of Rom. 8, keeping him company through all the troubles of recent months: 'I consider that what *we* suffer *at this present time* cannot be compared at all with the glory that is going to be revealed ...' (verse 18).

[72]Col. 1:7–8; 4:12. Epaphras may well have been converted at Ephesus, the nearby provincial capital; joined Paul's mission team; then returned as the pioneer missionary to his home town. This would make Paul the church's spiritual 'grandfather', and Timothy their 'uncle'.

[73]Col. 1:1. Although we have no record of Paul (or Timothy) visiting Colossae, it's perfectly likely that Timothy may have gone there during the long mission at Ephesus.

[74]Col. 1:3–4, 9. The authors' 'we' crops up again through the letter; but it seems there to refer to more people than the authors alone. 1:28 is a team policy statement, such as we have seen in earlier letters. The closing request for prayer in 4:2–4 and the introduction to the courier in 4:7–8 are both a mix of 'I' and 'we'. In 4:8 GNB changes the Greek 'we' to '*all of* us'. And as greetings immediately follow from Aristarchus, Mark, Joshua Justus, Epaphras, Luke and Demas, it's fair to assume that the 'we' goes wider than just Paul and Timothy.

[75]For more about this stage in Timothy's story, see chapter 3, pp. 75–76.

[76]Col. 1:23–25; 1:29 – 2:5; 4:10–13, 18.

[77]R. K. Harrison in *New Testament Introduction* (Tyndale Press, 3rd edn., 1970), p. 553, lists these as: (1) unusual genitive combinations in 1:27; 2:11, 19; 3:24; (2) more subsidiary clauses than in Paul's earlier letters; (3) a profusion of noun phrases beginning with 'in' in 1:9–23 and 2:9–15; (4) many words which do not appear in Paul's other letters; (5) more use of the liturgical hymn style, found in the prayers and thanksgivings in other letters.

[78]Although some of the earliest copies of the letter are addressed 'To God's people in Ephesus', others simply say 'To God's people'. Ephesus was capital of the province of Asia Minior. By the time of Revelation, a generation later, the province had churches in Smyrna, Pergamum, Thyatira, Sardis, Philadelphia and Laodicea (Rev. 2 – 3) as well as Ephesus and Colossae. The church at Laodicea had certainly started in Paul's time (Col. 4:15–16); others may have done so too. If

Ephesians was meant for Ephesus alone, the absence of any greeting from Timothy, who had worked there for three years, would be very strange.

[79](1) Col. 3:5–17; Eph. 4:17 – 5:20. (2) Col. 3:18 – 4:1; Eph. 5:21 – 6:9. (3) Col. 4:2–4; Eph 6:18–20.

[80]Col. 3:22 – 4:1; Eph. 6:5–9.

[81]Col. 3:18–19; Eph. 5:22–33. And in Ephesians the paragraph, and probably the whole household section, come under the important heading, missing in Colossians, of: 'Submit yourselves to one another because of your reverence for Christ' (5:21).

[82]Col. 3:16; Eph. 5:18–19.

[83]Col. 1:8; the Greek wording is simply 'your love in spirit'. The GNB also refers to God's Spirit in 1:9; but the Greek words there are 'spiritual understanding'.

[84]S. T. Coleridge (the poet) and A. C. Gaebelein, both quoted in H. L. Ellison, *The Mystery of Israel* (Paternoster, 1968 edn.), p. 97.

[85]It's only fair to admit that scholars have shown other ways in which *Ephesians* appears unlike the other Pauline letters. It's beyond my scope here to judge whether the claim to Pauline authorship is genuine in each case; I simply accept it at face value. My aim in this book is to take more seriously than others the claim, wherever it is made, to *Timothy*'s share in the authorship.

[86]The tags naming him are identical: Col. 4:7–8; Eph. 6:21–22. This is the only author's 'we' in Ephesians.

[87]Col. 4:9; Phm. 12.

[88]Col. 2:4–5.

[89]Once again F. F. Bruce has beaten me to this insight. He suggests that Timothy is responsible for the style of Colossians in his commentary on *The Epistles to the Colossians, to Philemon, and to the Ephesians* (Eerdmans, 1984), p. 30.

There is a possible sign that Timothy was regarded as Paul's active assistant writer in Rome long before F. F. Bruce and me, in the fourth-century *Apocalypse of Paul*. In this legend, Paul has a vision, and then 'The angel of the Lord took me up and brought me to the Mount of Olives and told them all I had seen. They praised God and commanded us, that is me, Mark *and Timothy*, to *write* the revelation' (M. R. James, *The Apocryphal New Testament*, Oxford University Press, 1924, p. 554.

[90]Col. 4:18. 'I, Paul' also appears in 1:23. The other general 'I' passages are listed in note 76.

[91]1 Cor. 4:17.

[92]Phil. 2:4–5, 20–21.

[93]They are not only 'jokers' within the Paul–Timothy sequence, but join Galatians and 1 Corinthians as deviants from all the other letters

surviving from the first century. These are the only ones from two named authors which then speak as 'I'.

[94]Phm. 4; Phil. 1:1, 3.

[95]Presumably, though, Paul may have varied his dictating style according to the identity of the secretary. If Tertius was a hired scribe, Paul probably dictated Romans word for word. By the time of Philippians, he could let Timothy – if Timothy was the secretary – use his own phrasing, at least in places. This would make him more of a collaborator than a mere dictating-machine. I suggest this in the opening episode of this chapter.

[96]Phil. 2:20–22. Anyone would find it awkward to write such things about himself; from all we have gathered about Timothy's self-effacing nature, it would have been peculiarly difficult for him. He may well have done it, protesting and disclaiming. Or perhaps Paul inserted this paragraph in his own hand. Or perhaps Timothy wasn't the secretary this time.

[97]See p. 109.

[98]Phm. 8–10.

[99]Phm. 15–16? Or Paul may be asking Philemon to loan Onesimus out to serve him in Rome, and perhaps beyond that, on the team (Phm. 13–14). I hint at both of these in the chapter's opening episode. Or perhaps, as I suspect, Paul is hoping for a third outcome as well: he may be asking Philemon to go one step further still and give Onesimus his freedom (Phm. 21?). As Dr Stephen Travis put it (speaking at Scripture Union's 'media workshop', held at St John's College, Nottingham, in August 1976), this one-page letter contains more revolutionary dynamite to abolish every form of slavery than all the writings of Karl Marx put together.

[100]Phm. 2.

[101]Phm. 23–24. There may be a further 'level 4' reason for Timothy's name at the head. We've already noted that Timothy may have made expeditions from Ephesus as Paul's envoy – to Colossae, for instance (see note 73 above). He may have known Philemon longer and better than Paul.

[102]I'm not suggesting that Paul the apostle 'needed' Timothy to boost his authority in any way, but simply that, here again, we misread the letters if we imagine Paul as a 'one-man leader' to his converts and supporting churches. He worked and wrote in association with the team. And at several times, his team *was* Timothy.

[103]Both letters offer indirect evidence for Timothy's high standing. Onesimus seems to have taken over the more lowly 'personal attendant to Paul' role which Timothy had in earlier days (Phm. 11, 13). And the two Philippians 'we's' which mean authors rather than readers point to Timothy's spiritual stature. In Phil. 3:15, 17 the 'us'

goes wider than just Paul and Timothy; it subconsciously includes any team members still with Paul in Rome, such as Epaphroditus (2:25–30), and deliberately includes some of the readers (presumably most of the church leaders) who already share Paul's mature attitude. But it certainly includes Timothy as well, identifying him as spiritually mature, sharing the gloriously Christ-centred outlook of verses 1–14, and setting the right example of Christian living.

[104]Phil. 1:4, 5, 7–8; 4:10, 15–16, 18. Many commentators have noted the exceptionally happy tone of the letter. Paul's relationship with the church seems uniquely unclouded. They are plagued with disagreements and false teaching like all the other churches Paul and Timothy wrote to (Phil. 2:2; 3:2; 4:2). But they seem to have supported Paul's mission in a way no other church could match. Timothy would feel equally warmly towards the Philippians, both as Paul's partner and on his own account. They were the first church he had a hand in planting.

[105]Some scholars believe that Paul came increasingly to look on Philippi as his home church. Antioch was the original base for the first missionary journey (Acts 13:1–2; 14:27–28). But Barnabas was more rooted in the church there than Paul was (11:20–26); the church may have 'sided' with Barnabas when the two of them split up (15:39–40).

[106]Phil. 1:12–19.

[107]Phil. 1:20–26; 2:24.

[108]Phil. 2:17–18.

[109]Phil. 2:19–20, 22.

[110]Phil. 2:23.

[111]The 'pastoral letters' to Timothy are the subject of chapters 7 and 8.

[112]The two letters look as if they were written at the same time. What Paul wanted to say to Timothy influenced what he said to Titus, and *vice versa* (see chapter 7, pp. 148–149).

[113]People who support the traditional view of Paul as sole author may not like what I'm saying here. But the burden is on them to prove that 'From Paul and Timothy' doesn't mean what it says.

[114]It would balance this if we could respect the other letters enough to say they're by whoever *they* say they're by! That would mean adding to the list Paul *and Timothy*'s letters to Philemon and the Philippians, and Paul *and Sosthenes*' letter to the Corinthians. Once again, this is not a maverick idea of my own. Michael Prior talks of the letters in exactly this way in his study of *Paul the Letter-Writer* (see note 18 above).

[115]A compelling case emerges from this train of thought for franker acknowledgments on modern book covers or at least title pages. Not

all major educational books are the one-author effort their by-line suggests. Many authors receive substantial help for whole sections or chapters from colleagues, editors or assistants. Their debt shouldn't be tucked away in the last paragraph of the Introduction.

Chapter 6: Go-between

[1]It's highly likely that Timothy wrote to Paul when he was away from him for extended periods. But no such letters have survived. So this one is 'level 4' hunch. But it's closely based on information in 1 Cor. 16:8–11 and 2 Cor. 8:1–5, as well as the 'level 1' facts about Timothy's 'go-between' missions to Macedonia and Corinth in AD 56/57, which are outlined in this chapter.

[2]There was nothing unusual about this 'shuttle diplomacy' (a good phrase to describe Timothy's work as Paul's go-between, coined by William Petersen, and quoted in Leslie B. Flynn, *The Other Twelve: Valuable Lessons in Ministry from the Partners of the Apostles*, Victor Books, 1988, p. 100). First-century rulers regularly sent envoys to keep in touch with their far-flung subjects, and maintain the relationship between them. Jesus spoke of his servants as his messengers (*e.g.* Jn. 13:16). Paul simply adopted the idea with a regular flow of *his* messengers to the many churches he'd helped to found. The convention, and Paul's use of it, are well explained in Margaret Mitchell's article 'New Testament Envoys in the Context of Greco-Roman Diplomatic and Epistolary Conventions: The Example of Timothy and Titus' (*Journal of Biblical Literature* 111/4, 1992), pp. 641–662.

[3]These go-between duties may have started almost at once. Several of Paul's 'biographers' state with complete assurance that Paul left Timothy temporarily at Philippi with Luke after the earthquake, because Acts 17:1 mentions only Paul and Silas moving on to Thessalonica. Similarly, they tend to have Timothy staying behind in Thessalonica to hold the infant church together, because Acts 17:10 records only Paul and Silas being sent to Berea. They may be right. We don't know, for Luke simply doesn't tell us what happened to Timothy. But his silence doesn't need to mean that Timothy stayed behind each time. Acts isn't about Timothy (see Introduction, note 3). My hunch is that Timothy remained humbly and 'invisibly' in attendance on Paul throughout the time at Thessalonica and Berea. It was still early days in their partnership, not yet a year old. And Timothy would have been very young to take on solo responsibility.

[4]Acts 17:14.
[5]Acts 17:15.
[6]Acts 17:10–12.

[7]The Jews had stirred up the mob against Paul (Acts 17:13), but we don't know whether this opposition carried on and turned directly against Silas and Timothy. It seems more than likely.

[8]Acts 14:22.

[9]Acts 17:12.

[10]Acts 17:11; 14:23. The church survived, and sent Sopater as their representative with the Jerusalem relief fund (Acts 20:4).

[11]Acts 19:21–22. This 'go-between' mission is during the three-year stay in Ephesus. It's likely that Timothy made other unrecorded journeys during this time. Acts 19:10 says that 'all the people in Asia heard the word' while Paul and Timothy worked in Ephesus. This doesn't mean that the entire population of the province came to Tyrannus' hall (although a large number of visiting tradesmen and Diana-worshippers probably did). Rather, as visitors from the neighbouring towns became Christians, they returned as missionaries to their own homes. We've seen that Epaphras probably helped to found the church in Colossae in this way (Col. 1:7; see chapter 5, note 72). And the other six churches of Rev. 2 and 3 (Smyrna, Pergamum, Thyatira, Sardis, Philadelphia and Laodicea) may well have started at this time. Timothy clearly helped to generate this ripple effect from Ephesus; it's more than likely that he visited some of these churches to help establish them as well.

[12]See chapter 3, p. 73.

[13]Phil. 1:5. See chapter 5, p. 119.

[14]2 Cor. 8:3–5. They wrote this report during their follow-up visit to Macedonia a year later. But some of this Macedonian generosity may have poured out at once at the feet of Timothy and Erastus. I follow this hunch in the 'letter' which opens this chapter.

[15]This 'helper' or team member Erastus is presumably the same as Paul's later companion Erastus who 'stayed in Corinth' (2 Tim. 4:20); but not necessarily, as the name was quite a common one. He's less likely to be the Erastus who was city treasurer in Corinth two years later at the time of the letter to the Romans (16:23). That would sound like unbelievably rapid upward (and geographical) mobility! The only way it would be just possible is if Erastus was a distinguished convert of Paul and Timothy's original mission to Corinth, who was then able to take time out from his work in the civil service to travel with them on the team for a few years before resuming it. This is an attractive fancy, because Timothy and Erastus' mission was to do with fund-raising.

[16]1 Thes. 3:1–2.

[17]1 Thes. 3:5.

[18]1 Thes. 3:2–3.

[19]1 Tim. 5:23.

[20]The letter is in effect Timothy's authorization from Paul to stay in Ephesus and tackle the problems there. See chapter 7, pp. 155–156.

[21]We mustn't overlook the harmful effects of bad water in first-century conditions. But Timothy's trouble can't have been just that he was a poor traveller. If that was all, he's unlikely to have remained Paul's travelling companion for so long; he would surely have moved to a settled ministry far sooner. It seems more likely his sickness was at least partly stress-related as well.

[22]1 Thes. 3:6. This is 'level 1' reportage.

[23]1 Thes. 3:10. This is 'level 2' deduction.

[24]1 Thes. 5:1–11; 2 Thes. 2.

[25]Death: 1 Thes. 4:13–18. Bed: 1 Thes. 4:1–8. Work: 1 Thes. 4:11–12; 2 Thes. 3:6–13. Church: 1 Thes. 4:9–10; 5:12–22 (love for fellow-believers, 4:9–10; 5:14–15; respect for leaders, 5:12–13; guidelines for church meetings, 5:16–22).

[26]1 Thes. 3:2. Here we come to 'level 3' inference. It's true that Paul regularly follows the practice of first-century diplomatic correspondence by including a phrase or sentence listing his messenger's credentials to represent him. But this is scarcely necessary after the messenger has already been and gone. And when he does list his envoys' credentials (*e.g.* 1 Cor. 4:17; Phil. 2:19–28), he doesn't follow a set formula; he chooses his words to fit the person and the circumstances. So, even if he and Silas threw in a 'credentials' reference to Timothy here almost by force of habit, they would still need to think *how* to describe him. And their choice would be determined by how the Thessalonians had reacted to Timothy's visit.

[27]1 Thes. 3:5. This is closely related to the writers' defensiveness about their attitude to the Thessalonians throughout chapter 2. Such strong pleading as we meet there shows that Timothy carried back with him some very harsh things that people had said.

[28]We've already seen both these principles emerge clearly: gradual progress, chapter 4, pp. 78–80; teamwork, chapter 3, pp. 56–57. In their desperation Paul and Silas took what they knew to be big risks.

[29]1 Cor. 4:7–8, 21. This is the scene of conflict Timothy will have to enter (verse 17).

[30]1 Cor. 4:16–17.

[31]It was conventional in the first century to list the credentials of your envoy. But of all the things Paul might have said about Timothy (brother, fellow-worker, *etc.*), he here chooses to stress his beloved sonship. It is a mute plea to treat gently someone they may feel inclined to treat roughly.

[32]1 Cor. 4:18–19.

[33]1 Cor. 16:10–11.

[34]The Greek word 'if' doesn't always imply doubt; its meaning here

is probably *'when* he arrives – but I can't tell exactly when that will be'. See Gordon Fee, *1 Corinthians*, New International Commentary (Eerdmans, 1987), p. 821. It could refer also to the dangers and uncertainties of travel in those days; and to the fact that Timothy was travelling the long way round from Ephesus, via Macedonia (Acts 19:22).

[35]2 Corinthians smarts with pain and distress. Some of this anguish comes in the 'I' sections by Paul. But some is in the 'we' sections, probably by Timothy (see chapter 5, p. 112). This may reflect the grief and shame he felt about his last contact with the Corinthians. My reconstruction here is no stronger than 'level 3' inference and 'level 4' hunch. J. B. Lightfoot thinks Timothy never got to Corinth, because Paul doesn't mention him in 2 Cor. 12:17–18 ('The Mission of Titus to the Corinthians' in *Biblical Essays*, Macmillan, 1893, pp. 271–284). As with most arguments from silence, I find this inconclusive. The fact that we now have 1 Corinthians in our Bibles suggests it was at least faithfully delivered.

[36]2 Cor. 2:4.

[37]Was it an example of the disunited pandemonium Paul slates in the letter (1 Cor. 11:20–21)? Perhaps Timothy had to trail round several different house-churches, some pro-Paul, but others aggressively pro-Peter or pro-Apollos (1 Cor. 1:12–13).

[38]To ill-treat the envoy was, in first-century etiquette, a direct insult to the one who had sent him. See Jesus' words in Lk. 10:16. Paul's plea in 1 Cor. 16:10–11 for a good reception for Timothy is a measure of how low his *own* relationship with the Corinthians has sunk.

[39]2 Cor. 7:8–9, 11.

[40]2 Cor. 7:13.

[41]Gal. 2:1–3. His greater age is 'level 2' deduction. His stronger character is 'level 3' inference. As a 'level 4' hunch he may have had the added advantage of being a stranger to the Corinthians, less easy to write off without a hearing.

[42]2 Cor. 7:15.

[43]Here again Timothy did better than Jonah who turned bitter at Nineveh's repentance (Jon. 3:5 – 4:4).

[44]2 Cor. 1:1. See chapter 3, p. 72, and chapter 5, p. 112.

[45]See chapter 5, note 104.

[46]Phil. 2:19, 23. The Greek of verse 19 underlines this idea of mutual sharing: it actually says, 'so that I *also* may be encouraged by news'. The implication is that the Philippians will first hear encouraging news about him.

[47]Phil. 1:27.

[48]Phil. 3:18–19, 2.

[49]See chapter 2, pp. 43–44.

[50]Phil. 2:12.

[51]Phil. 3:15, 17.

[52]Phil. 2:20, 22.

[53]Phil. 2:24.

[54]It's impossible to fit the events referred to in 1 Timothy and Titus into the time-scale of the Acts of the Apostles. So it's a fair 'level 2' deduction that Paul secured his release from this first Roman imprisonment (where Acts leaves him), and wrote those letters later.

[55]Phil. 2:25–28. Gordon Fee, whose opinion I usually revere only just short of idolatry, says that Phil. 2:19–23 marks *Timothy* as the courier (*1 Corinthians*, New International Commentary, Eerdmans, 1987, p. 189, note 36). But he must for once be wrong, because Paul says he *hopes* to send Timothy *in the future* when he knows his own fate. Epaphroditus is clearly the person Paul is sending at the same time as the letter.

[56]Phil. 2:29.

[57]Phil. 4:3.

[58]Timothy's relative lack of skill and success as a go-between gives me the feeling he didn't do it all that often. We've met hidden periods in his life when he *may* have been travelling elsewhere as Paul's envoy (see note 11 above, and chapter 3, p. 74). But my hunch is that he stayed with Paul more often than not. William Barclay is certainly off target when he says, 'Timothy must have spent most of his life going on expeditions on which Paul sent him' (*God's Young Church*, Saint Andrew Press, 1970 p. 105).

[59]Chapter 5, pp. 119–120. I realize I'm treading on holy ground in suggesting that Paul made mistakes. But did his apostolic accuracy extend to everything he did or planned for Timothy? Surely not, if he remained a fallible human.

Chapter 7: Wimp?

[1]I owe the idea of this 'false teaching course' to David Bell and George Lihou, who drew up a similar outline for a CYFA Pathfinders Ventures Training Weekend. The content of the course is based on 1 Tim. 1:4, 6–9, 19–20; 4:3; 5:5, 9–10, 20–21; 2 Tim. 2:16–18. The setting of this opening episode in Crete is based on Tit. 1:4, 12 and 1 Tim. 1:3, as explained later in the chapter.

[2]H. C. Kee in *The Interpreter's Dictionary of the Bible* (Abingdon, 1962), vol. 4, p. 651.

[3]J. C. Beker, in the next entry in *The Interpreter's Dictionary*, simply says, without any justifying evidence, that 1 and 2 Timothy 'are probably directed to churches in Asia Minor in the beginning of the second century'. The usual reasons for this view are that the style is

different from 'Paul's' other letters, and that the conditions of church life in Ephesus they imply couldn't have existed as early as Timothy's time. This chapter tries to demonstrate that both 'reasons' are wrong.

But it's worth noting here that unlike the other letters bearing Paul's name, his pastoral letters to Timothy and Titus claim neither a collaborator nor a secretary. They are personal letters to his friends and look as if he wrote them in his own hand. That is quite sufficient to explain any differences in style from letters that, say, Timothy helped him to write. But it also means, if true, that far from being *un*-Pauline, the pastoral letters are the *most* Pauline thing we've got. They may be the only letters in the New Testament purely by Paul alone. Their style and tone may be the truest echoes of Paul that have survived.

[4]Many commentaries on the pastoral epistles give us only occasional glimpses of Timothy. But he is there in virtually every verse of 2 Timothy, and his work features in every section of 1 Timothy.

[5]Part of the problem is the lack of precision in the English word 'you'. In 1 and 2 Timothy Paul writes 'you' in the singular; he's talking to Timothy. We tend to read the 'you' in the plural, as if Paul is talking directly to us or to churches in general. Similarly with 'we'. We naturally include ourselves when Paul says 'we', but he meant 'you, Timothy, and me, Paul. Just the two of us'. We're more likely to understand and learn God's lessons from these letters if we can train our ears to hear what Paul was really saying to Timothy.

[6]1 Tim. 1:3. Gordon Fee uses this verse as the key to unlock the meaning of the whole letter (and 2 Timothy and Titus as well) in his *1 and 2 Timothy, Titus*, New International Biblical Commentary (Hendrickson, 1988 – a revision of the earlier *Good News Commentary* of 1984). It is a major contribution to understanding.

[7]Phil. 1:25–26. See also chapter 6, note 54.

[8]We don't know whether he ever made it to Spain as he had long hoped (Rom. 15:24, 28), or to Colossae as he had more recently hinted to Philemon (Phm. 22).

[9]Tit. 1:5.

[10]He was presumably eager to pay the return visit he had promised the Philippians (Phil. 1:24–25; 2:24).

[11]Phil. 2:19, 23. See chapter 6, pp. 135–136.

[12]There *were* grounds for rejoicing in Paul's circumstances. Five years earlier he'd said a final goodbye to them all, convinced he was on his way to die (Acts 20:25, 38).

[13]Acts 20:30.

[14]Acts 20:20–21, 26–27, 31–32.

[15]1 Tim. 1:20.

[16] 1 Cor. 16:19.

[17] In reality it's probably impossible to reconcile the different strands of false teaching – despite the light-hearted attempt at the start of the chapter.

[18] 1 Tim. 1:4–11.

[19] 1 Tim. 2 (especially 9–10); 3:7; 5:8, 14; 6:1.

[20] 1 Tim. 4:3–4.

[21] 1 Tim. 6:5–10; compare 3:3, 8.

[22] Some are widespread attitudes or blind spots with little justification in the Bible. Others are exciting new ideas enthusiastically taught by so-called 'prophets', often given star treatment because they come from some other part of the country or the world, where we can't check their record.

[23] 1 Tim. 1:3. There's a fashionable slogan that Paul's counter-offensive to the false teaching in Ephesus was 'a man, not a plan'. It makes Timothy himself the remedy for the churches' ills. It contains the kernel of truth that God works primarily through people, rather than programmes or formulae. But it's not the whole truth. Careful reading of the letter shows that Paul had a clear three-point plan for Timothy to follow.

[24] 1 Tim. 1:5.

[25] 1 Tim. 5:20.

[26] 1 Tim. 5:22. Paul's Greek does not include the words 'in dedication to the Lord's service'; he merely says, 'Be in no hurry to lay hands on anyone.' But I join such modern commentators as Gordon Fee and George W. Knight III in following GNB's interpretation. This is because the immediately preceding words (verses 17–20) are about elders, and because elsewhere in the pastoral letters laying on hands is a sign of commissioning people to a church ministry. Paul's caution, 'Be in no hurry to lay hands', may on its own sound as if he is telling Timothy not to replace the false teachers. But his central concern to find suitable elders (3:1–13) to build up the church (3:15) shows that he has charged Timothy to make bad elders good by whatever means is necessary.

[27] 1 Tim. 5:24–25.

[28] 1 Tim. 3:2–7. Alfred Edersheim points out how similar Paul's list is to those of contemporary rabbis on the qualifications for members of the Jewish Sanhedrin or ruling Council (*Sketches of Jewish Social Life in the Days of Christ*, 1876: Eerdmans, 1990, p. 282). Some have concluded from this that Paul was merely echoing truisms about eldership from outside Christian circles. Their error is in the word 'merely'. He was probably perfectly aware that there was nothing uniquely Christian in many of the qualifications. But he was *also* sharply aware that these wise qualities were exactly what the Ephesus churches needed so as to stop the rot.

[29]1 Tim. 2:8; compare 1:4; 6:4.

[30]1 Tim. 5:17.

[31]1 Tim. 3:2.

[32]1 Tim. 3:15. This is how all the standard translations understand it. But F. W. Farrar points out that it could equally well be translated, '. . . in order that, if I am delayed, thou mayest know *how to bear thyself* in the house of God – seeing that it is the Church of God – *as a pillar and basis of the truth*' (*The Life and Work of St Paul*, Cassell, 1913, p. 654, my italics). This would charge *Timothy* to be the pillar and support of true faith in Ephesus. It would merely transfer this verse to the next part of Paul's task for Timothy, no. 3.

[33]1 Tim. 4:6, 11; 5:7; 6:2, 17–18; 4:16. 'Command' is the same military word as in 1:3. 'Teach' is basic instruction in the faith; 'preach' or exhort is stirring the will to obey the words of Scripture. Preaching and teaching have been Timothy's main work all through his time on Paul's team. See chapter 2, pp. 50–51.

At first glance it looks odd that Timothy should need to 'save' himself in 4:16. Most commentators take it in the sense of persevering to final safety in heaven; compare Paul's concern 'to keep myself from being disqualified after having called others to the contest' (1 Cor. 9:27). But as the rest of this chapter shows, there may be a more urgent need for Timothy to rescue himself.

[34]1 Tim. 4:12.

[35]1 Tim. 6:11–12. Paul's final word in the letter ties the two parts of this third task together: 'Timothy, keep safe what has been entrusted to your care' (6:20). Jesus and Paul have put the Good News into his hands; they're trusting him with their most precious treasure. And how can he – or anyone – keep the truth 'safe'? Quite simply, as Paul keeps telling him, by obeying it in daily life and by teaching it faithfully to others.

[36]Tit. 1:5–6, 10–11, 13; 2:1–3, 6–8, 15; 3:9–10.

[37]I haven't seen anyone else suggest this, so I may be wrong. But I wonder if two other unusual features of the greeting have the same effect as the lack of thanksgiving. Paul wishes Timothy not just the standard grace and peace, but *mercy* as well; he must want to stress God's warmth, patience and forgiveness. Forgiveness? Yes indeed. He and many of the elders have gone wrong and need forgiving. And what of the description of Jesus as 'our *hope*'? Does Paul want to lift the spirits of his reader(s) in view of the stiff task ahead? The stand that Timothy and the faithful elders are taking isn't a hopeless one, but has every chance of success with the encouragement of Jesus.

[38]On the 'South Galatian theory', which I'm following throughout, Timothy would of course have good reason to remember Galatians. See chapter 2, pp. 41–42, and chapter 2, note 24.

[39]'Order' and 'command' are the same word in Paul's Greek.

[40]Paul does more than merely repeat. He underscores and sharpens the command. In verse 3 Timothy was to do the ordering; now *he* is the one to obey.

[41]See chapter 2, p. 51. By the time of Paul's letter to him, Timothy may of course have received further words of encouragement from God.

[42]See chapter 2, p. 51.

[43]For the less worrying echoes in the opening words of verse 19, see chapter 2, p. 51, and chapter 2, note 74. It's *just* possible that the rest of verses 19 and 20 are intended as a warning to the elders. But as Paul says them straight after 'Timothy, my child', I can't filter out the clear note of warning to *him*.

[44]1 Tim. 4:6–11. The original Greek had no clear paragraph divisions. I have divided the passage one verse later than GNB's paragraph division, *i.e.* after verse 11 rather than verse 10.

[45]1 Tim. 5:11–13, 15.

[46]The recurring rhythm of the letter confirms that this is Paul's anxiety. He has just given a sketch of some of the false teaching in the previous paragraph (4:1–5); immediately he says to Timothy, 'Keep away from it.' It exactly repeats the pattern of chapter 1. There he outlined the false teaching (4–7), countered it (8–17), then said to Timothy, 'Keep your faith and a good conscience' (19). Timothy has been so badly unsettled by the erring elders, that Paul has to keep steadying him: 'This is what *they* say, but don't you believe it.'

[47]1 Tim. 4:12–16.

[48]Compare 1 Tim. 5:17.

[49]'What I write is true. God knows that [before God] I am not lying!' (Gal. 1:20).

[50]Acts 20:24. Interestingly, Timothy was present on almost all the recorded occasions when Paul used the word before. Together they 'solemnly witnessed' to the Thessalonians that the Lord will punish sexual sinners (1 Thes. 4:6). When Silas and Timothy arrived in Corinth, Paul gave his whole time to solemnly witnessing that Jesus is the Messiah (Acts 18:5). In their first ministry in Ephesus, Paul 'solemnly witnessed' to Jews and Gentiles that they should turn from their sins and believe in Jesus (Acts 20:21). Jesus commended Paul for solemn witness to him in Jerusalem and commissioned him to do the same in Rome (Acts 23:11), as indeed he did (Acts 28:23).

[51]Here again I have rearranged GNB's paragraphs into the two topics covered: verses 19–21 on disciplining erring elders, and verses 22–25 on appointing new elders.

[52]This is the force of the negative imperative in the present tense, which these are.

[53]This is the NIV's accurate translation.

[54]See p. 145.

[55]It has often been pointed out that this verse fatally torpedoes the view that Paul expected all Christians in his circle to be healed by some supernatural intervention. One of the most succinct comments on Paul's words is by Joni Eareckson, herself a quadriplegic woman confined to a wheelchair: 'He didn't say, "Pray more about it", or "Come and see me about it". He said, "Take something for it" ' (*A Step Further*, Pickering and Inglis, 1979, p. 158).

[56]1 Tim. 4:12.

[57]1 Tim. 1:18.

[58]See chapter 1, p. 30.

[59]This passage is also the third time Paul follows an exposé of the false teaching (verses 3–10) with an immediate warning to Timothy to avoid it (see note 46 above). He would surely not do this even once if it wasn't a real danger. But to do it three times within a single letter shows how deeply Paul feared Timothy might topple.

[60]Compare 1 Tim. 5:21.

[61]The combination of the shockingly strong language in 5:21; 6:13 and the negative present imperatives in 5:22–23 makes it so likely that Paul is confronting *what is really happening*. These are not just, as many have suggested, the unnecessarily exaggerated fears of a fond parent.

[62]1 Tim. 1:1. And by calling Timothy his *true* son in the faith, Paul publicly legitimizes him as his authorized representative (1 Tim. 1:2).

[63]Paul announced himself as apostle to the Galatians, Corinthians and Colossians where there were false teachers; and to the Romans and 'Ephesians' where not everybody knew him and acknowledged his authority. But he didn't bother with the apostle tag with the Thessalonians, Philippians or Philemon.

[64]This new perspective throws fresh light on many parts of the letter. Take 4:12, for example: 'Do not let anyone look down on you.' It's rather difficult for Timothy to *prevent* other people doing so. But once we hear the letter being read aloud in the erring house-churches, we realize *they* are being told not to look down their noses.

[65]2 Timothy has two items on its agenda. One is an immediate, urgent holding operation in a crisis; that's the subject of this chapter. The other is Paul's longer-term plan for Timothy; we come to that in chapter 8.

[66]2 Tim. 4:13.

[67]2 Tim. 2:9.

[68]2 Tim. 1:16.

[69]2 Tim. 1:15. Paul complains that even Phygelus and Hermogenes have deserted him; they were presumably two leaders he expected

better of. I've heard the point of view that Christianity has survived (and we are here today) only because Timothy obeyed Paul's appeal in this letter. But that is overstating things. Even if Timothy turned out to be the only remaining Christian in *Asia*, there's no hint that the churches in Galatia, Greece, Crete or Illyricum had deserted Paul. And Luke and Tychicus are still faithful members of the team (2 Tim. 4:11–12), not to mention all the non-Pauline churches in Jerusalem, Antioch, *etc.*

[70]In 2 Tim. 1:18, GNB translates 'you know very well how much he did for me in Ephesus', but Paul's exact words are 'you know *better*', implying 'you know better even than I do'. In other words, Timothy had seen at first hand Onesiphorus' firm stand for Paul in Ephesus while others all around were turning against him. And the clear, sad implication is that Timothy didn't join Onesiphorus' firm stand.

[71]2 Tim. 1:8, 16.

[72]Paul puts many of these imperatives as the first word in the sentence for emphasis.

[73]2 Tim. 1:8; 13–14; 2:1–3, 7–8, 14–16, 22–23; 3:1–2, 5, 14; 4:1–2, 5. There are a further further six commands in the second half of chapter 4, summoning Timothy to join Paul in Rome; these are part of the longer-term agenda waiting for the next chapter.

[74]Guy King, *To My Son* (Marshall, Morgan and Scott, 1944), pp. 7, 12.

[75]It's difficult to talk of the letter's sections and divisions without becoming confusing. Despite the letter's traditional division into chapters, its flow more naturally breaks at different points into four sections or, as I call them, 'movements': 1:3 – 2:13; 2:14 – 3:9; 3:10 – 4:5; 4:6–22.

[76]2 Tim. 2:18.

[77]2 Tim. 2:17.

[78]2 Tim. 3:2–4.

[79]2 Tim. 3:5.

[80]2 Tim. 3:6, 8.

[81]Positive imperatives in the present tense have this continuous sense. Greek uses the aorist tense for a command to take a single, once-for-all action.

[82]In fact it's almost certainly four times. See note 84 below.

[83]We eavesdropped on this sentence earlier (see chapter 4, note 81), but now its real meaning emerges with stark clarity.

[84]The evidence for reading 2 Tim. 2:15 in this light is the two verses it sits between. Verse 14 is misleading in all English translations, not just GNB: 'Remind your people of this, and give them a solemn warning in God's presence not to fight over words.' Paul's Greek words contain no 'your people' or 'them'. A sudden instruction to tell

other people not to squabble over trivial details sounds odd when the rest of the paragraph is telling Timothy himself what not to do. The words could be just as well translated, 'Keep remembering, as you do your job of preaching for God, not to fight.' The verse would then become a *fourth* plea in the passage for Timothy not to get bogged down in detailed arguments over the false teachers' use of words. And the sequence of the three verses with their three commands becomes: 'Never let Jesus and your union with him (verses 8–11) out of your mind as you do your proper work. Don't do it by fighting over words (which does no good but only ruins the hearers) (verse 14); but rather go flat out to please God by teaching his truth correctly (verse 15). I repeat and underline, get right away from the godless and empty discussions (which only drive people further away from God) (verse 16).' Paul is saying, twice over, 'Stop holding debates with the false teachers on their terms; get on with proclaiming God's truth.'

[85]This understanding of 2:14–25 brings Timothy to centre stage and focuses the spotlight on him throughout. Most commentaries switch Paul's focus hither and thither, and you wonder what these verses can have meant to Timothy. I suggest they're entirely about him.

[86]This is the GNB First Edition, which correctly translates Paul's actual words. But the Second Edition undoubtedly hits on his real meaning: 'As the Lord's servant, *you* must not quarrel. *You* must be . . . gentle as *you* correct *your* opponents . . .'

[87]2 Tim. 2:18.

[88]The inscription on this well-founded 'building' – 'The Lord knows who are his' – comes from the story in Numbers 16 of the rebellion against Moses and Aaron by Korah, Dathan and Abiram; Paul sees them as examples of false teachers. The second inscription – 'Whoever says that he belongs to the Lord must turn away from wrongdoing' – is common Old Testament teaching, but can also fit the same story, where God told Moses and Aaron and the rest of the Israelites to move away from the rebels who were then buried alive by the earth opening and swallowing them; the wrongdoing Paul is thinking of at Ephesus is clearly the false teaching.

[89]2 Tim. 2:22–25.

[90]2 Tim. 2:18–19.

[91]See pp. 145–146.

[92]There's almost certainly further emotional pressure here. Interwoven with these words is Paul's double prayer-wish, 'May the Lord show mercy to the family of Onesiphorus . . . May the Lord grant him his mercy on that Day!' (2 Tim. 1:16, 18). Onesiphorus is no longer either in Rome or with his family in Ephesus. Much the most likely explanation is that Onesiphorus has died. Paul has lost the only loyal person left in Asia. Come on now, Timothy, you're his last hope!

[93]In his letters with Timothy to Philippi and Philemon, Paul called Epaphras and Archippus 'fellow-soldiers' (Phil. 2:25; Phm. 2). They would now be examples to Timothy. Paul is having to tell *him* to *be* a soldier.

[94]The two words are, of course, related. 'Timothy' comes from the Greek for fearing God, the right sort of fear. 'Timid' comes from the Latin for a fearful disposition, fearing not just God but anything and everything.

[95]Peter Lee, Greg Scharf and Robert Willcox, *Food for Life* (IVP, 1977), p. 129.

[96]Colin Morris, *Epistles to the Apostle* (Hodder and Stoughton, 1974), pp. 131–132.

[97]See chapter 2, p. 44, and chapter 2, note 58.

[98]2 Tim. 1:4.

[99]Acts 20:19, 31.

[100]1 Tim. 5:23. See chapter 6, p. 129.

[101]1 Tim. 4:12.

[102]1 Tim. 5:1–2; 2 Tim. 2:22. See chapter 4, pp. 94–95 and note 81.

[103]Ranulph Fiennes, *Living Dangerously* (Macmillan, 1987), p. 18.

[104]All four commands in 1 Tim. 6:11–12 – 'avoid' (or 'flee'), 'strive', 'run' and 'win' – are athletic images. Christian self-mastery takes real energy and vigour.

[105]Michael Griffiths points out that the word and its relatives come thirty-four times in the New Testament – 'very significant when there was so little precedent for the idea beforehand. It is perhaps the most distinctive of Christian virtues' (*The Example of Jesus*, Hodder and Stoughton, 1985, p. 97). For a whole book exploring the word's history and significance, see Klaus Wengst, *Humility: Solidarity of the Humiliated* (English translation, SCM, 1988).

[106]2 Cor. 10:1. Paul uses it in the same sense when he calls our mortal bodies 'weak' (Phil. 3:21); or his own state as being at times 'in need' (4:12). He and Timothy use it to describe themselves as 'downhearted' (2 Cor. 7:6).

[107]Lk. 1:48.

[108]Mt. 11:29. The early Christians echoed him in one of their first hymns: 'He was humble and walked the path of obedience all the way to death – his death on the cross' (Phil. 2:8).

[109]Mt. 23:12; Lk. 14:11; 18:14.

[110]2 Cor. 11:7; Acts 20:19.

[111]Eph. 4:2; Col. 3:12.

[112]Mt. 18:4.

[113]2 Tim. 1:7–8.

[114]Mt. 8:26; compare Mk. 4:40.

[115]Jn. 14:27.

[116]Rev. 21:8.

[117]Mk. 8:38.

[118]2 Tim. 1:12.

[119]Because no letters from Timothy to Paul have survived, this is technically a 'level 4' hunch. But it's only human to want the right of reply. I've tried to explore Timothy's thoughts at the beginning of chapter 8. He may well have written to explain his point of view. But on the other hand he may have felt too ashamed, distressed and ambivalent to write. We've seen that Paul seems to be relying on Onesiphorus for his information in 2 Timothy. And, brooding alone in prison, he may have come to think worse of Timothy than was really fair. See chapter 6, note 59.

[120]1 Tim. 5:22; 3:10.

[121]From the first draft of the 'Ephesus' section of the *Marketplace Study Bible* (Inter-Varsity Christian Fellowship, 1989).

Chapter 8: Heir?

[1]This delving into Timothy's thoughts when he received Paul's second letter is, of course, 'level 4' hunch, based on chapter 7's exploration of his character. The words of Paul I hear him reacting to are 2 Tim. 2:14–16, 22–24; 3:5, 8–9.

[2]This is 2 Timothy's agenda item 2. See chapter 7, note 65.

[3]2 Tim. 4:9, 13, 21. Plans for Timothy's journey dominate this last movement of the letter (*e.g.* verses 11, 13). It's tremendously important to Paul that Timothy should make the journey safely. He warns him against Alexander the metalworker who almost certainly landed Paul in prison in Troas (see note 16 below); he might now do the same to Timothy, whose route couldn't avoid Troas (verses 14–15). Throughout the book I follow the vast majority of commentators in assuming that Timothy was still in Ephesus when he received Paul's second letter. But John Stirling in *An Atlas of the Acts* (George Philip and Son, 3rd edn., 1966, p. 27) suggests that 1:5; 3:11 and 4:12 could point to his having returned to Lystra. This would make picking up Mark (4:11) at Colossae (Col. 4:10) a more natural route. It would also deepen our suspicion that Timothy was falling down on the job by opening up the possibility that he'd actually run away from it.

[4]2 Tim. 4:6–8.

[5]2 Tim. 4:16–17.

[6]2 Tim. 4:18.

[7]2 Tim. 4:6.

[8]Some have suggested that Paul thinks of calling Timothy to Rome only at the end of the letter. But as the rest of this chapter tries to show, I think they've missed what he's really saying to Timothy throughout.

On their own the 'step' titles through the chapter might sound like 'level 4' hunches. With the evidence I produce in the main text and in the Notes, I believe they climb up the levels to inference, deduction and even observable fact.

[9]2 Tim. 2:2.

[10]See step 5 below.

[11]In Greek this is the aorist imperative. This makes step 1's understanding of the verse at least a 'level 3' inference, virtually a certain fact.

[12]Compare 1 Tim. 1:18; 6:20. See p. 15.

[13]Paul doesn't let on what he'll say to Timothy if and when he gets to Rome. So this step is no more than 'level 3' inference. But in light of the rest of 2 Timothy (and 1 Timothy) it's very clear inference indeed.

[14]2 Tim. 1:2–3.

[15]2 Tim. 1:4.

[16]Paul's word translated 'did me much harm' (2 Tim. 4:14) was a technical Roman legal term meaning 'filed the information against me'. This metalworking Alexander may be the same as the erring Ephesus church elder Alexander excommunicated by Paul in 1 Tim. 1:20. If so, Paul would understand the reason for this revenge, but bitterly regret that excommunication hadn't led him to repent.

[17]2 Tim. 4:10. Demas, named as one of the small band of fellow-workers by Paul in Phm. 24 and perhaps by Timothy in Col. 4:14, 'fell in love with this present world'. Paul's words are a deliberately echoing contrast to what he's just said in verse 8 about the victory prize in *the next world* awaiting 'those who wait with *love*' for Jesus to appear. To Demas, this life seemed more real and precious than the next.

[18]As we've seen, Paul was isolated in prison, perhaps thinking worse of Timothy than he needed to (chapter 7, note 119, and chapter 6, note 59). But we've also seen that fear of Timothy deserting the cause wasn't just a figment of Paul's anxious imagination. The news of Demas' defection was presumably one more unsettling influence on Timothy. Hence Paul's hard work to call him to heel.

[19]2 Tim. 4:16.

[20]Acts 28:15.

[21]2 Tim. 4:17.

[22]2 Tim. 4:10, 12, 20.

[23]2 Tim. 4:13. How he must have pined for his coat and books in the chilly isolation of his autumnal dungeon.

[24]This view of Paul at the end of his life should check our natural triumphalism at large numbers gathered for Christian celebrations or teach-ins. Some even tell us that God is somehow more tangible or more powerfully present there than in small, struggling churches.

They should reckon with Jesus. He didn't say, 'where two or three *thousand* come together in my name, I am there', but 'where two or three' (Mt. 18:20).

[25] 2 Tim. 4:11; presumably Luke was keeping Paul going medically, and would be the secretary for this letter, if Paul didn't write it all personally.

[26] 2 Tim. 4:11–12. Mark had already made his peace with Paul and rejoined the team (Col. 4:10). He would be able to encourage Timothy to do the same.

[27] 2 Tim. 4:21. Once again, 'brothers' may be in the technical sense of church leaders and/or missionaries rather than all the Christians. See chapter 4, p. 85.

[28] Col. 4:14.

[29] 2 Tim. 4:22. 1 Timothy was, in a sense, an open letter to all the Ephesus church members (see chapter 7, pp. 155–156). 2 Timothy is more restricted, but still not completely private to Timothy. At least Priscilla, Aquila and Onesiphorus' family would be likely to see it (4:19); probably also the other reliable church leaders Timothy was to work with (2:2).

[30] See chapter 7, p. 172, and the opening to this chapter.

[31] See chapter 7, pp. 172–173.

[32] 2 Tim. 1:3 – 2:13; see chapter 7, note 75.

[33] 2 Tim. 2:3.

[34] 2 Tim. 1:8.

[35] Apart from 'come', it's the only command in the letter repeated in the same words. Even GNB's threefold 'keep away' translates three different Greek words (2:16, 23; 3:5).

[36] Paul draws even more attention to it with the command in 2:7, 'Think about what I am saying, because the Lord will enable you to understand it all.' Here the imperative is in the present tense, meaning that Paul wanted Timothy to go on thinking about it, at length and in depth. The word means to pay careful attention so that you eventually grasp the point. We may comfort ourselves that if Timothy needed to scratch his head, it's small wonder we find it hard to unravel! Yet I suspect Timothy's problem wasn't a dim mind, but a sinking heart at what Paul was asking him to do. If Paul says, 'Think about *what I am saying*', he must want Timothy to chew over the words immediately before it. These are the trio of suffering images (soldier, athlete, farmer) illuminating the previous imperative verb ('take your part in suffering') (2:3–6).

[37] The NIV gets this right with its 'join with me in suffering' (1:8) and 'endure hardship with us' (2:3).

[38] 2 Tim. 1:8.

[39] 2 Tim. 1:16–17.

[40]On Onesiphorus' fate, see chapter 7, note 92. It's a fair 'level 3' inference – though not the only one possible – that he's dead, persecuted for his loyalty to Paul.

[41]2 Tim. 1:16.

[42]In this case the parchment books Paul wants (2 Tim. 4:13) may not be Old Testament Scriptures or the collected sayings of Jesus as many commentators suppose, but legal documents for the defence, such as his Roman citizen's certificate. They may not have proved enough to win an acquittal in a court so determined to find fault with Christian leaders. But Timothy's support would make all the difference to Paul's drooping spirit.

Our uncertainty whether Paul means witnessing in court is the only point where step 3 drops to inference or hunch (level 3 and 4). Everything else has been a close, deductive (level 2) reading of what Paul actually says (level 1).

[43]2 Tim. 2:7.

[44]Paul returns to this call to face danger in the third movement: 3:11–12; 4:5. Many have wondered why Paul specifies his sufferings in Galatia at the time of Timothy's conversion in 3:11. Surely it's all of a piece with Paul taking Timothy back to square one throughout the letter. 'You adopted suffering as your calling *then*; so why do I have to plead with you to stick to it *now*?'

[45]2 Tim. 1:7–8. Verse 7 is the first of a series of three reiterations of this point: (1) 'his Spirit fills us with power . . .'; (2) 'Through the power of the Holy Spirit . . . keep the good things . . . entrusted to you . . .' (1:14); (3) 'be strong through the grace that is ours in union with Christ Jesus' (2:1). Paul's threefold instructions are totally emphatic.

[46]2 Tim. 1:7, 13–14. Paul later winds up the first movement with the 'true saying' in 2:11–13; 'If we have died with him, we shall also live with him . . .' It's in verse, and so is probably the words of a hymn the early Christians sang. In the mind of the original author the 'we' in it must have meant all Christians. But in the setting of this letter and Paul's attempt to stiffen Timothy's resolve, he obviously applies the 'we' to the two of them.

Back in the chapter 1 passage Paul makes another, closely related point: 'I've been brave, so you must too.' To get the force of what he's saying, we must note the words he repeats to stress the contrast. '*I* am still full of confidence [implying that you should be too], because *I* know whom *I* have trusted, and *I* am sure that he is able to keep safe until that Day what he has *entrusted to me*. Hold firmly to the true words that I taught *you* . . . and . . . keep the good things that have been *entrusted to you*' (1:12–14). In his next breath Paul makes an exactly parallel contrast between *Onesiphorus* and Timothy. '*He* was not ashamed that I am in prison, but as soon as *he* arrived in Rome, *he* started looking for me until *he* found me . . . As for *you, my son*, be strong . . .' (1:16–17; 2:1). If Onesiphorus could suffer unashamed, how much more should you, who are my son!

[47]2 Tim. 1:10.

[48]2 Tim. 2:8, 11. Paul returns to this major concern at the end of the letter. He speaks of his own afterlife, and instantly reminds Timothy again that he can bank on the same bright future. 'And now there is waiting for me the victory prize . . . which the Lord . . . will give me on that Day – and not only to me, but to *all* those who wait with love for him to appear' (4:8).

[49]2 Tim. 2:4, 9–10.

[50]2 Tim. 2:5–6, 12.

[51]2 Tim. 2:12.

[52]2 Tim. 4:3.

[53]The first movement of the letter (1:3 – 2:13), which focuses mostly on calling Timothy to suffer with Paul in Rome (step 3), also includes step 4. '*Hold firmly* to the true words . . . *remain* in the faith and love . . . *keep* the good things that have been entrusted to you' (1:13–14). 'Hold . . . remain . . . keep' sound the distinct echo of this fourth footstep. We hear it again in 2:12: 'If we *continue to endure*, we shall also rule with him.'

The second movement of the letter (2:14 – 3:9) dwells mainly on the state of affairs in Ephesus, and so it featured in chapter 7 of this book. But it too gives Timothy two reminders of his continuing duty: (1) 'Do your best to win full approval . . . as a worker who . . . *correctly teaches the message of God's truth*' (2:15); (2) As the Lord's servant, you . . . must be . . . *a good and patient teacher* . . .' (2:24).

[54]The structure of the third movement is starkly simple. Backdrop: Christians will suffer (3:12) or turn away from the truth (3:13; 4:3–4). I, Paul, have persevered with my faith and ministry (3:10–11). You, Timothy, must persevere with yours (3:14 – 4:2, 5). Paul's command to Timothy to 'carry on teaching' is 'level 1' fact.

[55]Indeed I looked at it through this filter in chapter 2, pp. 38–39.

[56]The 'Scriptures' include Jesus' sayings and the apostles' writings as well as the Old Testament (2 Pet. 3:15–16); though as a child Timothy had, of course, known only the Old Testament.

[57]The GNB's phrase 'the person who serves God' is literally 'the man of God', an Old Testament technical term for God's messenger or minister; in this case Timothy (compare 1 Tim. 6:11), with his Bible-teaching ministry in Ephesus and beyond.

[58]Many of the words repeat what Paul has already told Timothy to do, some as recently as the previous sentence. He reckons it's impossible to remind Timothy too often of his lifelong job.

[59]In 2 Tim. 4:5 Paul inserts one phrase in the 'continuous' present

imperative, something Timothy must do for the rest of his life: 'you must keep control of yourself in all circumstances'. In other words, 'Keep a *permanent* grip on yourself and stay true to your ministry *for ever.*'

[60]2 Tim. 1:2; 2:1.

[61]The letter's structure adds to the impression of baton-passing. Near the beginning and again near the end, Paul seems in effect to say, 'I've done my job right up to the end; now you carry on with it.' This is the general drift of 1:11–14: 'God has appointed *me* as an apostle and teacher . . . and it is for this reason that *I* suffer . . . Hold firmly to the true words . . . remain in the faith and love . . . keep the good things that have been entrusted to *you.*' And, in reverse order ('*you* carry on with the work because *my* time's up'), it's also the impact of 4:5–7; 'do the work of a preacher . . . perform *your* whole duty . . . As for *me* . . . the time is here for *me* to leave this life . . . I have done *my* best . . . I have kept the faith.'

[62]2 Tim. 1:12.

[63]See chapter 5, pp. 119–120.

[64]Eusebius' *History of the Church from Christ to Constantine* was the first serious attempt at what we now call church history. He wrote it between AD 303 and 324. It contains only one reference to Timothy (and three to 'non-Timothy' details in the letters 1 and 2 Timothy). He records nothing beyond what's in the New Testament. So there's not the slightest hint that Timothy became Paul's 'replacement' apostle. On the other hand there *is* evidence elsewhere that Timothy did something else after Paul's death. See chapter 9.

[65]2 Tim. 1:11–12; 2:9; 3:10–11; 4:6, 17. This teasing out the exact sense in which Timothy was Paul's successor is a matter of deduction (level 2).

[66]2 Tim. 2:2.

[67]Chapter 4 mentioned 'the Timothy principle', which applies this verse to apprenticeship in Christian living. Billy Graham applies it to evangelism with the words, 'If every believer followed this pattern, the Church could reach the entire world with the gospel in one generation! Mass crusades, in which I believe and to which I have committed my life, will never finish the Great Commission; but a one-by-one ministry will' (*The Holy Spirit*, Collins, Fount Paperbacks edn.,1980, p. 147). But Paul's original reference, as in this chapter, was to teaching.

[68]2 Pet. 1:13–15.

[69]2 Tim. 1:13–14; 2:2, 15, 24; 3:14, 16; 4:2, 5.

[70]We get exactly the same result from another popular test. It's fashionable to explore 'what the Holy Spirit is doing or saying in the churches'. 2 Timothy has only one definite reference to the Holy Spirit (1:14). It says nothing of an apostolic 'succession' through ordination,

or of fresh revelations after the apostles. It simply promises the Spirit's power to help Timothy keep intact and pass on the true words Paul taught him. This is a major focus of the Spirit's activity in the post-apostolic church. (GNB also understands the 'spirit of power, love and self-control' in 1:7 as the Holy Spirit; it may well be right – and in any case the meaning comes to much the same – but Paul's word may equally mean the human spirit.)

This perception of Timothy as bridge between the apostles and the rest of us is 'level 2' deduction throughout. It involves reading the New Testament, not as some paper dart God threw at us from outer space without reference to conditions on earth at the time of writing, but as the memorandum from Jesus' inner circle in the first century to all succeeding generations of Christians.

[71]2 Tim. 2:2; 4:2. The only Bible character I know of who has so far given his name to a Bible-distribution agency is Gideon (the Gideons International, who place Bibles in hotels, hospitals and schools). He seems to me a far less obvious Bible 'patron saint' than Timothy. The Gideons chose him, in fact, because he was called to do an unusual work of faith and obedience for God.

[72]1 Tim. 4:13. This is no plea or excuse for unimaginatively presenting the Bible 'the way we've always done it'. All Paul insists on is that the Scriptures should be *the content*. No one *method* is prescribed for the reading, preaching and teaching. It's a grave impoverishment to persist with a diet of nothing but monologue readings and lectures. In an age when fewer and fewer people are used to passive listening to the spoken word or to silent reading of the written word, we have to devise varied and multi-media ways of conveying the Bible to people.

[73]Some might claim 'evangelist' as a third title on the strength of 2 Tim. 4:5. (It's interesting that Philip is the only other person in the New Testament called an 'evangelist'; Acts 21:8.) But it's only one occurrence, and it isn't certain from Paul's phrasing, '*do the work of* a preacher of the Good News', that he considers Timothy a naturally gifted evangelist (see chapter 4, note 17).

[74]Acts 1:21–22.

[75]E.g. Gal. 1:1, 11–19; 2:6–9; 1 Cor. 15:8–10; Eph. 1:1; 3:1–10; 2 Tim. 1:1, 11. Paul saw the risen Jesus in a special, startling way. This perhaps marked him, rather than Matthias, as God's choice.

[76]Eph. 2:20; 3:5.

[77]Mt. 19:28; Rev. 21:14.

[78]1 Thes. 2:6–7.

[79]2 Cor. 11:4–5, 13; compare 1:19, 24, where Paul names Silas and Timothy as co-founders of the church, with apostolic authority which they exercise gently and sensitively.

[80]In fact, I've gone beyond the New Testament in giving the impression he was any sort of apostle in his own right. Paul and Silas refer to the three of them *together* as 'apostles'. They made up an apostolic team.

[81]The earliest post-New Testament reference to these 'deacons' is in the letter known as *1 Clement*, from the church at Rome to that at Corinth, probably written before AD 100. Ignatius also refers to them in his letters to the Magnesians and the Trallians, written before his death in about AD 115. By his time the role of deacons is becoming more fixed and regulated.

[82]Phil. 1:1.

[83]1 Tim. 3:1–7; 8–13.

[84]Even when the New Testament writers were thinking of specially appointed office-holders, the office was probably very different from what it has become in various denominations today. So it's usually misleading to translate as 'deacon' in a modern English Bible. E. E. Ellis argues that 'servant'/'deacon' was a name for a group of Paul's co-workers who specialized in preaching and teaching (*Prophecy and Hermeneutic in Early Christianity*, J. C. B. Mohr, 1978, pp. 7–13).

[85]1 Cor. 3:5; 2 Cor. 11:23; Acts 20:24; 1 Tim. 1:12; 2 Tim. 4:11. He also uses it a few times in a more technical sense.

[86]For the argument that Timothy wrote this part of 2 Corinthians, see chapter 5.

[87]2 Cor. 3:2–3, 5–6; 4:1; 5:18; 6:3–4; 8:3–4. We should look not only at the single word *diakonos* or *diakonia*. These chapters of 2 Corinthians breathe the spirit of servanthood. If Timothy wrote them for and with Paul, they presumably reflect his servant nature as much as Paul's self-humbling love for his spiritual children.

[88]Acts 19:22. This makes Timothy (with Erastus) the first person in the New Testament to receive the 'title' deacon (or servant); AD 56/57. Some manuscripts of 1 Thes. 3:2 include the word 'deacon' to describe Timothy there; that would be earlier still, AD 50/51.

[89]1 Tim. 4:6.

[90]2 Tim. 4:5.

[91]Paul can hardly have failed to cast a glance at Timothy's own track record as he wrote, 'Those [deacons] who do their [deaconing] well win for themselves a good standing and are able to speak boldly about their faith in Christ Jesus' (1 Tim. 3:13).

[92]2 Tim. 4:5, my translation.

[93]Timothy is the bridge from apostles to deacons in church leadership, much as he earlier embodied the move from Jews to Gentiles in Christian mission (see chapter 2, p. 46).

[94]Insofar as the title 'deacon' settled on a more junior job in churches, it fails in that specialized sense to cover the whole of

Timothy's identity. After all, he was responsible for appointing *elders*, the more senior post. But his relation to Paul and his attitude to Christian service make him a model for all deacons/ministers/servants.

[95]It was the genius of the early Christians – and Timothy may have contributed to it – when they needed a word to describe their church work, to call themselves simply 'servants'. They understood their job simply to be core Christians, or Christians *par excellence*; they were to be *in fact* what every Christian *ought* to be.

[96]Lk. 22:27.

[97]Jn. 13:4–5, 14–17.

[98]I think this is one reason for the fact (noted in chapter 1) that Timothy is the only New Testament character apart from Jesus about whose childhood any information is recorded. We need a typical Christian there; we can identify with his development from childhood through youth to maturity.

[99]Mk. 10:42–44.

[100]Many Christian communities, from the Vatican to independent house-churches, have discovered the power of this action and made it an annual or even more frequent event.

[101]2 Cor. 4:5.

[102]2 Tim. 4:5 (see note 92 above); 1 Tim. 4:12; 1 Tim. 4:13; 2 Tim. 2:2; 2 Cor. 6:4.

Chapter 9: Saint and martyr?

[1]Priscilla and Aquila are one of the unexplained mysteries of 2 Timothy. Although Paul greets them (4:19), he doesn't instruct Timothy to work with them. This is strange when they were such old associates of Paul (Acts 18:2–3, 18–19). I assume they were still reliable. (This is perhaps supported by the fact that the only other people he greets are the family of Onesiphorus, who had been a byword for loyalty; 1:15–18.) But who knows? Perhaps Priscilla and Aquila had been another sad casualty of the desertion of Paul.

[2]Paul was probably *en route* to Ephesus for his planned visit (1 Tim. 3:14) when he was arrested. See chapter 7, p. 156.

[3]It's virtually certain Timothy wasn't a Roman citizen. Speaking of Timothy's father, Sir William Ramsay wrote, 'The Greek-educated inhabitants . . . would not be fully qualified citizens: only the Roman Coloni were burgesses of Lystra at this period' (*The Cities of St Paul*, Hodder and Stoughton, 1907, pp. 417–418).

[4]There is, of course, no solid evidence for either opening scene.' They don't even rate as 'level 4' hunches, as I make no choice between them. How Timothy responded to 2 Timothy is an

unanswered question of history. The parts of 2 Timothy I quote or refer to are: 1:4–8; 2:2, 11–12; 4:8, 11–16, 18–19, 21.

[5]The early 'saints' didn't become so by formal canonization. They simply received popular veneration, usually on account of their holy living and martyrdom.

[6]Acts 17:34. But the letter isn't from the real Dionysius. The writer is a Syrian Christian teacher in the sixth century. It became the custom to use the names of Bible characters as pseudonyms.

[7]'The Epistle of S. Dionysius the Areopagite to S. Timothy' in *Gadla Hawariyat* (*Conflicts of the Apostles*), translated by S. C. Malan (D. Nutt, 1871), pp. 231–232.

[8]See p. 91.

[9]Heb. 13:23. This cryptic verse gives Timothy yet another unique distinction, to add to all the others we've found in the New Testament. He's the only person alive at the time Hebrews was written to be mentioned by name in the letter.

[10]Technically, perhaps, we can't be 100% certain it was the same Timothy. But there's no other Timothy known to first-century church history. And the one in this verse is clearly known to the readers; or, at the very least, they know *about* him. And the writer calls him 'our brother', just as Paul did in their letter-headings. As we saw in chapter 4, 'brother' may have been the special title for members of Paul's mission team (see p. 85). That didn't include two Timothys. We can be as sure as makes no odds that this is *our* Timothy.

[11]But Hebrews can't date from long after Paul's death. It talks a lot about the Jewish sacrifices, and would surely have mentioned the destruction of the Jerusalem temple in AD 70 if that had already happened. The most likely date of the letter seems to be in the late 60s after Paul's death.

[12]We don't know whether he suffered willingly; or whether he was alone, or perhaps with Mark. Just possibly, if Hebrews was *not* sent to readers in Rome, Timothy literally suffered *with* Paul and joined him in prison.

[13]See chapter 3, p. 70.

[14]Phil. 1:28–29.

[15]Phil. 1:22.

[16]2 Cor. 4:16.

[17]1 Tim. 4:16.

[18]In particular, Hippolyte Delehaye, 'Les Actes de S. Timothée' in *Mélanges d'Hagiographie Grecque et Latine* (Subsidia Hagiographica 42, 1966), pp. 408–415.

[19]Polycrates' Life of Timothy must surely have been written before 356 at the very latest, as it makes no mention of the transfer of

Timothy's relics from Ephesus to Constantinople which happened in
that year (see p. 213).

[20]Polycrates' Life of Timothy is preserved in the first volume of a
seventeenth-century project called *Acta Sanctorum* (*The Deeds of the
Saints*). This is the work of a society of Belgian Jesuit priests called the
Bollandists, after their founder Jean Bolland. He and his colleagues set
out to publish the lives of all the officially recognized saints, checked
for historical accuracy and purged of all their later, legendary fables.
They started working through the saints in calendar order through the
year, sifting all the old martyrologies and medieval accounts. It was
long, slow work and reached December only in the 1960s. But
Timothy's 'saint's day' is (or was until recently) 22 January, the
traditional date of his death. So he appears in volume 1, published in
1643, the work of Bolland himself, with his collaborator Godfrey
Henschenius. They supplied a long and careful introduction, discussing the many documents they had considered. Then they printed two
Lives of Timothy in full: Polycrates' and that of Symeon Metaphrastes,
a tenth-century collector of Lives of the saints. They consider both of
these Lives of Timothy basically reliable, and they give their reasons
for thinking Polycrates to be genuinely the second-century bishop.

[21]See note 20 above for further information about Metaphrastes.

[22]All my quotations from Bolland, Polycrates and Metaphrastes
come from the S. Timothy section of *Acta Sanctorum*, translated for me
by Rosalind Love in 1992.

[23]Acts 8:14–17, 25: John's journey with Peter to seal the arrival of the
Good News in Samaria.

[24]Gal. 2:9.

[25]I follow tradition in believing this to be John's description of
himself in his gospel. See references in chapter 4, note 65.

[26]See chapter 7, pp. 145–148.

[27]Bolland and Henschenius, *Acta Sanctorum*, vol. 1 (1643), p. 562.
This is referring to the rather strange account of John's gospel in
Polycrates. 'At that time also, those who followed the disciples of Our
Lord Jesus Christ, coming together at the city of Ephesus, unan-
imously decided to offer to John the favoured Theologian, the things
which had been recorded everywhere in their midst and written down
in various languages, about the miracles done by Our Lord Jesus
Christ, since they did not know how to put them in order. He
considered all the accounts carefully, and, moved to joy by them, he
arranged the things they had said in three Gospels, according to order,
that is, of Matthew, Mark and Luke, and wrote down their names and
applied each to each Gospel. He found that they recounted the
manifestations of Christ's humanity, and so he himself fully described
those things which he had imbibed from the divine breast and which

had not been narrated by the others, supplying also chapters on the divine miracles, which had been mentioned less by the others. Hence, when it was complete, he added his own name to a work not previously attempted by any other man, to wit, his holy Gospel.'

[28]We're now in a position to review the Timothy factor in the New Testament:

Written to Timothy

Level 1 – directly stated
1 and 2 Timothy
Level 3 – inferrable from the theories or traditions accepted in this book
Galatians
Revelation 2:1–7 (perhaps also 2:8 – 3:22, and by implication 4:1 – 22:21)

Written with Timothy's collaboration

Level 1 – directly stated (in association with Paul)
2 Corinthians
Philippians
Colossians
1 and 2 Thessalonians
Philemon
Level 3 – inferrable from tradition accepted in this book (giving assistance to John)
John's gospel
John's letters?
In addition, Timothy was probably one of the sources of information for Acts 17 – 20 (see chapter 3, note 131).

Written about Timothy

Level 1 – directly stated
Acts 16:1–3; 17:14–16; 18:5; 19:22; 20:4–6
Romans 16:21
1 Corinthians 4:17; 16:10–11
Philippians 2:19–23
1 Thessalonians 3:2, 5–6
Hebrews 13:23
Level 2 – clearly deducible
Acts 16:4–15; 17:2–13; 18:6–17; 20:7 – 21:17
Level 3 – reasonably inferrable
Acts 18:18–23; 19:1–21; 28:30–31

Known by Timothy

Level 2 – clearly deducible
Romans
1 Corinthians

Level 3 – reasonably inferrable from theories or traditions accepted in this book

The rest of Acts

Ephesians

Matthew, Mark, Luke

On the other hand, I do not believe one other tradition of Timothy's years in Ephesus. St John of Damascus, an eighth-century theologian, claimed that Timothy witnessed the Virgin Mary being taken up to heaven from Ephesus at the end of her life. (The Roman Catholic Church officially believes that Mary was taken physically into heaven in much the same way as Jesus was.) But it's only based on much later claims, like this one by John of Damascus. He presumably mentions Timothy only as a supporting detail, because he was widely known as the bishop of Ephesus at that time. In any case, it's far from certain that Mary was even in Ephesus. Neither Polycrates nor Metaphrastes mentions the story at all. There's a common tradition that she accompanied John there, presumably because Jesus entrusted her to John from the cross (Jn. 19:26–27). But if, as we've seen, John can't have gone to Ephesus much before AD 70, she would by then have been approaching ninety and may well have already died.

[29]Metaphrastes earlier called Timothy bishop of Ephesus under John's oversight (see p. 205). Now he says Timothy *became* bishop of Ephesus in place of John on the latter's exile to Patmos!

[30]Tit. 1:5–7.

[31]See chapter 2, p. 37.

[32]For more on Timothy as Paul's go-between, see chapter 6. For his lack of 'episcopal' authority, see chapter 8, p. 188. It's true that Polycrates and Metaphrastes *thought* of Timothy as the diocesan bishop, but that only shows how quickly titles changed their meaning after New Testament times. It's never helpful to assume that our modern structures and titles are the same as in the New Testament. We should try to understand the structures and titles it recommends, and then feel free to question and reform our modern attempts to achieve the same results.

[33]To those who would claim Timothy as the prototype vicar or bishop, one has to point out that he was, until this last chapter just before his death, a very poor one.

[34]As with most details of this book that don't directly involve Timothy, I'm following the traditional dating and origin of Revelation, while aware that some scholars have other theories.

[35]Timothy may well have been the stand-in bishop and messenger to all the Asian churches. The repeated refrain, 'He who has an ear, let *him* hear what the Spirit says to the churches' (Rev. 2:7, 11, 17, 29; 3:6, 13, 22, NIV) may be a coded message from John (and Jesus) to Timothy.

[36]The Bollandist commentary quotes them and agrees with them (*Acta Sanctorum*, vol. 1, 1643, p. 564).

[37]Verses 1–6 are second person singular, addressed to the 'angel'. Verse 7 is third person singular masculine, addressed to one male listener. See note 51 below.

[38]Rev. 2:1.

[39]Rev. 2:2–3.

[40]Rev. 2:2, 6.

[41]Rev. 2:14–15. The Greek wording of these two verses can mean that the followers of Balaam and the Nicolaitans taught much the same things; even that they're two names for the same group.

[42]Ignatius, *To the Ephesians IX*, in Edward Burton, *The Apostolic Fathers*, vol. 2 (John Grant, 1909), p. 76.

[43]The words quoted so far come from the beginning and end of Jesus' 'letter'. He wraps his whole message round with strong approval of what the church (and Timothy?) have achieved. The full wording of verse 6 reads: '*But this is what you have in your favour:* you hate what the Nicolaitans do, *as much as I do.*'

[44]Rev. 2:4.

[45]John's Greek doesn't have the word 'me'; he simply says, 'you do not love as you did'. It certainly includes love for Jesus, but probably love for other people as well.

[46]Rev. 2:5.

[47]Ignatius, *To the Ephesians IX*, in Burton, p. 76.

[48]These early Lives of the Saints were first known as 'martyrologies' because they gave most of their attention to their heroes' glorious deaths. The gospels, of course, have this same stress on the death of their central character.

[49]2 Cor. 5:2. See chapter 3, pp. 71–72; and chapter 5, p. 112.

[50]2 Tim. 3:10–12.

[51]Rev. 2:7, NIV. The words are not in the plural, as in GNB, but pointedly in the singular. They may refer generally to all who would be martyred, but Timothy would have heard in them a special message for him. See also note 35 above.

[52]2 Cor. 4:7.